The O'Leary Series

Microsoft® Office PowerPoint® 2003

Brief Edition

The O'Leary Series

Microsoft® Office PowerPoint® 2003

Brief Edition

Timothy J. O'Leary
Arizona State University

Linda I. O'Leary

Boston   Burr Ridge, IL   Dubuque, IA   Madison, WI   New York   San Francisco   St. Louis
Bangkok   Bogotá   Caracas   Kuala Lumpur   Lisbon   London   Madrid   Mexico City
Milan   Montreal   New Delhi   Santiago   Seoul   Singapore   Sydney   Taipei   Toronto

Technology Education

MICROSOFT® OFFICE POWERPOINT® 2003, BRIEF EDITION
Published by McGraw-Hill Technology Education, an imprint of the McGraw-Hill Companies, Inc. 1221 Avenue of the Americas, New York, NY, 10020. Copyright © 2004 by the McGraw-Hill Companies, Inc. All rights reserved. No part of this publication may be reproduced or distributed in any form or by any means, or stored in a database or retrieval system, without the prior written consent of The McGraw-Hill Companies, Inc., including, but not limited to, in any network or other electronic storage or transmission, or broadcast for distance learning.

Some ancillaries, including electronic and print components, may not be available to customers outside the United States.

This book is printed on acid-free paper.

2 3 4 5 6 7 8 9 0 QPD/QPD 0 9 8 7 6 5

ISBN 0-07-283613-X

Editor-in-Chief: *Bob Woodbury*
Sponsoring editor: *Don Hull*
Developmental editor: *Jennie Yates*
Marketing manager: *Andy Bernier*
Media producer: *Mark Christianson*
Project manager: *Jim Labeots*
Manager, new book production: *Heather D. Burbridge*
Coordinator freelance design: *Artemio Ortiz Jr.*
Photo research coordinator: *Ira C. Roberts*
Supplement producer: *Matthew Perry*
Senior digital content specialist: *Brian Nacik*
Cover design: *Asylum Studios*
Interior design: *Artemio Ortiz Jr.*
Typeface: *10.5/13 New Aster*
Compositor: *Rogondino & Associates/Cecelia G. Morales*
Printer: *Quebecor World Dubuque Inc.*

Library of Congress Control Number 2003108663

www.mhhe.com

McGraw-Hill Technology Education

At McGraw-Hill Technology Education, we publish instructional materials for the technology education market—in particular, for computer instruction in post secondary education that ranges from introductory courses in traditional four-year universities to continuing education and proprietary schools. McGraw-Hill Technology Education presents a broad range of innovative products—texts, lab manuals, study guides, testing materials, and technology-based training and assessment tools.

We realize that technology has created and will continue to create new mediums for professors and students to use in managing resources and communicating information to one another. McGraw-Hill Technology Education provides the most flexible and complete teaching and learning tools available and offers solutions to the changing needs of the classroom. McGraw-Hill Technology Education is dedicated to providing the tools for today's instructors and students, which will enable them to successfully navigate the world of Information Technology.

- McGraw-Hill/Osborne—This division of The McGraw-Hill Companies is known for its best-selling Internet titles, Harley Hahn's *Internet & Web Yellow Pages* and the *Internet Complete Reference*. For more information, visit Osborne at www.osborne.com.

- Digital Solutions—Whether you want to teach a class online or just post your "bricks-n-mortar" class syllabus, McGraw-Hill Technology Education is committed to publishing digital solutions. Taking your course online doesn't have to be a solitary adventure, nor does it have to be a difficult one. We offer several solutions that will allow you to enjoy all the benefits of having your course material online.

- Packaging Options—For more information about our discount options, contact your McGraw-Hill Sales representative at 1-800-338-3987 or visit our website at **www.mhhe.com/it**.

McGraw-Hill Technology Education is dedicated to providing
the tools for today's instructors and students.

Brief Contents

Detailed Contents

Acknowledgments

The new edition of The O'Leary Series has been made possible only through the enthusiasm and dedication of a great team of people. Because the team spans the country, literally from coast to coast, we have utilized every means of working together including conference calls, FAX, e-mail, and document collaboration. We have truly tested the team approach and it works!

Leading the team from McGraw-Hill are Don Hull, Sponsoring Editor, and Jennie Yates, Developmental Editor. Their renewed commitment, direction, and support have infused the team with the excitement of a new project.

The production staff is headed by James Labeots, Project Manager, whose planning and attention to detail has made it possible for us to successfully meet a very challenging schedule. Members of the production team include: Artemio Ortiz, Designer; Pat Rogondino and Cecelia Morales, Compositors; Susan Defosset, Copy Editor; Heather Burbridge, Production Supervisor; Matthew Perry, Supplement Coordinator; and Mark Christianson, Media Producer. We would particularly like to thank Pat, Cecelia, and Susan—team members for many past editions whom we can always depend on to do a great job.

Finally, we are particularly grateful to a small but very dedicated group of people who helped us develop the manuscript. Colleen Hayes, Susan Demar, and Kathy Duggan have helped on the last several editions and continue to provide excellent developmental support. To Steve Willis, Carol Cooper, and Sarah Martin who provide technical expertise, youthful perspective, and enthusiasm, our thanks for helping get the manuscripts out the door and meeting the deadlines.

Preface

Introduction

The 20th century not only brought the dawn of the Information Age, but also rapid changes in information technology. There is no indication that this rapid rate of change will be slowing— it may even be increasing. As we begin the 21st century, computer literacy will undoubtedly become prerequisite for whatever career a student chooses. The goal of the O'Leary Series is to assist students in attaining the necessary skills to efficiently use these applications. Equally important is the goal to provide a foundation for students to readily and easily learn to use future versions of this software. This series does this by providing detailed step-by-step instructions combined with careful selection and presentation of essential concepts.

About the Authors

Tim and Linda O'Leary live in the American Southwest and spend much of their time engaging instructors and students in conversation about learning. In fact, they have been talking about learning for more than 25 years. Something in those early conversations convinced them to write a book, to bring their interest in the learning process to the printed page. Today, they are as concerned as ever about learning, about technology, and about the challenges of presenting material in new ways, both in terms of content and the method of delivery.

A powerful and creative team, Tim combines his years of classroom teaching experience with Linda's background as a consultant and corporate trainer. Tim has taught courses at Stark Technical College in Canton, Ohio, Rochester Institute of Technology in upper New York state, and is currently a professor at Arizona State University in Tempe, Arizona. Tim and Linda have talked to and taught students from ages 8 to 80, all of them with a desire to learn something about computers and the applications that make their lives easier, more interesting, and more productive.

About the Book

Times are changing, technology is changing, and this text is changing, too. Do you think the students of today are different from yesterday? There is no doubt about it—they are. On the positive side, it is amazing how much effort students will put toward things they are convinced are relevant to them. Their effort directed at learning application programs and exploring the Web seems at times limitless. On the other hand, students can often be shortsighted, thinking that learning the skills to use the application is the only objective. The mission of the series is to build upon and extend this interest by not only teaching the specific application skills but by introducing the concepts that are common to all applications, providing students with the confidence, knowledge, and ability to easily learn the next generation of applications.

Same Great Features as the Office XP Edition with some new additions!

- **Introduction to Computer Essentials**—A brief introduction to the basics of computer hardware and software (appears in Office Volume I only).

- **Office Outlook 2003**—A lab devoted to Microsoft Office Outlook 2003 basics (appears in Office Volume I only).

- **Introduction to Microsoft Office 2003**—Presents an overview to the Microsoft Office 2003 components: Office Word, Excel, Access, Power-Point, and Outlook. Includes a hands-on section that introduces the features that are common to all Office 2003 applications, including using menus, task panes, and the Office Help system.

- **Lab Organization**—The lab text is organized to include main and subtopic heads by grouping related tasks. For example, tasks such as changing fonts and applying character effects appear under the "Formatting" topic head. This results in a slightly more reference-like approach, making it easier for students to refer back to the text to review. This has been done without losing the logical and realistic development of the case.

- **Relevant Cases**—Four separate running cases demonstrate the features in each application. Topics are of interest to students—At Arizona State University, over 600 students were surveyed to find out what topics are of interest to them.

- **Focus on Concepts**—Each lab focuses on the concepts behind the application. Students learn the concepts, so they can succeed regardless of the software package they might be using. The concepts are previewed at the beginning of each lab and summarized at the end of each lab.

- All **Numbered Steps** and bullets appear in left margin space making it easy not to miss a step.

- **Clarified Marginal Notes**—Marginal notes have been enhanced by more clearly identifying the note content with box heads and the use of different colors.

  Additional Information—Brief asides with expanded discussion of features.

  Having Trouble?—Procedural tips advising students of possible problems and how to overcome them.

  Another Method—Alternative methods of performing a procedure.

- **Focus on Careers**—A new feature, appearing at the end of each lab, which provides an example of how the material covered may be applied in the "real world."

- A **Microsoft Office Specialist Skills** table, appearing at the end of each lab, contains page references to Microsoft Office Specialist skills learned in the lab.

- **End-of-Chapter Material**

  - Screen Identification (appears in the first lab of each application)

  - Matching

  - Multiple Choice

  - Fill-In

  - True/False

  Hands-On Practice Exercises—Students apply the skills and concepts they learned to solve case-based exercises. Many cases in the practice exercises tie to a running case used in another application lab. This helps to demonstrate the use of the four applications across a common case setting. For example, the Adventure Travel Tours case used in the Word labs is continued in practice exercises in Excel, Access, and PowerPoint.

  - Step-by-Step

  - On Your Own

- **Rating System**—The 3-star rating system identifies the difficulty level of each practice exercise in the end-of-lab materials.

rating system
★ Easy
★ ★ Moderate
★ ★ ★ Difficult

- **Continuing Exercises**—A continuing exercise icon identifies exercises that build off of exercises completed in earlier labs.

- **Working Together Labs**—At the completion of the brief and introductory texts, a final lab demonstrates the integration of the MS Office applications.

- **References**

  Command Summary—Provides a able of all commands used in the labs.

  Glossary of Key Terms—Includes definitions for all bolded terms used in the labs and included in the Key Terms list at the end of each lab.

  Data File List—Helps organize all data and solution files.

  Microsoft Office Specialist Certification Guide—Links all Microsoft Office Specialist objectives to text content and end-of-chapter exercises.

Instructor's Guide

We understand that, in today's teaching environment, offering a textbook alone is not sufficient to meet the needs of the many instructors who use our books. To teach effectively, instructors must have a full complement of supplemental resources to assist them in every facet of teaching from preparing for class, to conducting a lecture, to assessing students' comprehension. *The O'Leary Series* offers a fully-integrated supplements package and Web site, as described below.

Instructor's Resource Kit

The **Instructor's Resource Kit** contains a computerized Test Bank, an Instructor's Manual, and PowerPoint Presentation Slides. Features of the Instructor's Resource Kit are described below.

- **Instructor's Manual** The Instructor's Manual contains lab objectives, concepts, outlines, lecture notes, and command summaries. Also included are answers to all end-of chapter material, tips for covering difficult materials, additional exercises, and a schedule showing how much time is required to cover text material.

- **Computerized Test Bank** The test bank contains over 1,300 multiple choice, true/false, and discussion questions. Each question will be accompanied by the correct answer, the level of learning difficulty, and corresponding page references. Our flexible Diploma software allows you to easily generate custom exams.

- **PowerPoint Presentation Slides** The presentation slides will include lab objectives, concepts, outlines, text figures, and speaker's notes. Also included are bullets to illustrate key terms and FAQs.

Online Learning Center/Web Site

Found at **www.mhhe.com/oleary**, this site provides additional learning and instructional tools to enhance the comprehension of the text. The OLC/Web Site is divided into these three areas:

- **Information Center** Contains core information about the text, supplements, and the authors.

- **Instructor Center** Offers instructional materials, downloads, and other relevant links for professors.

- **Student Center** Contains data files, chapter competencies, chapter concepts, self-quizzes, flashcards, additional Web links, and more.

Skills Assessment

SimNet (Simulated Network Assessment Product) provides a way for you to test students' software skills in a simulated environment.

- Pre-testing options
- Post-testing options
- Course placement testing
- Diagnostic capabilities to reinforce skills
- Proficiency testing to measure skills
- Web or LAN delivery of tests.
- Computer-based training tutorials

For more information on skills assessment software, please contact your local sales representative, or visit us at **www.mhhe.com/it**.

Digital Solutions to Help You Manage Your Course

PageOut is our Course Web Site Development Center that offers a syllabus page, URL, McGraw-Hill Online Learning Center content, online exercises and quizzes, gradebook, discussion board, and an area for student Web pages.

Available free with any McGraw-Hill Technology Education product, PageOut requires no prior knowledge of HTML, no long hours of coding, and a way for course coordinators and professors to provide a full-course Web site. PageOut offers a series of templates—simply fill them with your course information and click on one of 16 designs. The process takes under an hour and leaves you with a professionally designed Web site. We'll even get you started with sample Web sites, or enter your syllabus for you! PageOut is so straightforward and intuitive, it's little wonder why over 12,000 college professors are using it. For more information, visit the PageOut Web site at www.pageout.net.

Online courses are also available. Online Learning Centers (OLCs) are your perfect solutions for Internet-based content. Simply put, these Centers are "digital cartridges" that contain a book's pedagogy and supplements. As students read the book, they can go online and take self-grading quizzes or work through interactive exercises. These also provide students appropriate access to lecture materials and other key supplements.

Online Learning Centers can be delivered through any of these platforms:

- Blackboard.com
- WebCT (a product of Universal Learning Technology)

McGraw-Hill has partnerships with WebCT and Blackboard to make it even easier to take your course online. Now you can have McGraw-Hill content delivered through the leading Internet-based learning tool for higher education.

Computing Concepts

Computing Essentials 2004 and *Computing Today* offer a unique, visual orientation that gives students a basic understanding of computing concepts. *Computing Essentials* and *Computing Today* are some of the few books on the market that are written by a professor who still teaches the courses every semester and loves it. The books encourage "active" learning with their exercises, explorations, visual illustrations, and inclusion of screen shots and numbered steps. While combining the "active" learning style with current topics and technology, these texts provide an accurate snapshot of computing trends. When bundled with software application lab manuals, students are given a complete representation of the fundamental issues surrounding the personal computing environment.

Select features of these texts include:

- **Using Technology**—Engaging coverage of hot, high-interest topics, such as phone calls via the Internet, using the Internet remotely with a Personal Digital Assistant (PDA), and Client and Server operating systems. These Web-related projects direct the student to explore current popular uses of technology.

- **Expanding Your Knowledge**—Geared for those who want to go into greater depth on a specific topic introduced within the chapter. These projects meet the needs of instructors wanting more technical depth of coverage.

- **Building Your Portfolio**—Develops critical thinking and writing skills while students examine security, privacy, and ethical issues in technology. By completing these exercises, students will be able to walk away from the class with something to show prospective employers.

- **Making IT Work for You**—Based on student surveys, *Computing Essentials* identified several special interest topics and devoted a two-page section on each in the corresponding chapter. Making IT Work for You sections engage students by presenting high interest topics that directly relate to the concepts presented in the chapter. Topics include downloading music from the Internet, creating personal Web sites, and using the Internet to make long-distance phone calls. Many of these are supported by short video presentations that will be available via CD and the Web.

- **On the Web Explorations**—Appear throughout the margins of the text and encourage students to go to the Web to visit several informative and established sites in order to learn more about the chapter's featured topic.

- **A Look to the Future Sections**—Provide insightful information about the future impact of technology and forecasts of how upcoming enhancements in the world of computing will play an important and powerful role in society.

- **End-of-Chapter Material**—A variety of material including objective questions (key terms, matching, multiple choice, and short answer completion) and critical thinking activities. This will help to reinforce the information just learned.

STUDENT'S GUIDE

As you begin each lab, take a few moments to read the **Case Study** and the Concept Preview. The case study introduces a real-life setting that is interwoven throughout the entire lab, providing the basis for understanding the use of the application. Also, notice the Additional Information, Having Trouble?, and Another Method boxes scattered throughout the book. These tips provide more information about related topics, help get you out of trouble if you are having problems, and offer suggestions on other ways to perform the same task. Finally, read the text between the steps. You will find the few minutes more it takes you is well worth the time when you are completing the practice exercises.

Many learning aids are built into the text to ensure your success with the material and to make the process of learning rewarding. The pages that follow call your attention to the key features in the text.

Objectives

Appear at the beginning of the lab and identify the main features you will be learning.

Case Study

Introduces a real-life setting that is interwoven throughout the lab, providing the basis for understanding the use of the application.

Creating and Editing a Document LAB 1

Objectives

After you have read this chapter, you should be able to:

1. Develop a document as well as enter and edit text.
2. Insert and delete text and blank lines.
3. Reveal formatting marks.
4. Use AutoCorrect, AutoText, and AutoComplete.
5. Use automatic spelling and grammar checking.
6. Save, close, and open files.
7. Select text.
8. Undo and redo changes.
9. Change fonts and type sizes.
10. Bold and color text.
11. Change alignment.
12. Insert, size, and move pictures.
13. Preview and print a document.
14. Set file properties.

WD1.1

Case Study

Adventure Travel Tours

As a recent college graduate, you have accepted a job as advertising coordinator for Adventure Travel Tours, a specialty travel company that organizes active adventure vacations. The company is headquartered in Los Angeles and has locations in other major cities throughout the country. You are responsible for coordination of the advertising program for all locations. This includes the creation of many kinds of promotional materials: brochures, flyers, form letters, news releases, advertisements, and a monthly newsletter. You are also responsible for creating Web pages for the company Web site.

Adventure Travel is very excited about four new tours planned for the upcoming year. They want to promote them through informative presentations held throughout the country. Your first job as advertising coordinator will be to create a flyer advertising the four new tours and the presentations about them. The flyer will be modified according to the location of the presentation.

The software tool you will use to create the flyer is the word processing application Microsoft Word Office 2003. It helps you create documents such as letters, reports, and research papers. In this lab, you will learn how to enter, edit, and print a document while you create the flyer (shown right) to be distributed in a mailing to Adventure Travel Tours clients.

© PhotoDisc

WD1.2

Concept Preview

Provides an overview to the concepts that will be presented throughout the lab.

Another Method

Offers additional ways to perform a procedure.

Having Trouble

Helps resolve potential problems as you work through each lab.

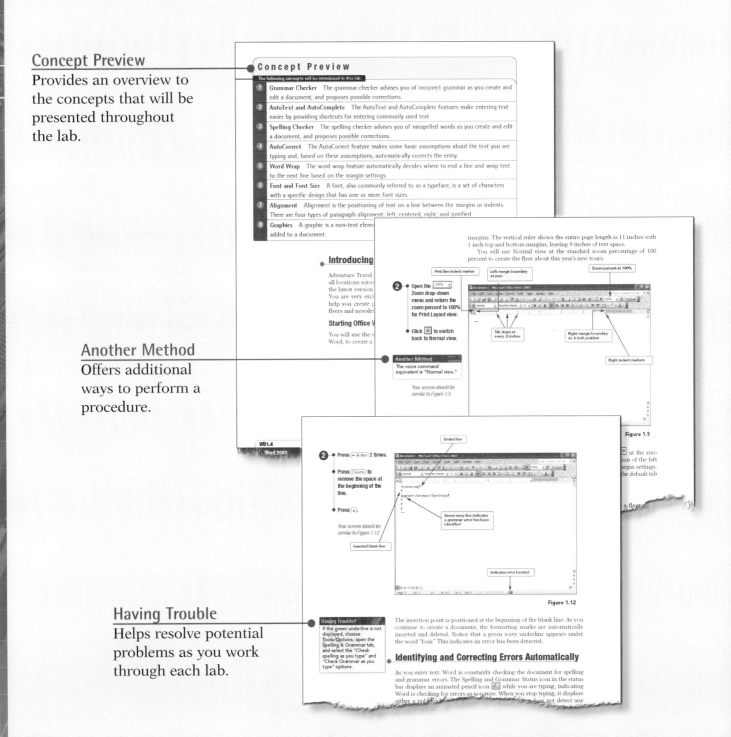

Numbered and Bulleted Steps, Additional Information

Numbered and Bulleted Steps

Provide clear Step-by-Step Instructions on how to complete a task, or series of tasks.

Additional Information

Offers brief asides with expanded coverage of content.

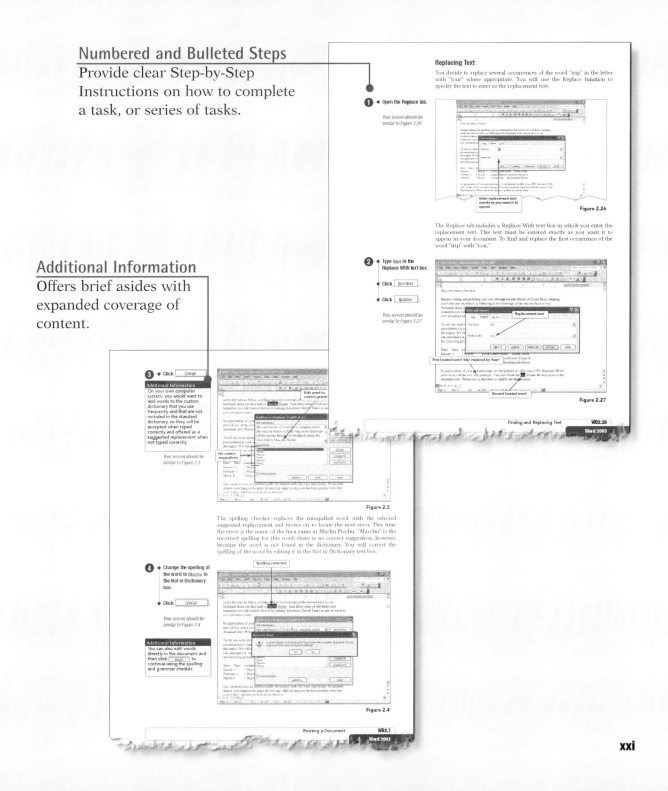

Replacing Text

You decide to replace several occurrences of the word "trip" in the letter with "tour" where appropriate. You will use the Replace function to specify the text to enter as the replacement text.

1 ● Open the Replace tab.

Your screen should be similar to Figure 2.26

Enter replacement text exactly as you want it to appear

Figure 2.26

The Replace tab includes a Replace With text box in which you enter the replacement text. This text must be entered exactly as you want it to appear in your document. To find and replace the first occurrence of the word "trip" with "tour,"

2 ● Type tour in the Replace With text box.
● Click Find Next.
● Click Replace.

Your screen should be similar to Figure 2.27

Replacement text

First located word 'trip' replaced by 'tour'

Second located word

Figure 2.27

Finding and Replacing Text WD2.25

Word 2003

3 ● Click Change.

Additional Information
On your own computer system, you would want to add words to the custom dictionary that you use frequently and that are not included in the standard dictionary, so they will be accepted when typed correctly and offered as a suggested replacement when not typed correctly.

Your screen should be similar to Figure 2.3

Edit word to correct grammar

No correct suggestions

Figure 2.3

The spelling checker replaces the misspelled word with the selected suggested replacement and moves on to locate the next error. This time the error is the name of the Inca ruins at Machu Picchu. "Macchu" is the incorrect spelling for this word; there is no correct suggestion, however, because the word is not found in the dictionary. You will correct the spelling of the word by editing it in the Not in Dictionary text box.

4 ● Change the spelling of the word to Machu in the Not in Dictionary box.
● Click Change.

Your screen should be similar to Figure 2.4

Additional Information
You can also edit words directly in the document and then click to continue using the spelling and grammar checker.

Spelling corrected

Figure 2.4

Revising a Document WD2.7

Word 2003

Figures and Callouts, Tables

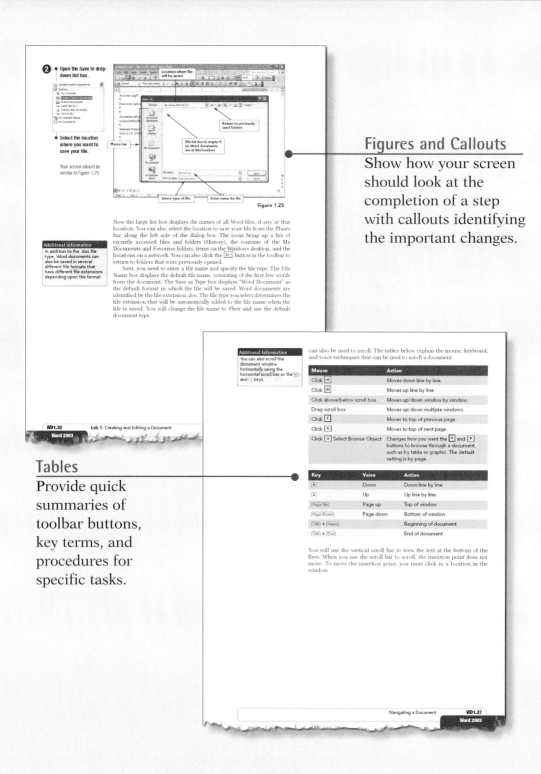

Figures and Callouts
Show how your screen should look at the completion of a step with callouts identifying the important changes.

Tables
Provide quick summaries of toolbar buttons, key terms, and procedures for specific tasks.

• Focus on Careers, Concept Summary

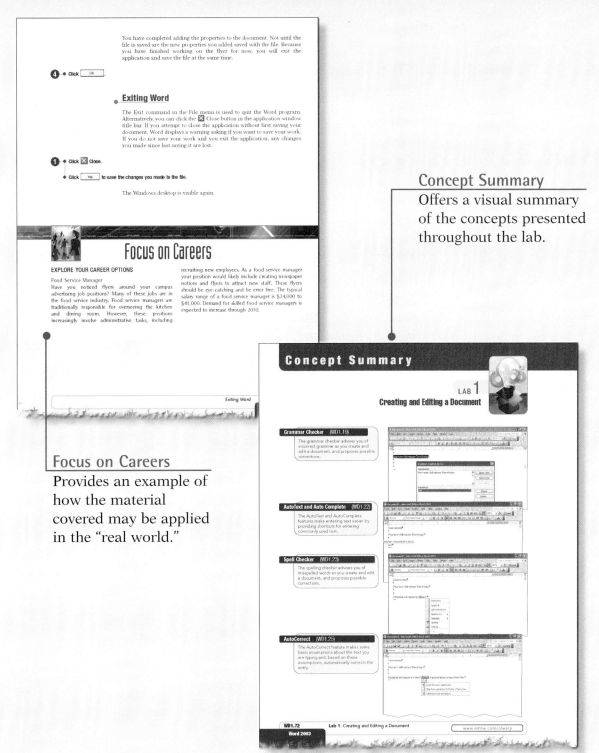

Concept Summary
Offers a visual summary of the concepts presented throughout the lab.

Focus on Careers
Provides an example of how the material covered may be applied in the "real world."

Key Terms and Microsoft Office Specialist Skills, Command Summary

Key Terms and Microsoft Office Specialist Skills
Includes a list of all bolded terms with page references and a table showing the Microsoft Office Specialist certification skills that were covered in the lab.

Command Summary
Provides a table of commands and keyboard and toolbar shortcuts for all commands used in the lab.

---

lab review

LAB 3
Creating Reports and Tables

key terms

alignment WD1.58	font size WD1.51	sans serif font WD1.51
AutoComplete WD1.22	format WD1.11	select WD1.6
AutoCorrect WD1.25	formatting mark WD1.14	selection rectangle WD1.65
AutoText WD1.22	Formatting toolbar WD1.5	serif font WD1.51
character formatting WD1.50	grammar checker WD1.16	sizing handles WD1.65
cursor WD1.5	graphic WD1.60	Smart Tag WD1.29
custom dictionary WD1.23	Insert mode WD1.40	soft space WD1.58
default WD1.68	insertion point WD1.5	source program WD1.60
document window WD1.5	main dictionary WD1.23	spelling checker WD1.23
drawing object WD1.60	object WD1.60	Standard toolbar WD1.5
edit WD1.11	Overtype mode WD1.41	thumbnail WD1.62
embedded object WD1.60	pane WD1.6	TrueType WD1.52
end-of-file marker WD1.5	paragraph formatting WD1.50	typeface WD1.51
file property WD1.69	picture WD1.60	word wrap WD1.28
font WD1.51	ruler WD1.5	

microsoft office specialist skills

The Microsoft Office Specialist (MOS) certification program is designed to measure your proficiency in performing basic tasks using the Office 2003 applications. Getting certified demonstrates that you have the skills and provides a valuable industry credential for employment. After completing this lab, you have learned the following Microsoft Office Specialist skills:

Skill	Description	Page
Creating Content	Insert and edit text, symbols, and special characters	WD1.XX
	Insert frequently used and predefined text	WD1.XX,
	Insert, position, and size graphics	WD1.XX
Formatting Content	Format text	WD1.XX
	Format paragraphs	WD1.XX
Formatting and Managing Documents	Preview and print documents	WD1.XX
	Review and modify document properties	WD1.XX
	Save documents in appropriate formats for different uses	WD1.XX
	Print documents, envelopes, and labels	WD1.XX
	Preview documents and Web pages	WD1.XX
	Change and organize document views and windows	WD1.XX

WD1.74   Lab 1: Creating and Editing a Document

Word 2003   www.mhhe.com/oleary

---

command summary

Command	Shortrtcut Key	Button	Voice	Action
File/Page Setup				Changes layout of page including margins, paper size, and paper source
File/Versions				Saves, opens, and deletes document versions
Edit/Cut	Ctrl + X		Cut	Cuts selection to Clipboard
Edit/Copy	Ctrl + C		Copy	Copies selection to Clipboard
Edit/Paste	Ctrl + V		Paste	Pastes item from Clipboard
Edit/Find	Ctrl + F			Locates specified text
Edit/Replace	Ctrl + H			Locates and replaces specified text
Insert/Break/Page break	Ctrl + ←Enter			Inserts hard page break
Insert/Date and Time				Inserts current date or time, maintained by computer system, in selected format
Insert/AutoText				Enters predefined text
Insert/AutoText/AutoText				Create new AutoText entries
Insert/Picture/AutoShapes		AutoShapes ▾		Inserts selected AutoShape
Format/Font/Font/ Underline style/Single	Ctrl + U	U		Underlines selected text with a single line
Format/Paragraph/Indents and Spacing/Special/First Line				Indents first line of paragraph from left margin
Format/Paragraph/Indents and Spacing/Line Spacing	Ctrl + #			Changes amount of white space between lines
Format/Bullets and Numbering				Creates a bulleted or numbered list
Format /Tabs				Specifies types and position of tab stops
Format/Styles and Formatting				Displays the Styles and Formatting Task pane

Lab Review   WD2.71

Word 2003

Lab Exercises

Reinforce the terminology and concepts presented in the lab through Screen Identification, Matching, Multiple Choice, True/False, and Fill-in questions.

lab exercises

screen identification

1. In the following Word screen, letters identify important elements. Enter the correct term for each screen element in the space provided.

a. _____ d. _____ g. _____ j. _____
b. _____ e. _____ h. _____ k. _____
c. _____ f. _____ i. _____

Lab Exercises   WD2.73
Word 2003

matching

Match the item on the left with the correct description on the right.

1. [icon] _____ a. new text writes over existing text
2. font _____ b. moves to the top of the document
3. [Del] _____ c. feature that automatically begins a new line when text reaches the right margin
4. alignment _____ d. images that enhance a document
5. [Ctrl] + [Home] _____ e. displays the Print Preview window
6. graphics _____ f. type style that can be applied to text
7. [icon] _____ g. font size measurement
8. word wrap _____ h. controls paragraph positioning between the margins
9. point _____ i. saves a document using the same file name
10. sans serif _____ j. font without a flair at the base of each letter

multiple choice

Circle the correct response to the questions below.

1. Document development follows these steps.
   a. plan, edit, enter, format, preview, and print
   b. enter, edit, format, preview, and print
   c. plan, enter, edit, format, preview, and print
   d. design, enter, edit, format, preview, and print

2. The Word feature that makes some basic assumptions about the text makes changes based on those assumptions is _____
   a. AutoChange
   b. AutoCorrect
   c. AutoText
   d. AutoFormat

3. Words that are not contained in the main dictionary can be added to
   a. custom
   b. additional
   c. add to
   d. user defined

4. The feature that allows you to preview a document before it is printed
   a. print review
   b. page review
   c. page preview
   d. print preview

lab exercises

true/false

Circle the correct answer to the following questions.

1. The spelling checker identifies synonyms for common words.   True   False
2. Formatting and text editing can be done in the Print Preview window.   True   False
3. Indents are used to set paragraphs off from the rest of the text.   True   False
4. The Find and Replace feature is used to locate misspelled words in a document.   True   False
5. A bulleted list conveys a sequence of events.   True   False
6. A source is the location from which text is moved or copied.   True   False
7. Soft page breaks are automatically inserted whenever the text reaches the bottom margin.   True   False
8. Using Document versions creates separate files of different versions of a document.   True   False
9. AutoCorrect entries are used to insert commonly used words or phrases into a document.   True   False
10. A hyperlink is a connection to a location in the current document, another document, or to a Web site.   True   False

fill-in

1. As you add or remove text from a page, Word automatically _____ the placement of the soft page break.

2. A(n) _____ code instructs Word to insert the current date in the document using the selected format whenever the document is printed.

3. Standard single-sided documents have four _____: top, bottom, left, and right.

4. Double-sided documents with facing pages typically use _____ margins in which the left page

Lab Exercises: Step-by-Step, On Your Own

Lab Exercises

Provide hands-on practice and develop critical thinking skills through step-by-step and on-your-own practice exercises. These exercises have a rating system from easy to difficult and test your ability to apply the knowledge you have gained in each lab. Exercises that build off of previous exercises are noted with a Continuing Exercise icon.

On Your Own

The O'Leary Series

Microsoft® Office PowerPoint® 2003

Brief Edition

Introduction to Microsoft Office 2003

Objectives

After completing the Introduction to Microsoft Office 2003, you should be able to:

Describe Office System 2003.

Describe the Office 2003 applications.

Start an Office 2003 application.

Recognize the basic application window features.

Use menus, shortcut menus, and shortcut keys.

Use toolbars and task panes.

Use Office Help.

Exit an Office 2003 application.

What Is Microsoft Office System 2003?

Microsoft Office System 2003 is a comprehensive, integrated system of programs, servers and services designed to solve a wide array of business needs. Although the programs can be used individually, they are designed to work together seamlessly making it easy to connect people and organizations to information, business processes and each other. The applications include tools used to create, discuss, communicate, and manage projects. If you share a lot of documents with other people, these features facilitate access to common documents. This version has expanded and refined the communication and collaboration features and integration with the World Wide Web. In addition, several new interface features are designed to make it easier to perform tasks and help users take advantage of all the features in the applications.

The Microsoft Office System 2003 is packaged in different combinations of components. The major components and a brief description are provided in the following table.

Component	Description
Microsoft Office 2003	
Office Word 2003	Word Processor
Office Excel 2003	Spreadsheet
Office Access 2003	Database manager
Office PowerPoint 2003	Presentation graphics
Office Outlook 2003	Desktop information manager
Office FrontPage 2003	Web site creation and management
Office InfoPath 2003	Creates XML forms and documents
Office OneNote 2003	Note-taking
Office Publisher 2003	Desktop publishing
Office Visio 2003	Drawing and diagramming
Office SharePoint Portal Server v2.0 and Services	

The five components of Microsoft Office 2003—Word, Excel, Access, PowerPoint, and Outlook—are the applications you will learn about in this series of labs. They are described in more detail in the following sections.

Office Word 2003

Office Word 2003 is a word processing software application whose purpose is to help you create text-based documents. Word processors are one of the most flexible and widely used application software programs. A word processor can be used to manipulate text data to produce a letter, a report, a memo, an e-mail message, or any other type of correspondence.

Two documents you will produce in the first two Word labs, a letter and flyer, are shown here.

A letter containing a tabbed table, indented paragraphs, and text enhancements is quickly created using basic Word features.

March 25, 2005

Dear Adventure Traveler:

Imagine hiking and paddling your way through the rain forests of Costa Rica, camping under the stars in Africa, or following in the footsteps of the ancient Inca as you backpack along the Inca trail to Machu Picchu. Turn these dreams of adventure into memories you will cherish forever by joining Adventure Travel Tours on one of our four new adventure tours.

To tell you more about these exciting new adventures, we are offering several presentations in your area. These presentations will focus on the features and cultures of the region. We will also show you pictures of the places you will visit and activities you can participate in, as well as a detailed agenda and package costs. Plan to attend one of the following presentations:

Date	Time
January 5 ----- 7:00 p.m. ---------	
February 3 ---- 7:30 p.m. ---------	
March 8 ------- 7:00 p.m. ---------	

In appreciation of your past patr[...] price of any of the new tour packages. [...] departure date. Please turn in this letter t[...]

Our vacation tours are profession[...] almost everything in the price of your t[...] dollar. All tours include these features:

- **Professional tour manager and**
- **All accommodations and meal[...]**
- **All entrance fees, excursions, t[...]**

We hope you will join us this ye[...] Your memories of fascinating places an[...] long, long time. For reservations, please[...] directly at 1-800-777-0004.

Announcing

New Adventure Travel Tours

Attention adventure travelers! Attend an Adventure Travel presentation to learn about some of the earth's greatest unspoiled habitats and find out how you can experience the adventure of a lifetime. This year we are introducing four new tours and offering you a unique opportunity to combine many different outdoor activities while exploring the world.

India Wildlife Adventure
Inca Trail to Machu Picchu
Safari in Tanzania
Costa Rica Rivers and Rain Forests

Presentation dates and times are January 5 at 7:00 p.m., February 3 at 7:30 p.m., and March 8 at 7:00 p.m. All presentations are held at convenient hotel locations. The hotels are located in downtown Los Angeles, in Santa Clara, and at the airport.

Call 1-800-777-0004 for presentation locations, a full color brochure, and itinerary information, costs, and trip dates.

Visit our
Web site at
www.AdventureTravelTours.com

A flyer incorporating many visual enhancements such as colored text, varied text styles, and graphic elements is both eye-catching and informative.

The beauty of a word processor is that you can make changes or corrections as you are typing. Want to change a report from single spacing to double spacing? Alter the width of the margins? Delete some paragraphs and add others from yet another document? A word processor allows you to do all these things with ease.

Word 2003 includes many group collaboration features to help streamline how documents are developed and changed by group members. You can also create and send e-mail messages directly from within Word using all its features to create and edit the message. In addition, you can send an entire document as your e-mail message, allowing the recipient to edit the document directly without having to open or save an attachment.

Word 2003 is closely integrated with the World Wide Web, detecting when you type a Web address and automatically converting it to a hyperlink. You can also create your own hyperlinks to locations within documents, or to other documents, including those at external locations such as a Web site or file server. Its many Web-editing features, including a Web Page Wizard that guides you step by step, help you quickly create a Web page.

Office Excel 2003

Office Excel 2003 is an electronic worksheet that is used to organize, manipulate, and graph numeric data. Once used almost exclusively by accountants, worksheets are now widely used by nearly every profession. Marketing professionals record and evaluate sales trends. Teachers record grades and calculate final grades. Personal trainers record the progress of their clients.

Excel includes many features that not only help you create a well-designed worksheet, but one that produces accurate results. Formatting features include visual enhancements such as varied text styles, colors, and graphics. Other features help you enter complex formulas and identify and correct formula errors. You can also produce a visual display of data in·the form of graphs or charts. As the values in the worksheet change, charts referencing those values automatically adjust to reflect the changes.

Excel also includes many advanced features and tools that help you perform what-if analysis and create different scenarios. And like all Office 2003 applications, it is easy to incorporate data created in one application into another. Two worksheets you will produce in Labs 2 and 3 of Excel are shown on the next page.

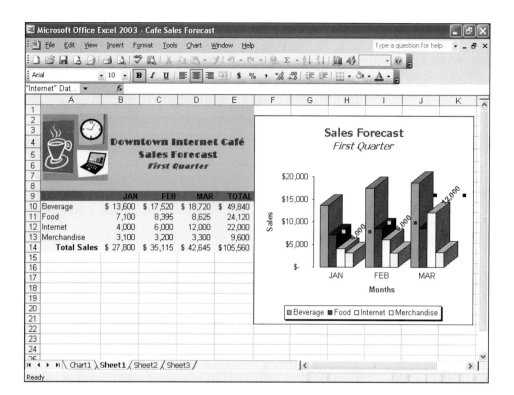

A worksheet showing the quarterly sales forecast containing a graphic, text enhancements, and a chart of the data is quickly created using basic Excel features.

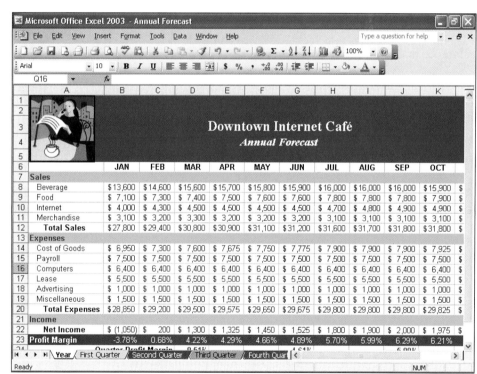

A large worksheet incorporating more complex formulas, visual enhancements such as colored text, varied text styles, and graphic elements is both informative and attractive.

You will see how easy it is to analyze data and make projections using what-if analysis and what-if graphing in Lab 3 and to incorporate Excel data in a Word document as shown in the following figures.

Changes you make in worksheet data while performing what-if analysis are automatically reflected in charts that reference that data.

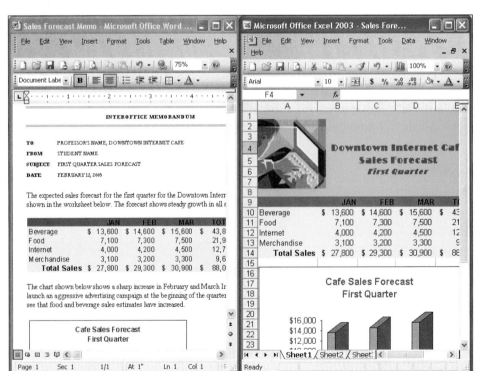

Worksheet data and charts can be copied and linked to other Office documents such as a Word document.

Office Access 2003

Office Access 2003 is a relational database management application that is used to create and analyze a database. A database is a collection of related data. In a relational database, the most widely used database structure, data is organized in linked tables. Tables consist of columns (called fields) and rows (called records). The tables are related or linked to one another by a common field. Relational databases allow you to create smaller and more manageable database tables, since you can combine and extract data between tables.

The program provides tools to enter, edit, and retrieve data from the database as well as to analyze the database and produce reports of the output. One of the main advantages of a computerized database is the ability to quickly add, delete, and locate specific records. Records can also be easily rearranged or sorted according to different fields of data, resulting in multiple table arrangements that provide more meaningful information for different purposes. Creation of forms makes it easier to enter and edit data as well. In the Access labs you will create and organize the database table shown below.

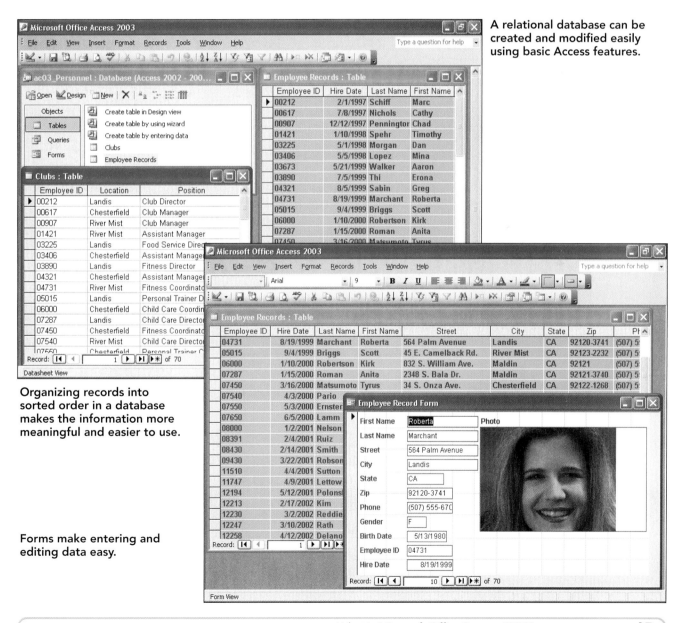

A relational database can be created and modified easily using basic Access features.

Organizing records into sorted order in a database makes the information more meaningful and easier to use.

Forms make entering and editing data easy.

Another feature is the ability to analyze the data in a table and perform calculations on different fields of data. Additionally, you can ask questions or query the table to find only certain records that meet specific conditions to be used in the analysis. Information that was once costly and time-consuming to get is now quickly and readily available. This information can then be quickly printed out in the form of reports ranging from simple listings to complex, professional-looking reports in different layout styles, or with titles, headings, subtotals, or totals.

A database can be queried to locate and display only specified information.

A professional-looking report can be quickly generated from information contained in a database.

Office PowerPoint 2003

Office PowerPoint 2003 is a graphics presentation program designed to help you produce a high-quality presentation that is both interesting to the audience and effective in its ability to convey your message. A presentation can be as simple as overhead transparencies or as sophisticated as an on-screen electronic display. In the first two PowerPoint labs you will create and organize the presentation shown on the next page.

A presentation consists of a series of pages or "slides" presenting the information you want to convey in an organized and attractive manner.

When running an on-screen presentation, each slide of the presentation is displayed full-screen on your computer monitor or projected onto a screen.

Office Outlook 2003

Office Outlook 2003 is a personal information manager (PIM) program that is designed to get you organized and keep you organized. PIMs, also known as desktop managers, are designed to maximize your personal productivity by making it efficient and easy to perform everyday tasks such as scheduling meetings, recording contact information, and communicating with others, to name a few. Outlook 2003 includes an integrated e-mail program, a calendar, and contact and task management features.

The opening Outlook window provides quick access to all the tools to keep you organized.

The Outlook calendar and scheduling component not only allow you to create an appointment, but will remind you of appointments by playing a sound or displaying a message.

Common Office 2003 Features

Additional Information

Please read the Before You Begin and Instructional Conventions sections in the Overview to Office PowerPoint 2003 (PPO.5) before starting this section.

Additional Information

It is assumed that you are already familiar with basic Windows operating system features. To review these features, refer to your Windows text or if available, the O'Leary Series *Introduction to Windows* text.

Now that you know a little about each of the applications in Microsoft Office 2003, we will take a look at some of the features that are common to all Office 2003 applications. This is a hands-on section that will introduce you to the features and allow you to get a feel for how Office 2003 works. Although Word 2003 will be used to demonstrate how the features work, only common features will be addressed. These features include using menus, Office Help, task panes, toolbars, and starting and exiting an application. The features that are specific to each application will be introduced individually in each application text.

Starting an Office 2003 Application

There are several ways to start an Office 2003 application. The two most common methods are by using the Start menu or by clicking a desktop shortcut for the program if it is available. If you use the Start menu, the steps will vary slightly depending on the version of Windows you are using.

1 • Click **start** to display the Start menu.

• Select All Programs.

Having Trouble?

If you are using Windows 2002 or earlier, select Programs.

• Select
  Microsoft Office ▶.

• Choose
  Microsoft Office Word 2003 .

OR

1 • Double-click the shortcut on the desktop.

2 • If necessary, click ☐ Maximize in the title bar to maximize the window.

Additional Information

Your window may appear with olive green or silver colors, depending upon the Windows settings on your computer.

Your screen should be similar to Figure 1

Figure 1

The Word program is started and displayed in a window on the desktop. The left end of the application window title bar displays the file name followed by the program name, Microsoft Office Word 2003. The right end of the title bar displays the ▬ Minimize, ⧉ Restore Down, and ☒ Close buttons. They perform the same functions and operate in the same way as all Windows versions.

The **menu bar** below the title bar displays the application's program menu. The right end displays the document window's ☒ Close Window button. As you use the Office applications, you will see that the menu bar contains many of the same menus, such as File, Edit, and Help. You will also see several menus that are specific to each application.

The **toolbars** located below the menu bar contain buttons that are mouse shortcuts for many of the menu items. Commonly, the Office applications will display two toolbars when the application is first opened: Standard and Formatting. They may appear together on one row (as in Figure 1), or on separate rows.

The large center area of the program window is the **document window** where open application files are displayed. Currently, there is a blank Word document open. In Word, the mouse pointer appears as I when positioned in the document window and as a ⇖ when it can be used to select items. The **task pane** is displayed on the right side of the document window. Task panes provide quick access to features as you are using the application. As you perform certain actions, different task panes automatically open. In this case, since you just started an application, the Getting Started task pane is automatically displayed, providing different ways to create a new document or open an existing document.

The **status bar** at the bottom of the window displays location information and the status of different settings as they are used. Different information is displayed in the status bar for different applications.

On the right and bottom of the document window, are vertical and horizontal scroll bars. A **scroll bar** is used with a mouse to bring additional lines of information into view in a window. The vertical scroll bar is used to move up or down, and the horizontal scroll bar moves side to side in the window.

As you can see, many of the features in the Word window are the same as in other Windows applications. The common user interface makes learning and using new applications much easier.

Using Menus

A menu is one of many methods you can use to accomplish a task in a program. When opened, a menu displays a list of commands. When an Office program menu is first opened, it may display a short version of commands. The short menu is a personalized version of the menu that displays basic and frequently used commands and hides those used less often. An expanded version will display automatically after the menu is open for a few seconds.

① Click **File** to open the File menu.

● Point to each menu in the menu bar to see the full menu for each.

Additional Information

Once one menu is expanded, others expand automatically until you choose a command or perform another action.

● Point to the **View** menu.

Your screen should be similar to Figure 2

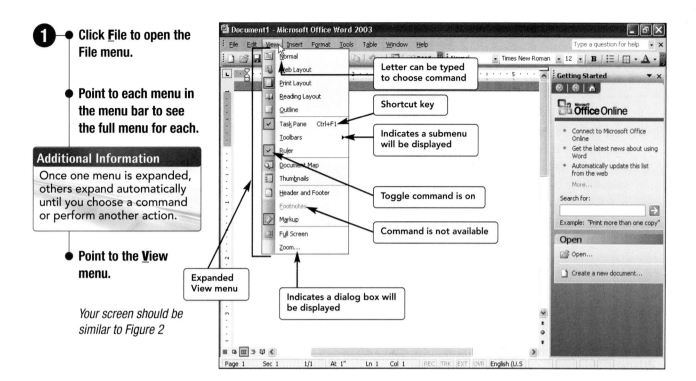

Figure 2

Additional Information

If you do not want to wait for the expanded menu to appear, you can click [⮟] at the bottom of the menu or double-click the menu name to display the full menu immediately.

Many commands have images next to them so you can quickly associate the command with the image. The same image appears on the toolbar button for that feature. Menus may include the following features (not all menus include all features):

Feature	Meaning
Ellipsis (…)	Indicates a dialog box will be displayed.
[▸]	Indicates a submenu will be displayed.
Dimmed	Indicates the command is not available for selection until certain other conditions are met.
Shortcut key	A key or key combination that can be used to execute a command without using the menu.
Checkmark	Indicates a toggle type of command. Selecting it turns the feature on or off. A checkmark indicates the feature is on.
Underlined letter	Indicates the letter you can type to choose the command.

Additional Information

If underlined command letters are not displayed, this feature is not active on your system.

On the View menu, two options, Task Pane and Ruler, are checked, indicating these features are on. The Task Pane option also displays the shortcut key combination, [Ctrl] + [F1], after the option. This indicates the command can be chosen by pressing the keys instead of using the menu. The Footnotes option is dimmed because it is not currently available. The Toolbars option will display a submenu when selected, and the Zoom command a dialog box of additional options.

Once a menu is open, you can select a command from the menu by pointing to it. A colored highlight bar, called the **selection cursor**, appears over the selected command.

Standard toolbar **Toolbar submenu** **Formatting toolbar**

2 ● **Point to the Toolbars command to select it and display the submenu.**

Your screen should be similar to Figure 3

Figure 3

Currently there are three selected (checked) Toolbar options: Standard, Formatting, and although not technically a toolbar, the Task Pane. If other toolbars are selected in your menu, this is because once a toolbar has been turned on, it remains on until turned off.

To choose a command, you click on it. When the command is chosen, the associated action is performed. You will close the task pane and any other open toolbars and display the Drawing toolbar.

3 • **Click on Task Pane to turn off this feature.**

• **Open the View menu again, select Toolbars, and if it is not already selected, click on the Drawing toolbar option to turn it on.**

• **If necessary, choose View/Toolbars again and deselect any other toolbar options (there should be 3 selected toolbar options).**

Your screen should be similar to Figure 4

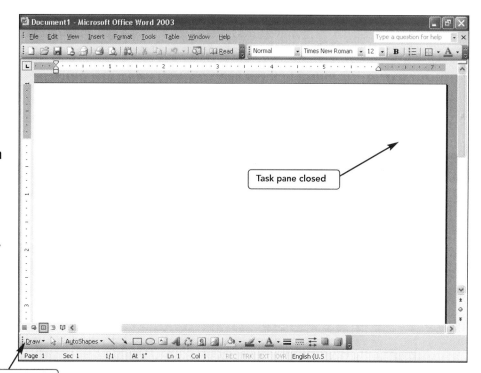

Task pane closed

Drawing toolbar displayed

Figure 4

The task pane is closed and the Drawing toolbar is displayed above the status bar. Any other toolbars that were open which you deselected are closed.

Using Shortcut Menus

Another way to access menu options is to use the **shortcut menu**. The shortcut menu is opened by right-clicking on an item on the screen. This menu displays only those options associated with the item. For example, right-clicking on any toolbar will display the toolbar menu options only. You will use this method to hide the Drawing toolbar again.

1 • **Point to the Drawing toolbar and right-click.**

Your screen should be similar to Figure 5

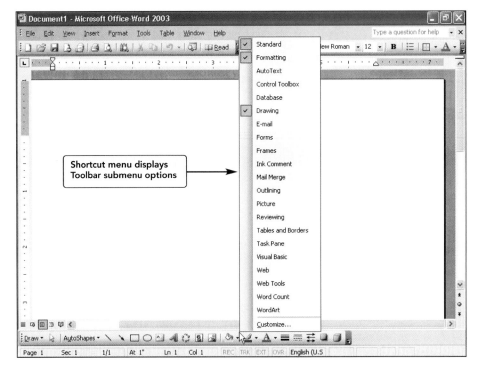

Shortcut menu displays Toolbar submenu options

Figure 5

Additional Information

The Customize option can be used to change features of toolbars and menus.

The shortcut menu displays only the Toolbar submenu options on the View menu. Using a shortcut menu saves time over selecting the main menu command sequence.

2 • **Choose Drawing to turn off this feature.**

Your screen should be similar to Figure 6

Drawing toolbar closed

Figure 6

The Drawing toolbar is no longer displayed.

Using Shortcut Keys

A third way to perform a command is to use the shortcut key or key combination associated with a particular command. If you will recall, the shortcut key associated with the **V**iew/Tas**k** Pane command is Ctrl + F1 . To use the key combination, you hold down the first key while pressing the second.

1 ─● Hold down Ctrl and press the F1 function key.

Your screen should be similar to Figure 7

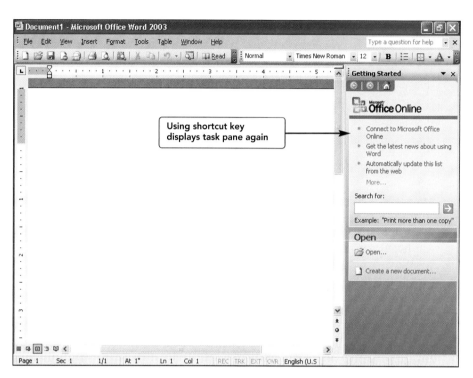

Using shortcut key displays task pane again

Figure 7

The task pane is displayed again. Using shortcut keys is the quickest way to perform many actions; however, you need to remember the key combination in order to use it.

Using Toolbars

Initially, Word displays two toolbars, Standard and Formatting, below the menu bar (see Figure 3). The **Standard toolbar** contains buttons that are used to complete the most frequently used menu commands. The **Formatting toolbar** contains buttons that are used to change the appearance or format of the document. There are many features that can be used to make working with toolbars easier.

Displaying Toolbars on Separate Rows

The default toolbar arrangement is to display both toolbars on one row. Because there is not enough space to display all the buttons on both toolbars on a single row, many buttons are hidden. The Toolbar Options button located at the end of a toolbar displays a drop-down button list of those buttons that are not displayed. Toolbars initially display the basic buttons. Like menus, they are personalized automatically, displaying those buttons you use frequently and hiding others. When you use a button from this list, it then is moved to the toolbar, and a button that has not been used recently is moved to the Toolbar Options list. It also contains an option to display the toolbars on separate rows. You will use this option to quickly see all the toolbar buttons.

1 ● Click Toolbar Options.

● Choose S**h**ow Buttons on Two Rows.

Toolbars displayed on two rows

Toolbar options button

Figure 8

Another Method

You can also use **T**ools/**C**ustomize/**O**ptions, or choose **C**ustomize/**O**ptions from the toolbar shortcut menu and select "Show Standard and Formatting toolbars on two rows."

Your screen should be similar to Figure 8

Additional Information

The Add or Remove Buttons option allows you to customize existing toolbars by selecting those buttons you want to display and by creating your own customized toolbars.

The two toolbars now occupy separate rows, providing enough space for all the buttons to be displayed. Now using Toolbar Options is no longer necessary, and when selected only displays the options to return the toolbars display to one row and the Add or Remove Buttons option.

When a toolbar is open, it may appear docked or floating. A **docked toolbar** is fixed to an edge of the window and displays a vertical bar, called the move handle, on the left edge of the toolbar. Dragging this bar up or down allows you to move the toolbar. If multiple toolbars share the same row, dragging the bar left or right adjusts the size of the toolbar. If docked, a toolbar can occupy a row by itself, or several can be on a row together. A **floating toolbar** appears in a separate window and can be moved anywhere on the desktop.

2 ● Point to the move handle of the Standard toolbar and, when the mouse pointer appears as ✛, drag the toolbar into the document window.

Your screen should be similar to Figure 9

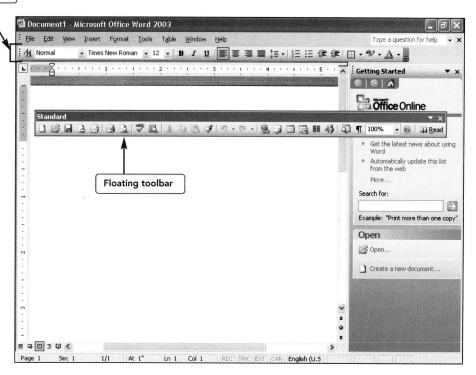

Docked toolbar

Floating toolbar

Figure 9

The Standard toolbar is now a floating toolbar and can be moved to any location in the window by dragging the title bar. If you move a floating toolbar to the edge of the window, it will attach to that location and become a docked toolbar. A floating toolbar can also be sized by dragging the edge of toolbar.

3 ● Drag the title bar of the floating toolbar (the mouse pointer appears as ✛) to move the toolbar to the row below the Formatting toolbar.

● Move the Formatting toolbar below the Standard toolbar.

● Align both toolbars with the left edge of the window by dragging the move handle horizontally.

Your screen should be similar to Figure 10

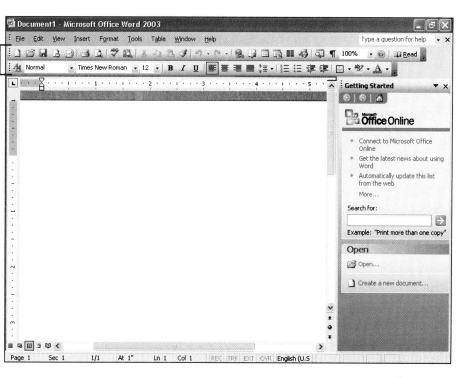

Toolbars docked and displayed on two rows again

Figure 10

The two toolbars again occupy two rows. To quickly identify the toolbar buttons, you can display the button name by pointing to the button.

4 ● **Point to any button on the Standard toolbar.**

Your screen should be similar to Figure 11

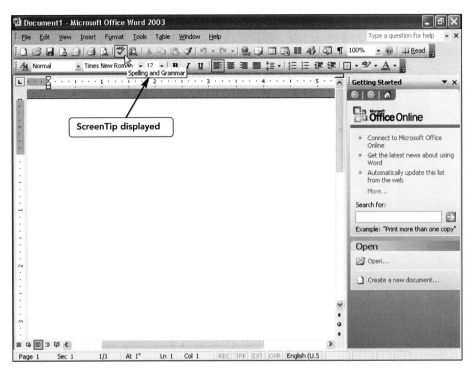

ScreenTip displayed

Figure 11

A ScreenTip containing the button name appears next to the mouse pointer. Clicking on a button will perform the associated action. You will use the ⊚ Help button to access Microsoft Word Help.

Accesses Word Help

Click title bar to open task pane menu

5 ● **Click ⊚ Microsoft Office Word Help.**

Another Method
You can also choose **H**elp/ Microsoft Office Word **H**elp, or press F1 to access Help.

Your screen should be similar to Figure 12

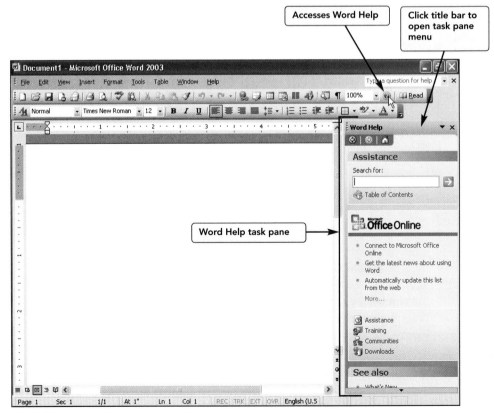

Word Help task pane

Figure 12

The Getting Started task pane is replaced by the Microsoft Word Help task pane. The name of the task pane appears in the task pane title bar.

Using Task Panes

Additional Information

You can drag the pane divider line to adjust the width of the pane. When there is more information in the pane than can be displayed, [▲] and [▼] appear to scroll the information into view.

Task panes appear automatically when certain features are used. They can also be opened manually from the task pane menu. Clicking the task pane title bar displays a drop-down menu of other task panes you can select. In Word there are 14 different task panes. You will redisplay the Getting Started task pane. Then you will quickly return to the previously displayed task pane using the ⊕ Back toolbar button in the task pane.

1 ● Click on the task pane title bar.

Word Help ▼

- Getting Started
- ✓ Help
- Search Results
- Clip Art
- Research
- Clipboard
- New Document
- Shared Workspace
- Document Updates
- Protect Document
- Styles and Formatting
- Reveal Formatting
- Mail Merge
- XML Structure

● Choose Getting Started.

Another Method

You can also click the 🏠 Home button to quickly display the Getting Started task pane.

● Click ⊕ Back.

Your screen should be similar to Figure 13

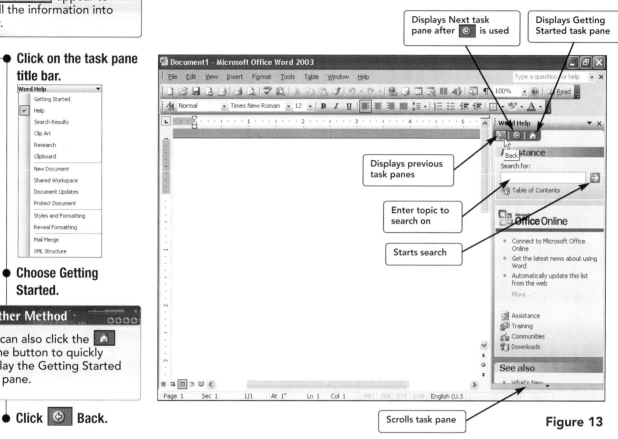

Displays Next task pane after ⊕ is used

Displays Getting Started task pane

Displays previous task panes

Enter topic to search on

Starts search

Scrolls task pane

Figure 13

The Help task pane is displayed again. Likewise, clicking the ⊕ Forward button will display the task pane that was viewed before using ⊕ Back.

Using Office Help

Additional Information

Although you can also simply enter a word or phrase in the Search box, the best results occur when you type a complete sentence or question.

There are several ways you can get help. One method is to conduct a search of the available help information by entering a sentence or question you want help on in the Search text box of the Help task pane. Notice the insertion point is positioned in the Search text box. This indicates it is ready for you to type an entry. You will use this method to learn about getting Help while you work.

1 • Type **How do I get help?** in the Search box.

Having Trouble?
If the insertion point is not displayed in the Search box, simply click in the box to activate it.

• Click ➡ Start Searching.

Your screen should be similar to Figure 14

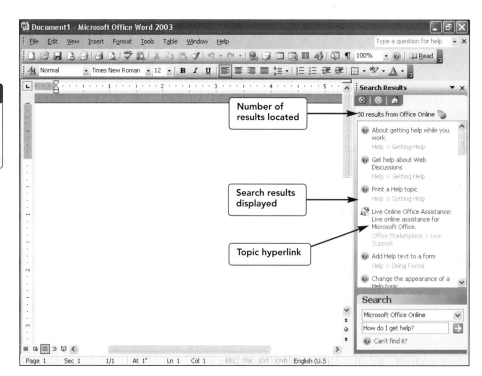

Number of results located

Search results displayed

Topic hyperlink

Figure 14

Additional Information
In addition to being connected to the Internet, the Online Content settings must be selected. Click Online Content Settings in the Help task pane and select all the options to turn on these features.

Additional Information
The number of results located and where they were found is displayed at the top of the list.

If you are connected to the Internet, the Microsoft Office Online Web site is searched and the results are displayed in the Search Results task pane. If you are not connected, the offline help information that is provided with the application and stored on your computer is searched. Generally the search results are similar, but fewer in number.

The Search Results pane displays a list of located results. The results are shown in order of relevance, with the most likely matches at the top of the list. Each result is a **hyperlink** or connection to the information located on the Online site or in Help on your computer. Clicking the hyperlink accesses and displays the information associated with the hyperlink.

You want to read the information in the topic "About getting help while you work."

2 • From the Search Results list click the "About getting help while you work" hyperlink.

Additional Information
When you point to the hyperlink, it appears underlined and the mouse pointer appears as 🖑.

Your screen should be similar to Figure 15

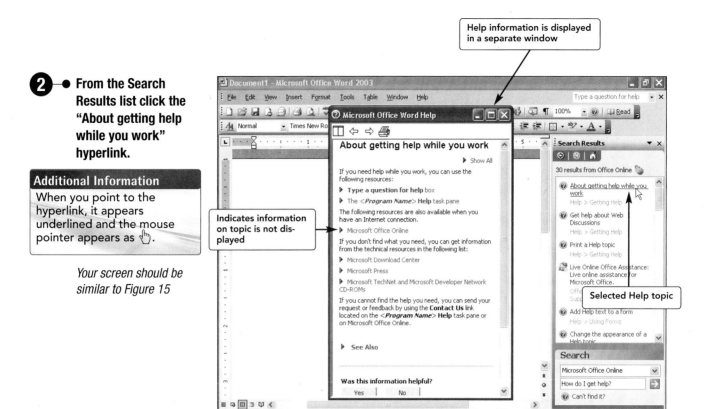

Figure 15

The information on the selected topic is displayed in a separate Help window. The Help window on your screen will probably be a different size and arrangement than in Figure 15. Depending on the size of your Help window, you may need to scroll the window to see all the Help information provided. As you are reading the help topic, you will see many subtopics preceded with ▶. This indicates the information in the subtopic is not displayed. Clicking on the subtopic heading displays the information about the topic.

3 • If necessary, use the
scroll bar to scroll the
Help window to see
the information on this
topic.

• Scroll back up to the
top of the window.

Additional Information
Clicking the scroll arrows
scrolls the text in the window
line by line, and dragging the
scroll bar up or down moves
to a general location within
the window area.

• Click the "Type a
question for help box"
subtopic.

• Click the "The
<Program name> Help
task pane" subtopic.

• Read the information
on both subtopics.

*Your screen should be
similar to Figure 16*

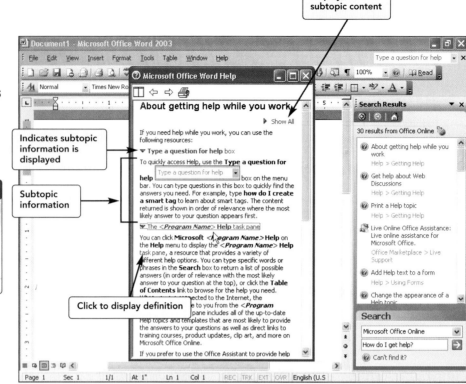

Figure 16

The ▶ preceding the subtopic has changed to ▼ indicating the subtopic
content is displayed. The selected subtopics provide information about
accessing Help using the "Type a question for help" box and the Help task
pane. Notice the blue words "task pane" within the subtopic content. This
indicates that clicking on the text will display a definition of the term. You
can continue to click on the subtopic headings to display the information
about each topic individually, or you can click Show All to display all the
available topic information.

4 Click "task pane" to see the definition.

● Click Show All at the top of the Help window.

● Scroll the window to see the Microsoft Office Online subtopic.

● Read the information on this subtopic.

Your screen should be similar to Figure 17

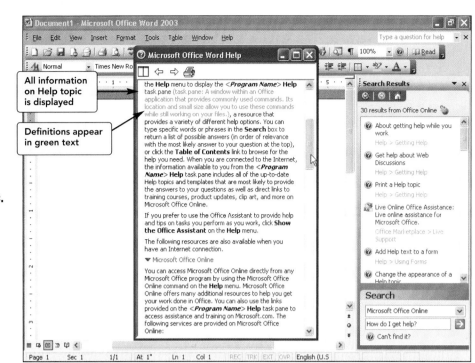

Figure 17

The information under all the subtopics is fully displayed, including definitions.

Using the Help Table of Contents

Another source of help is to use the Help table of contents. Using this method allows you to browse the Help topics to locate topics of interest to you.

1 Click ✕ Close in the Help window title bar to close the Help window.

● Click ⊕ Back in the task pane.

● Click Table of Contents (below the Search box).

Your screen should be similar to Figure 18

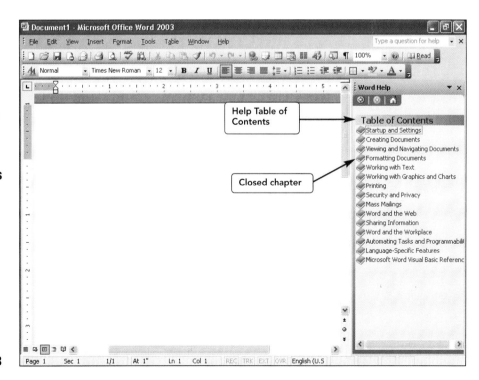

Figure 18

The entire Word Help Table of Contents is displayed in the Help task pane. Clicking on an item preceded with a 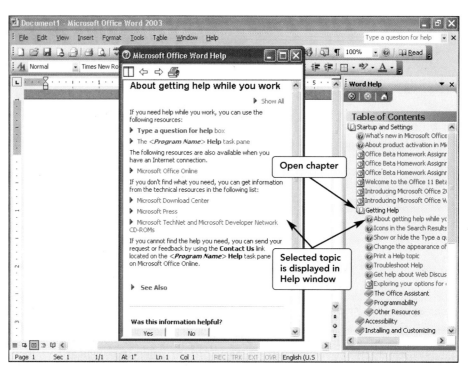 Closed Book icon opens a chapter, which expands to display additional chapters or topics. The 📖 Open Book icon identifies those chapters that are open. Clicking on an item preceded with 📄 displays the specific Help information.

2 ● Click "Startup and Settings" to open this chapter.

● Click "Getting Help."

● Click "About getting help while you work."

Additional Information

Pointing to an item in the Table of Contents that is not entirely visible in the pane displays a ScreenTip of the entire topic heading.

Your screen should be similar to Figure 19

Figure 19

The Help window opens again and displays the information on the selected topic. To close a chapter, click the 📖 icon.

Exiting an Office 2003 Application

Now you are ready to close the Help window and exit the Word program. The Exit command on the File menu can be used to quit most Windows programs. Alternatively, you can click the ⊠ Close button in the program window title bar.

1 ● Click ⊠ Close in the Help window title bar to close the Help window.

● Click ⊠ Close in the Task pane title bar to close the task pane.

Another Method

You could also use Ctrl + F1 to close a task pane.

● Click ⊠ Close in the Word window title bar to exit Word.

The program window is closed and the desktop is visible again.

lab review

Introduction to Microsoft Office 2003

key terms

docked toolbar   I.18

document window   I.12

floating toolbar   I.18

Formatting toolbar   I.17

hyperlink   I.22

menu bar   I.12

scroll bar   I.12

selection cursor   I.14

shortcut menu   I.15

Standard toolbar   I.17

status bar   I.12

task pane   I.12

toolbar   I.12

command summary

Command	Shortcut Key	Button	Voice	Action
start /All Programs				Opens program menu
File/E**x**it	Alt + F4	✕		Exits Office program
View/**T**oolbars			View toolbars	Hides or displays toolbars
View/Tas**k** Pane	Ctrl + F1		Task pane Show task pane View task pane Hide task pane	Hides or displays task pane
Tools/**C**ustomize/**O**ptions				Changes settings associated with toolbars and menus
Help/Microsoft Word **H**elp	F1	②		Opens Help window

lab exercises

step-by-step

Using an Office Application ★

1. All Office 2003 applications have a common user interface. You will explore the Excel 2003 application and use many of the same features you learned about while using Word 2003 in this lab.

    a. Use the Start menu or a shortcut icon on your desktop to start Office Excel 2003. Close the Getting Started Task Pane.

    b. What shape is the mouse pointer when positioned in the document window area? _____

    c. Excel also has nine menus. Which menu is not the same as in Word? _____ Open the Tools Menu. How many commands in the Tools menu will display a submenu when selected? _____ How many commands are listed in the Formula Auditing submenu? _____

    d. Click on a blank space near the Formatting toolbar to open the toolbar shortcut menu. How many toolbars are available in Excel? _____

    e. Display the Chart toolbar. Dock the Chart toolbar above the Status bar. Change it to a floating toolbar. Close the Chart toolbar.

    f. Use the shortcut key combination to display the Task Pane. How many Task Panes are available? _____

    g. Display the Help Task Pane and search for help information on "worksheet." How many search results were returned? _____ Read the "About viewing workbooks and worksheets" topic. What is the definition of a worksheet? _____
    _____

    h. Close the Help window. Close the Excel window to exit the program.

on your own

Exploring Microsoft Help ★

1. In addition to the Help information you used in this lab, Office 2003 Online Help also includes many interactive tutorials. Selecting a Help topic that starts a tutorial will open the browser program on your computer. Both audio and written instructions are provided. You will use one of these tutorials to learn more about using Office 2003. Start Word 2003 and search for Help on "shortcut keys." Then select the "Work with the Keyboard in Office" topic. Follow the directions in the tutorial to learn about this feature. When you are done, close the browser window and the Word window.

Overview of Microsoft Office PowerPoint 2003

What Is a Presentation Program?

You are in a panic! Tomorrow you are to make a presentation to an audience and you want it to be good. To the rescue comes a powerful tool: graphics presentation programs. These programs are designed to help you create an effective presentation, whether to the board of directors of your company or to your fellow classmates. An effective presentation gets your point across clearly and in an interesting manner.

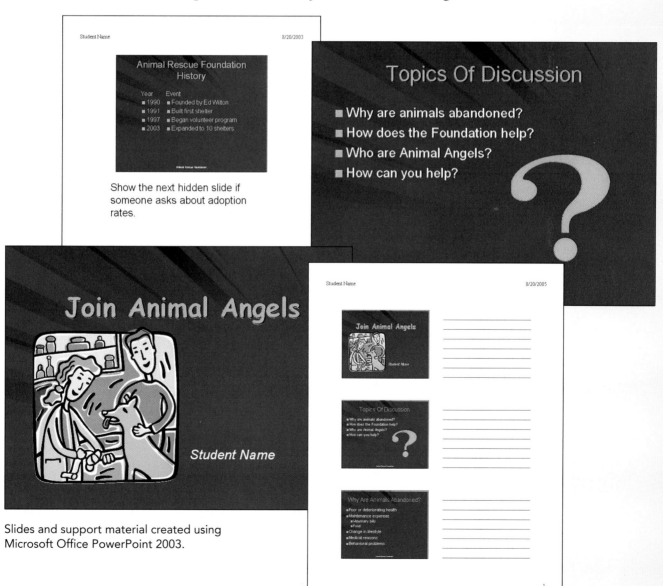

Slides and support material created using Microsoft Office PowerPoint 2003.

Graphics presentation programs are designed to help you produce a high-quality presentation that is both interesting to the audience and effective in its ability to convey your message. A presentation can be as simple as overhead transparencies or as sophisticated as an onscreen electronic display. Graphics presentation programs can produce black-and-white or color overhead transparencies, 35mm slides, onscreen electronic presentations called screen shows, Web pages for Web use, and support materials for both the speaker and the audience.

The graphics presentation program includes features such as text handling, outlining, graphing, drawing, animations, clip art, and multimedia support. With a few keystrokes, the user can quickly change, correct, and update the presentation. In addition, graphics presentation programs suggest layouts for different types of presentations and offer professionally designed templates to help you produce a presentation that is sure to keep your audience's attention.

Office PowerPoint 2003 Features

Creating an effective presentation is a complicated process. Graphics presentation programs help simplify this process by providing assistance in the content development phase, as well as in the layout and design phase. In addition, these programs produce the support materials you can use when making a presentation to an audience.

The content development phase includes deciding on the topic of your presentation, the organization of the content, and the ultimate message you want to convey to the audience. As an aid in this phase, PowerPoint 2003 helps you organize your thoughts based on the type of presentation you are making. Several common types of presentations sell a product or idea, suggest a strategy, or report on the progress of a program. Based on the type of presentation, the program suggests ideas and organization tips. For example, if you are making a presentation on the progress of a sales campaign, the program would suggest that you enter text on the background of the sales campaign as the first page, called a slide; the current status of the campaign as the next slide; and accomplishments, schedule, issues and problems, and where you are heading on subsequent slides.

The layout for each slide is the next important decision. Again, PowerPoint 2003 helps you by suggesting text layout features such as title placement, bullets, and columns. You can also incorporate graphs of data, tables, organizational charts, clip art, and other special text effects in the slides.

PowerPoint 2003 also includes professionally designed templates to further enhance the appearance of your slides. These templates include features that standardize the appearance of all the slides in your presentation. Professionally selected combinations of text and background colors, common typefaces and sizes, borders, and other art designs take the worry out of much of the design layout.

After you have written and designed the slides, you can then have the slides made into black-and-white or color overhead transparencies or 35mm slides. Alternatively, you can use the slides in an onscreen electronic presentation or a Web page for use on the Web. An electronic presentation uses the computer to display the slides on an overhead projection screen. When you use this type of presentation, many programs also include a rehearsal feature, allowing you to practice and time your presentation. The length of time to display each slide can be set and your entire presentation can be completed within the allotted time. A presentation can be modified to display on a Web site and to run using a Web browser.

Finally, with PowerPoint 2003 you can also print out the materials you have created. You can print an outline of the text showing the titles of the slides and main text but not the art. The outline allows you to check the organizational logic of your presentation. You can also print speaker notes to which you can refer to while making your presentation. These notes generally consist of a small printout of each slide with any notes on topics you want to discuss while the slides are displayed. Finally, you can create printed handouts of the slides for the audience. The audience can refer to the slide and make notes on the handout page as you speak.

Case Study for Office PowerPoint 2003 Labs

You have volunteered at the Animal Rescue Foundation, a nonprofit organization that rescues unwanted animals from local animal shelters and finds foster homes for them until a suitable adoptive family can be found. With your computer skills, you have been asked to create a powerful and persuasive presentation to entice the community to volunteer.

The organization has recently purchased the graphics presentation program Microsoft Office PowerPoint 2003. You will use this application to create the presentation.

Lab 1: You use PowerPoint to enter and edit the text for your presentation. You also learn how to reorganize the presentation and enhance it with different text attributes and by adding a picture. Finally, you learn how to run a slide show and print handouts.

Lab 2: You learn about many more features to enhance the appearance of your slides. These include changing the slide design and color scheme and adding clip art, animation, and sound. You also learn how to add transition effects to make the presentation more interesting. Finally, you create speaker notes to help you keep your cool during the presentation.

Working Together: Demonstrates the sharing of information between applications. First you learn how to copy and embed a table created in Word into a slide. Then you learn how to link a chart created in Excel to another slide.

Before You Begin

To the Student

The following assumptions have been made:

- The Microsoft Office PowerPoint 2003 program has been installed on your computer system.

- You have the data files needed to complete the series of PowerPoint 2003 Labs and practice exercises. These may be supplied by your instructor and are also available at the online learning center Web site found at www.mhhe.com/oleary.

- You have completed the McGraw-Hill Windows Labs or you are already familiar with how to use Windows and a mouse.

To the Instructor

It is assumed that the complete version of the program has been installed prior to students using the labs. In addition, please be aware that the following settings are assumed to be in effect for the PowerPoint 2003 program. These assumptions are necessary so that the screens and directions in the text are accurate.

- The Getting Started task pane is displayed on startup (use Tools/Options/View).

- The status bar is displayed (use Tools/Options/View).

- The vertical ruler is displayed (use Tools/Options/View).

- The Paste Options buttons are displayed (use Tools/Options/Edit).

- The Standard, Formatting, Drawing, and Outlining toolbars are on (use Tools/Customize/Toolbars).

- The Standard and Formatting toolbars are displayed on separate rows (use Tools/Customize/Options).

- Full menus are always displayed (use Tools/Customize/Options).

- The Office Assistant feature is enabled but not on (right-click on the Assistant, choose Options, and clear the Use the Office Assistant option).

- Normal view is on (use View/Normal).

- The Clip Organizer is installed on the local disk or network.

- The automatic spelling check feature is on (use Tools/Options/Spelling and Style/Check spelling as you type).

- The style check feature is off (use Tools/Options/Spelling and Style and clear the Check Style option).

- All the options in the View tab are selected (use Tools/Options/View).

- All slide design templates have been installed.

- The feature to access Online Help is on (choose Online Content Settings from the Help task pane and select the Show content and links from Microsoft Office Online option).

In addition, all figures in the manual reflect the use of a standard VGA display monitor set at 800 by 600. If another monitor setting is used, it may display more or fewer lines of text displayed in the windows than in the figures. This setting can be changed using Windows setup.

Microsoft Office Language Bar

The Microsoft Office Language bar may be displayed when you start the application. Commonly, it will appear in the title bar, however, it may appear in other locations depending upon your setup. The Language bar provides buttons to access and use the Speech Recognition and Hand-writing recognition features of Office. To display the Language bar, choose Toolbars/Language bar from the Taskbar Shortcut menu.

Instructional Conventions

Hands-on instructions that you are to perform appear as a sequence of numbered steps. Within each step, a series of bullets identifies the specific actions that must be performed. Step numbering begins over within each topic heading throughout the lab.

Command sequences that you are to issue appear following the word "Choose." Each menu command selection is separated by a /. If the menu command can be selected by typing a letter of the command, the letter will appear underlined and bold. Items that need to be selected will follow the word "Select" and will appear in black text. You can select items with the mouse or directional keys. (See Example A.)

Example A

1 Choose **File/Open.**

Select 3½ Floppy (A:) from the Look In drop-down list.

Commands that can be initiated using a button and the mouse appear following the word "Click." The icon (and the icon name if the icon does not include text) is displayed following "Click." The menu equivalent, keyboard shortcut and/or voice command appear in an Another Method margin note when the action is first introduced. (See Example B.)

Example B

1 Click 🗁 Open.

> **Another Method**
>
> The menu equivalent is **File/Open,** the keyboard shortcut is Ctrl + O, and the voice command is "Open."

Plain blue text identifies file names. Information you are asked to type appears in blue and bold. (See Example C.)

Example C

1 Click Open.

Select Volunteer.

2 Move to slide 1.

Type How Do I become an Animal Angel?.

Creating a Presentation

LAB 1

Objectives

After completing this lab, you will know how to:

1 Use the AutoContent wizard to create a presentation.

2 View and edit a presentation.

3 Save, close, and open a presentation.

4 Check spelling.

5 Delete, move, and insert slides.

6 Size and move placeholders.

7 Run a slide show.

8 Change fonts and formatting.

9 Insert pictures and clip art.

10 Preview and print a presentation.

Case Study

Animal Rescue Foundation

You are the Volunteer Coordinator at the local Animal Rescue Foundation. This nonprofit organization rescues unwanted pets from local animal shelters and finds foster homes for them until a suitable adoptive family can be found. The agency has a large volunteer group called the Animal Angels that provides much-needed support for the foundation.

The agency director has decided to launch a campaign to increase community awareness about the Foundation. As part of the promotion, you have been asked to create a powerful and persuasive presentation to entice more members of the community to join Animal Angels.

The agency director has asked you to preview the presentation at the weekly staff meeting tomorrow and has asked you to present a draft of the presentation by noon today.

Although we would all like to think that our message is the core of the presentation, the presentation materials we use can determine whether the message reaches the audience. To help you create the presentation, you will use Microsoft Office PowerPoint 2003, a graphics presentation application that is designed to create presentation materials such as slides, overheads, and handouts. Using Office PowerPoint 2003, you can create a high-quality and interesting onscreen presentation with pizzazz that will dazzle your audience.

© Andy Sotiriou/Getty Images

Each main topic in your presentation should have a supporting slide with a title and bulleted points.

The presentation can be reorganized easily by adding, deleting, and moving slides.

Enhance the presentation with the addition of graphics and text colors.

Concept Preview

The following concepts will be introduced in this lab:

1. **Template**   A template is a file containing predefined settings that can be used as a pattern to create many common types of presentations.

2. **Presentation Style**   A PowerPoint presentation can be made using five different styles: onscreen presentations, Web presentations, black-and-white or color overheads, and 35mm slides.

3. **Slide**   A slide is an individual "page" of your presentation.

4. **AutoCorrect**   The AutoCorrect feature makes some basic assumptions about the text you are typing and, based on these assumptions, automatically corrects the entry.

5. **Spelling Checker**   The spelling checker locates all misspelled words, duplicate words, and capitalization irregularities as you create and edit a presentation, and proposes possible corrections.

6. **Layout**   The layout controls the way items are arranged on a slide.

7. **Font and Font Size**   A font, also commonly referred to as a typeface, is a set of characters with a specific design. Each font has one or more sizes.

8. **Graphics**   A graphic is a non-text element or object, such as a drawing or picture, that can be added to a slide.

9. **Stacking Order**   Stacking order is the order in which objects are inserted into different layers of the slide.

Introducing Office PowerPoint 2003

The Animal Rescue Foundation has just installed the latest version of the Microsoft Office Suite of applications, Office 2003, on their computers. You will use the graphics presentation program, Microsoft Office PowerPoint 2003, included in the office suite to create your presentation. Using this program, you should have no problem creating the presentation in time for tomorrow's staff meeting.

Starting Office PowerPoint 2003

Figure 1.1

① ● **Start the Office PowerPoint 2003 application.**

Having Trouble?

See "Introduction to Office System 2003" for information on starting the application and for a discussion of features that are common to all Office 2003 applications.

Your screen should be similar to Figure 1.1

Additional Information

Because the Office 2003 applications remember settings that were on when the program was last exited, you screen may look slightly different.

Additional Information

If you have installed the Speech Recognition feature the voice command to display toolbars is "View Toolbars" and to display the task pane is "Task pane."

The PowerPoint application window is displayed. The menu bar below the title bar displays the PowerPoint program menu. It consists of nine menus that provide access to the commands and features you will use to create and modify a presentation.

Located below the menu bar are the Standard and Formatting toolbars. The Standard toolbar contains buttons that are used to complete the most frequently used menu commands. The Formatting toolbar contains buttons that are used to change the appearance or format of the document. The **Drawing toolbar** is displayed along the bottom edge of the window. It contains buttons that are used to enhance text and create shapes. In addition, the **Outlining toolbar** may be displayed along the left edge of the window. It is used to enter and modify the content of the presentation. PowerPoint 2003 has 13 different toolbars. Many of the toolbars appear automatically as you use different features. Other toolbars may be displayed if they were on when the program was last exited.

② ● **If necessary, make the following changes to your screen to make it look like Figure 1.1:**

- **Use View/Toolbars and select or deselect the appropriate toolbar to display or hide it. There should be four toolbars displayed.**

- **The Standard, Formatting, Drawing and Outlining toolbars should be displayed.**

- **If your task pane is not displayed, choose View/Task Pane.**

The large area containing the blank slide is the **workspace** where your presentations are displayed as you create and edit them. Because you just started the program, the Getting Started task pane is automatically displayed on the right side of the window. It is used to open an existing presentation or create new presentations. The status bar at the bottom of the PowerPoint window displays messages and information about various PowerPoint settings.

Developing New Presentations

During your presentation you will present information about the Animal Rescue Foundation and why someone should want to join the Animal Angels volunteer group. As you prepare to create a new presentation, you should follow several basic steps: plan, create, edit, enhance, and rehearse.

Step	Description
Plan	The first step in planning a presentation is to understand its purpose. You also need to find out the length of time you have to speak, who the audience is, what type of room you will be in, and what kind of audiovisual equipment is available. These factors help to determine the type of presentation you will create.
Create	To begin creating your presentation, develop the content by typing your thoughts or notes into an outline. Each main idea in your presentation should have a supporting slide with a title and bulleted points.
Edit	While typing, you are will probably make typing and spelling errors that need to be corrected. This is one type of editing. Another type is to revise the content of what you have entered to make it clearer, or to add or delete information. To do this, you might insert a slide, add or delete bulleted items, or move text to another location.
Enhance	You want to develop a presentation that grabs and holds the audience's attention. Choose a design that gives your presentation some dazzle. Wherever possible add graphics to replace or enhance text. Add effects that control how a slide appears and disappears, and that reveal text in a bulleted list one bullet at a time.
Rehearse	Finally, you should rehearse the delivery of your presentation. For a professional presentation, your delivery should be as polished as your materials. Use the same equipment that you will use when you give the presentation. Practice advancing from slide to slide and then back in case someone asks a question. If you have a mouse available, practice pointing or drawing on the slide to call attention to key points.

After rehearsing your presentation, you may find that you want to go back to the editing phase. You may change text, move bullets, or insert a new slide. Periodically, as you make changes, rehearse the presentation again to see how the changes affect your presentation. By the day of the presentation, you will be confident about your message and at ease with the materials.

During the planning phase, you have spoken with the Foundation director regarding the purpose of the presentation and the content in general. The purpose of your presentation is to educate members of the community about the organization and to persuade many to volunteer. In addition, you want to impress the director by creating a professional presentation.

Creating a Presentation

When you first start PowerPoint, a new blank presentation is opened. It is like a blank piece of paper that already has many predefined settings. These settings, called **default** settings, are generally the most commonly used settings and are stored as a presentation template.

Concept 1
Template

1   A **template** is a file containing predefined settings that can be used as a pattern to create many common types of presentations. Every PowerPoint presentation is based on a template. The default settings for a basic blank presentation are stored in the default design template file. Whenever you create a new presentation using this template, the same default settings are used.

Many other templates that are designed to help you create professional-looking presentations are also available within PowerPoint and in the Microsoft Office Template Gallery on the Microsoft Office Web site. They include design templates, which provide a design concept, fonts, and color scheme; and content templates, which suggest content for your presentation based on the type of presentation you are making. You can also design and save your own presentation templates.

The Getting Started task pane is used to specify how you want to start using the PowerPoint program. It provides a variety of ways to start a new presentation or to open an existing presentation. More options for starting a new presentation are available in the New Presentation task pane.

1 ● **Click Create a new presentation in the Getting Started task pane.**

Another Method

You could also select the task pane to open from the Other Task Panes drop-down menu.

Your screen should be similar to Figure 1.2

Figure 1.2

Four methods can be used to create a presentation. The first method is to start with a blank presentation that has minimal design elements and add your own content and design changes. Another is to use one of the many design templates as the basis for your new presentation. The third method is to use the AutoContent wizard. A **wizard** is an interactive approach that guides you through the process of performing many complicated tasks. The AutoContent wizard creates a presentation that contains suggested content and design based on the answers you provide. Finally, you can use an existing presentation as the base for your new presentation by making the design or content changes you want for the new presentation.

Using the AutoContent Wizard

Because this is your first presentation created using PowerPoint, you decide to use the AutoContent wizard.

2 ● **From the New Presentation task pane, select From AutoContent wizard.**

Your screen should be similar to Figure 1.3

Figure 1.3

The opening dialog box of the AutoContent wizard briefly describes how the feature works. As the AutoContent wizard guides you through creating the presentation, it shows your progress through the steps in the outline on the left side of the dialog box. The green box identifies the current step.

2 ● Click [Next >].

Additional Information

You can also click the outline box on the left side to move directly to any step.

Your screen should be similar to Figure 1.4

Figure 1.4

In the Presentation Type step, you are asked to select the type of presentation you are creating. PowerPoint offers 24 different types of presentations, each with a different recommended content and design. Each type is indexed under a category. Currently, only the names of the six presentation types in the General category appear in the list box. You will use the Generic presentation option.

3 ● Click on each category button to see the different presentation types in each category.

● Select Generic from the General category.

Additional Information

The Generic option is also available under the All category.

● Click [Next >].

Your screen should be similar to Figure 1.5

Figure 1.5

In the Presentation Style step, you select the type of output your presentation will use.

Concept 2
Presentation Style

2 A PowerPoint presentation can be made using five different styles: onscreen presentations, Web presentations, black-and-white or color overheads, and 35mm slides. The type of equipment that is available to you will affect the style of presentation that you create.

If you have computer projection equipment that displays the current monitor image on a screen, you should create a full-color onscreen presentation. You can also design your onscreen presentation specifically for the World Wide Web, where a browser serves as the presentation tool. Often you will have access only to an overhead projector, in which case you can create color or black-and-white transparencies. Most laser printers will print your overheads directly on plastic transparencies, or you can print your slides and have transparencies made at a copy center. If you have access to a slide projector, you may want to use 35mm slides. You can send your presentation to a service bureau that will create the slides for you.

The room in which you will be using to make your presentation is equipped with computer projection equipment, so you will create an onscreen presentation. The Wizard selects the color scheme best suited to the type of output you select. Because On-screen Presentation is the default selection, you will accept it and move to the next step.

4 ➞ • **Click** .

Your screen should be similar to Figure 1.6

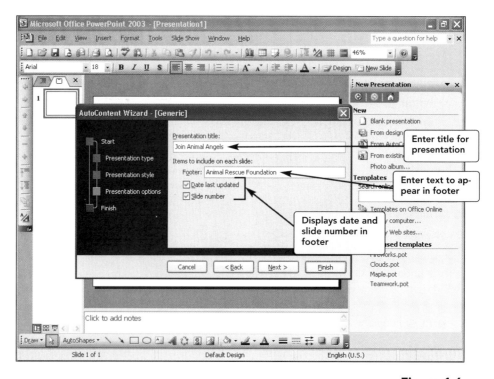

Figure 1.6

In the Presentation Options step, you are asked to enter some basic information that will appear on the title slide and in the footer of each slide in the presentation.

Concept 3

Slide

3 A **slide** is an individual "page" of your presentation. The first slide of a presentation is the title slide which is used to introduce your presentation. Additional slides are used to support each main point in your presentation. The slides give the audience a visual summary of the words you speak, which helps them understand the content and keeps them entertained. The slides also help you, the speaker, organize your thoughts, and prompt you during the presentation.

You would like to have the name of the presentation appear as the title on the first slide, and to have the name of the organization, date of the presentation, and the slide number appear on the footer of each slide. A **footer** consists of text or graphics that appear at the bottom of each slide. Because the options to display the date that the presentation was last updated and slide number are already selected, you only need to enter the title text and footer text.

5
● Click in the Presentation title text box to display the insertion point.

● Type **Join Animal Angels.**

Having Trouble?

If you make a typing error, use the [Backspace] key to delete the characters to the left of the insertion point and then retype the current text.

● Press [Tab ↹].

● Type **Animal Rescue Foundation** in the Footer text box.

Your screen should be similar to Figure 1.7

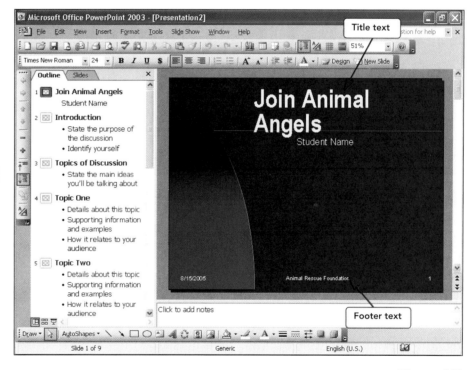

Figure 1.7

You have entered all the information PowerPoint needs to create your presentation.

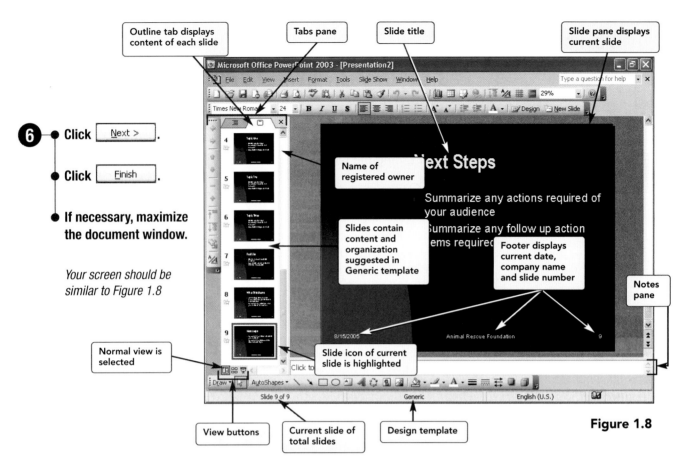

Outline tab displays content of each slide

Tabs pane

Slide title

Slide pane displays current slide

6 ● Click `Next >`.

● Click `Finish`.

● If necessary, maximize the document window.

Your screen should be similar to Figure 1.8

Name of registered owner

Slides contain content and organization suggested in Generic template

Footer displays current date, company name and slide number

Notes pane

Normal view is selected

Slide icon of current slide is highlighted

View buttons

Current slide of total slides

Design template

Figure 1.8

Viewing the Presentation

Based on your selections and entries, the AutoContent wizard creates a presentation and displays it in the workspace. The colors and design were selected by the wizard when you selected the Generic presentation type.

The presentation is initially displayed in Normal view showing the Outline tab. A **view** is a way of looking at a presentation. PowerPoint provides several views you can use to look at and modify your presentation. Depending on what you are doing, one view may be preferable to another. The commands to change views are located on the View menu. In addition, the three view buttons to the left of the horizontal scroll bar can be used to switch quickly from one view to another. The menu commands, buttons, and voice commands for the three main views are described in the table on the next page.

View	Command	Button	Voice	Description
Normal	**V**iew/**N**ormal	⊞	Normal or Normal view	Provides three working areas of the window that allow you to work on all aspects of your presentation in one place.
Slide Sorter	**V**iew/Sli**d**e Sorter	⊞	Slide sorter	Displays a miniature of each slide to make it easy to reorder slides, add special effects such as transitions, and set timing between slides.
Slide Show	**V**iew/Slide Sho**w**	⬚	View show, Begin slide show, Start slide show, or Slide show view	Displays each slide in final form using the full screen space so you can practice or present the presentation.

Using Normal View

Additional Information

Normal view is often referred to as a tri-pane view because it displays three panes simultaneously.

Additional Information

You will learn about speaker notes in Lab 2.

Additional Information

You can adjust the size of each pane by dragging the splitter bar that borders each pane.

Normal view is displayed by default because it is the main view you use while creating a presentation. In Normal view, three working areas, called **panes**, are displayed. These panes allow you to work on all components of your presentation in one convenient location. The pane on the left side includes tabs that alternate between viewing the presentation in outline format and as slide miniatures. The pane on the right displays the selected slide. The notes pane below the slide pane includes space for you to enter speaker notes.

Currently, the Outline tab is open and displays the title and text for each slide in the presentation. It is used to organize and develop the content of your presentation. To the left of each slide title in the Outline tab is a slide icon ▣ and a number that identifies each slide (see Figure 1.8). The icon of the current slide is highlighted, and the current slide is displayed in the main working area, called the slide pane. The text for the first slide consists of the title and the footer text you specified when using the AutoContent wizard. Below the title, the name of the registered owner of the application program is displayed automatically. The other slides shown in the Outline tab contain sample text that is included by the Wizard based upon the type of presentation you selected. The sample text suggests the content for each slide to help you organize your presentation's content. Because the current view is Normal, the ⊞ button is highlighted. The status bar displays the number of the current slide and total number of slides, and the name of the design template used.

The Slides tab is used to display each slide in the presentation as a thumbnail. A **thumbnail** is a miniature representation of a picture, in this case of a slide. Clicking on the thumbnail selects the slide, making it the current slide, and displays it in the slide pane.

1 • **Click on the Slides tab to open it.**

Another Method

You can also press Ctrl + ⇧ Shift + Tab⇄ to switch between the Slide and Outline tabs. The voice commands are "Slides" or "Outline."

• **Scroll the tabs pane to view the rest of the slides.**

• **Click on the last slide in the Slides tab.**

Your screen should be similar to Figure 1.9

Tab name replaced by icon

Drag splitter bar to adjust size of pane

Slide tab displays thumbnails of slides

Next Steps

■ Summarize any actions required of your audience
■ Summarize any follow up action items required of you

8/15/2005   Animal Rescue Foundation   9

Current slide is surrounded by a border and displayed in the slide pane

Current slide

Figure 1.9

Additional Information

You can make the thumbnails larger by increasing the width of the tabs pane.

The size of the tabs pane adjusted to be just large enough to display the thumbnails. In addition, because the pane is narrower, the tab names are replaced by icons. The presentation has a total of nine slides. The status bar displays the number of the current slide.

Using Slide Sorter View

The second main view that is used while creating a presentation is Slide Sorter view. This view also displays thumbnails of the slides.

1 Click 🔲 Slide Sorter View.

Having Trouble?
Pointing to a view button displays its name in a ScreenTip.

Your screen should be similar to Figure 1.10

All slides have the same design style

Slide Sorter view displays miniatures of all slides in presentation

Border surrounds current slide

Slide Sorter view is selected

Figure 1.10

This view displays a miniature of each slide in the window. All the slides use the same design style, associated with a generic presentation. The design style sets the background design and color, as well as the text style, color, and layout. The currently selected slide, slide 9, appears with a blue border around it. Clicking on a thumbnail selects the slide and makes it the **current slide**, or the slide that will be affected by any changes you make.

2 Click on slide 1.

Your screen should be similar to Figure 1.11

Current slide is affected by any changes you make

Figure 1.11

Editing a Presentation

After creating a presentation using the AutoContent wizard, you need to replace the sample content with the appropriate information for your presentation. Editing involves making text changes and additions to the content of your presentation. It also includes making changes to the organization of content. This can be accomplished quickly by rearranging the order of bulleted items on slides as well as the order of slides.

While editing, you will need to move to specific locations in the text. You can use the mouse to move to selected locations simply by clicking on the location. An insertion point appears to show your location in the text. You can also use the arrow keys located on the numeric keypad or the directional keypad to move the insertion point. The keyboard directional keys and voice commands used to move within text are described in the following table.

Key	Voice	Movement
→	Right	One character to right
←	Left	One character to left
↑	Up	One line up
↓	Down	One line down
Ctrl + →	Next word	One word to right
Ctrl + ←	Back word	One word to left
Home	Home	Left end of line
End	Go end	Right end of line

Additional Information

You can use the directional keys on the numeric keypad or the dedicated directional keypad area. If you use the numeric keypad, make sure the Num Lock feature is off, otherwise numbers will be entered in the document. The Num Lock indicator light above the keypad is lit when on. Press Num Lock to turn it off.

Holding down a directional key or key combination moves the insertion point quickly in the direction indicated, saving multiple presses of the key. Many of the insertion point movement keys can be held down to execute multiple moves.

While editing you will also need to select text. To select text using the mouse, first move the insertion point to the beginning or end of the text to be selected, and then drag when the mouse pointer is an I-beam to highlight the text you want selected. You can select as little as a single letter or as much as the entire document. To remove highlighting and deselect text, simply click anywhere in the document.

You can also quickly select a block of text, such as a word or line. The following table summarizes the mouse techniques used to select standard blocks.

To Select	Procedure
Word	Double-click in the word.
Sentence	Press Ctrl and click within the sentence.
All text in a bullet	Triple-click in the bulleted text.
Multiple lines and bullets	Drag up or down across the lines

You can also select text with the keyboard or using voice commands shown in the following table.

Keyboard	Voice	Action
⇧Shift + →		Selects the next space or character.
⇧Shift + ←		Selects the previous space or character.
Ctrl + ⇧Shift + →	Select next word	Selects the next word.
Ctrl + ⇧Shift + ←	Select last word	Selects the last word.
Ctrl + ⇧Shift + ↑	Select last line	Selects text going backward.
Ctrl + ⇧Shift + ↓	Select next line	Selects text going forward.
Ctrl + A	Select all	Selects the entire document.

Using the Outline Tab

The easiest way to make text-editing changes is to use the Outline tab in Normal view. When working in the Outline tab, the Outlining toolbar is displayed. It is used to modify the presentation outline.

● Click ☐ Normal View to switch to Normal view again.

● Click the Outline tab.

Your screen should be similar to Figure 1.12

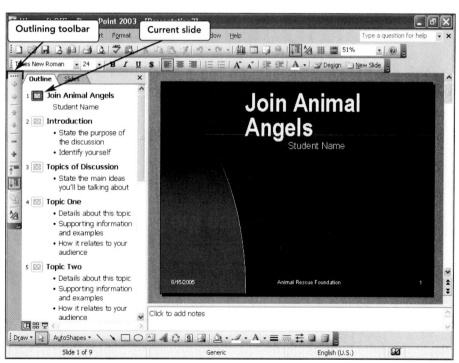

Figure 1.12

Slide 1 is still the current slide. The first change you want to make is to select the owner name on the first slide and delete it.

2 ● Triple-click on the user name on slide 1 in the Outline tab.

● Press [Delete].

Having Trouble?

If you accidentally drag selected text, it will move. To return it to its original location, use Edit/Undo or click [↩·] Undo immediately, or use the voice command "Undo."

● Type **Animal Rescue Foundation**.

Having Trouble?

If you make a typing error, press [Backspace] to delete the characters to the error and retype the entry.

Your screen should be similar to Figure 1.13

Additional Information

If you click the slide icon [▦] to the right of the slide number, all text on the slide is selected.

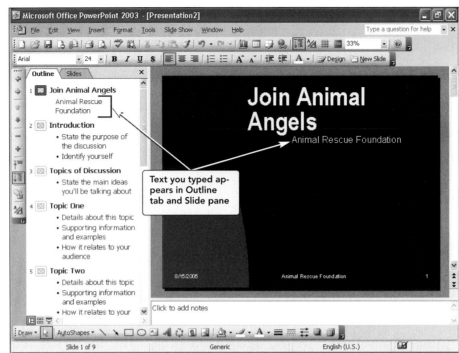

Figure 1.13

The selected text is removed and the new text is entered in the Outline tab as well as in the slide displayed in the slide pane. As you make changes in the Outline tab, the slide pane updates immediately.

The next change you want to make is in the Introduction slide. The sample text in this slide recommends that you enter an opening statement to explain the purpose of the discussion and to introduce yourself. You must replace the sample text next to the first bullet with the text for your slide. In the Outline tab, you can also select an entire paragraph and all subparagraphs by pointing to the left of the line and clicking when the mouse pointer is a ✛.

3 ● **Click on the slide 2 icon.**

● **Click to the left of the sample text "State the purpose of the discussion" in the Outline tab when the mouse pointer is a ⊕.**

● **Type volunter (this word is intentionally misspelled).**

● **Press** [Spacebar].

Your screen should be similar to Figure 1.14

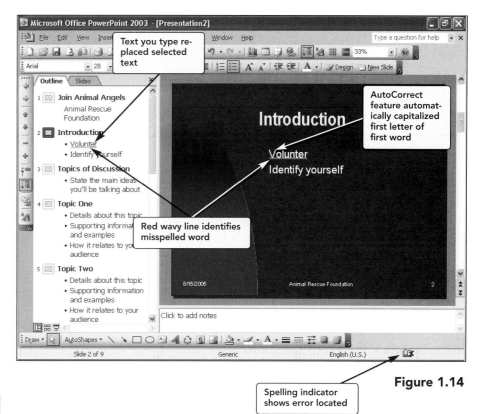

Text you type replaced selected text

AutoCorrect feature automatically capitalized first letter of first word

Red wavy line identifies misspelled word

Spelling indicator shows error located

Figure 1.14

Additional Information

Bulleted items in a presentation are capitalized in sentence case format. Ending periods, however, are not included.

As soon as you pressed a key, the selected text was deleted and replaced by the new text you typed. Also, as you enter text, the program checks words for accuracy. First, PowerPoint capitalized the first letter of the word. This is part of the AutoCorrect feature of PowerPoint.

Concept 4
AutoCorrect

4   The AutoCorrect feature makes some basic assumptions about the text you are typing and, based on these assumptions, automatically corrects the entry. The AutoCorrect feature automatically inserts proper capitalization at the beginning of sentences and in the names of days of the week. It will also change to lowercase letters any words that were incorrectly capitalized due to the accidental use of the [Caps Lock] key. In addition, it also corrects many common typing and spelling errors automatically.

One way the program makes corrections automatically is by looking for certain types of errors. For example, if two capital letters appear at the beginning of a word, the second capital letter is changed to a lowercase letter. If a lowercase letter appears at the beginning of a sentence, the first letter of the first word is capitalized. If the name of a day begins with a lowercase letter, the first letter is capitalized.

Another way the program makes corrections is by checking all entries against a built-in list of words that are commonly spelled incorrectly or typed incorrectly. If it finds the entry on the list, the program automatically replaces the error with the correction. For example, the typing error "aboutthe" is automatically changed to "about the" because the error is on the AutoCorrect list. You can also add words to the AutoCorrect list that you want to be corrected automatically. Any such words are added to the list on the computer you are using and will be available to anyone who uses the machine after you.

Next, PowerPoint identified the word as misspelled by underlining it with a wavy red line. In addition, the spelling indicator in the status bar appears as 🖳, indicating that the automatic spelling check feature has found a spelling error.

Concept 5
Spelling Checker

5 The **spelling checker** locates all misspelled words, duplicate words, and capitalization irregularities as you create and edit a presentation, and proposes possible corrections. This feature works by comparing each word to a dictionary of words. If the word does not appear in the main dictionary or in a custom dictionary, it is identified as misspelled. The **main dictionary** is supplied with the program; a **custom dictionary** is one you can create to hold words you commonly use, such as proper names and technical terms, but that are not included in the main dictionary.

If the word does not appear in either dictionary, the program identifies it as misspelled by displaying a red wavy line below the word. You can then correct the misspelled word by editing it. Alternatively, you can display a list of suggested spelling corrections for that word and select the correct spelling from the list to replace the misspelled word in the presentation.

Additional Information

The spelling checker works just as it does in the other Microsoft Office 2003 applications.

Because you have discovered this error very soon after typing it, and you know that the correct spelling of this word is "volunteer," you can quickly correct it by using the Backspace key. The Backspace key removes the character or space to the left of the insertion point; therefore, it is particularly useful when you are moving from right to left (backward) along a line of text. You will correct this word and continue entering the text for this slide.

4 ● **Press** Backspace **twice.**

● **Type er.**

● **Press** Spacebar.

● **Type recrutment.**

Additional Information

As you type, an animated pen appears over the spelling indicator while the spelling checker is in the process of checking for errors. When no spelling errors are located, the indicator appears as 🖳.

Your screen should be similar to Figure 1.15

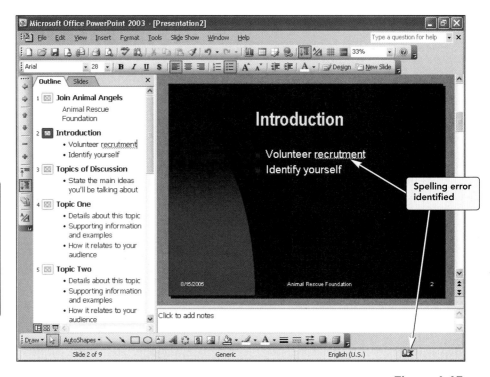

Figure 1.15

Again, the program has identified a word as misspelled. Another way to quickly correct a misspelled word is to select the correct spelling from a list of suggested spelling corrections displayed on the shortcut menu.

5 Right-click on the misspelled word in the Outline tab to display the shortcut menu.

Your screen should be similar to Figure 1.16

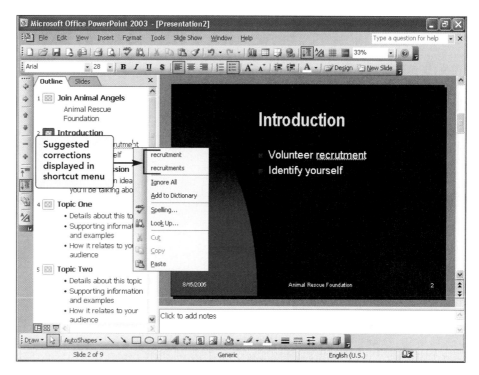

Figure 1.16

The shortcut menu displays two suggested correct spellings. The menu also includes several related menu options described below.

Option	Effect
Ignore All	Instructs PowerPoint to ignore the misspelling of this word throughout the rest of this session.
Add to Dictionary	Adds the word to the custom dictionary list. When a word is added to the custom dictionary, PowerPoint will always accept that spelling as correct.
Spelling	Starts the spelling checker to check the entire presentation.
Look Up	Checks the spelling of text in another language.

Additional Information

If only one suggested spelling correction is offered, the correction is automatically inserted.

Sometimes no suggested replacements are offered because PowerPoint cannot locate any words in its dictionary that are similar in spelling, or the suggestions offered are not correct. If either situation happens, you must edit the word manually. In this case, you will replace the word with the correct spelling and enter your name on this slide.

6 ● Choose "recruitment."

● Select "Identify yourself" in the Outline tab.

● Type your name.

Your screen should be similar to Figure 1.17

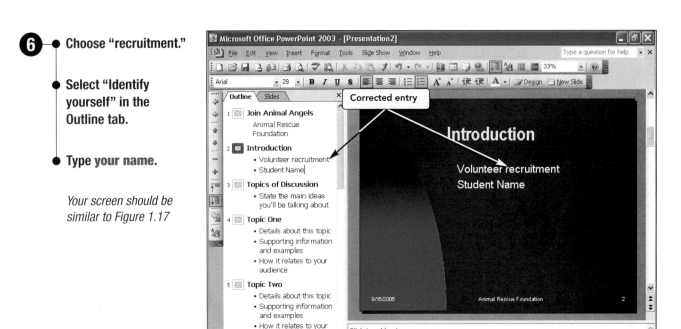

Figure 1.17

You are now ready to update the third slide in your presentation by entering the three main topics you will be discussing. You want to enter each topic on a separate bulleted line. The first bullet is already displayed and contains sample text that you will replace. To add additional lines and bullets, you simply press ←Enter.

7 ● In slide 3 of the Outline tab, select "State the main ideas you'll be talking about."

● Type **Why are pets abandoned?**.

● Press ←Enter.

● Type **How can you help?**.

● Press ←Enter.

● Type **How does the Foundation help?** (do not press ←Enter).

Having Trouble?
If you accidentally insert an extra bullet and blank line, press Backspace twice to remove them.

Your screen should be similar to Figure 1.18

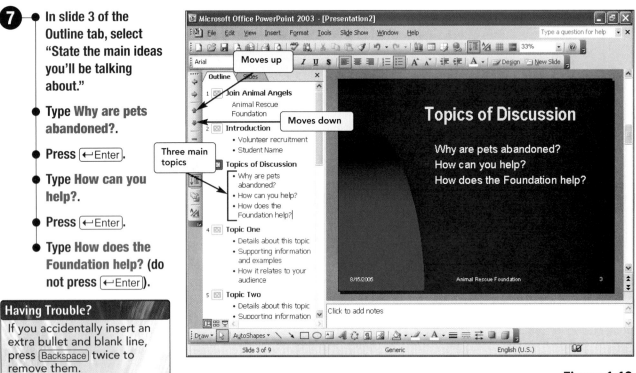

Figure 1.18

You realize that you entered the topics in the wrong order. You want the last item to be the second item in the list. A bulleted point can be moved easily by selecting it and dragging it to a new location, or by using the ⬆ Move Up or ⬇ Move Down buttons in the Outlining toolbar. When using the buttons, the insertion point must be on the bulleted item you want to move. You will move the bulleted item on the current line up one line.

8 ● **Click ⬆ Move Up.**

Your screen should be similar to Figure 1.19

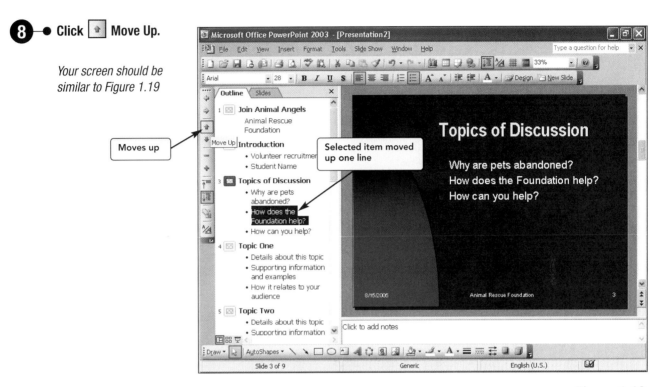

Figure 1.19

Editing in the Slide Pane

Next, you want to update the content of the fourth slide. The fourth slide contains the title "Topic One" and a list of three bulleted items. The title and the bulleted list are two separate elements or placeholders on the slide. **Placeholders** are boxes that are designed to contain specific types of items or **objects** such as the slide title text, bulleted item text, charts, tables, and pictures. Each slide can have several different types of placeholders. To indicate which placeholder to work with, you must first select it. You will change the sample text in the title placeholder first in the slide pane.

1 ● Click on slide 4 in the Outline tab to display it in the slide pane.

● Click anywhere on the slide title text in the slide pane.

Your screen should be similar to Figure 1.20

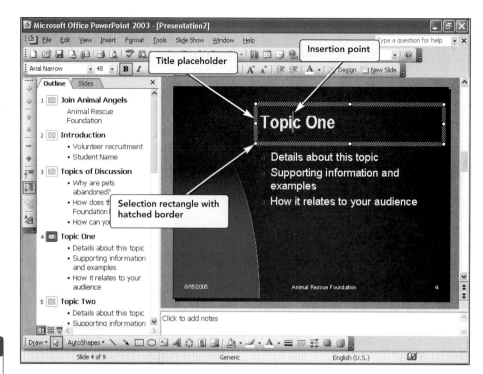

Figure 1.20

The title placeholder is now a selected object and is surrounded by a **selection rectangle**. The hatch-marked border of the selection rectangle indicates that you can enter, delete, select, and format the text inside the placeholder. An insertion point is displayed to show your location in the text and to allow you to select and edit the text. The mouse pointer appears as an I-beam to be used to position the insertion point. You will enter the new title for this slide.

2 ● Select the title text.

● Type **Why Are Pets Abandoned?**.

Your screen should be similar to Figure 1.21

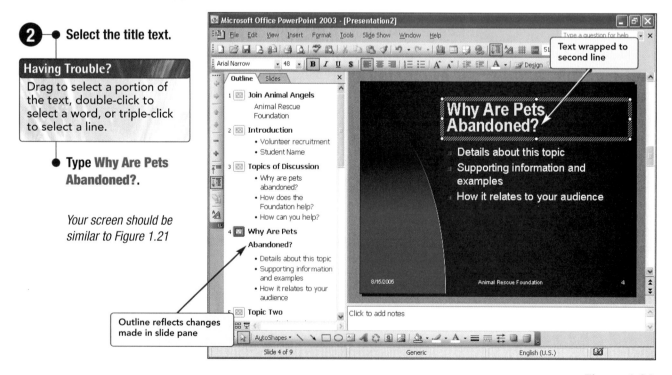

Figure 1.21

Notice that the text automatically wrapped to a second line when the length exceeded the width of the box. The Outline tab reflects the changes as they are made in the slide pane. Next, you need to replace the sample text in the bulleted list.

3 ● Click on any of the bulleted items to select the placeholder.

● Select all three items in the placeholder box.

Having Trouble?
Drag to select multiple lines of text, or use **E**dit/Select All or the shortcut key Ctrl + A to select everything in the placeholder box.

● Type **Poor or deteriorating health**.

● Press ←Enter.

Another Method
Using voice dictation you would say "Enter" to start a new line.

● Enter the following text for the next three bullets:

Maintenance expenses

Change in lifestyle

Behavioral problems

Your screen should be similar to Figure 1.22

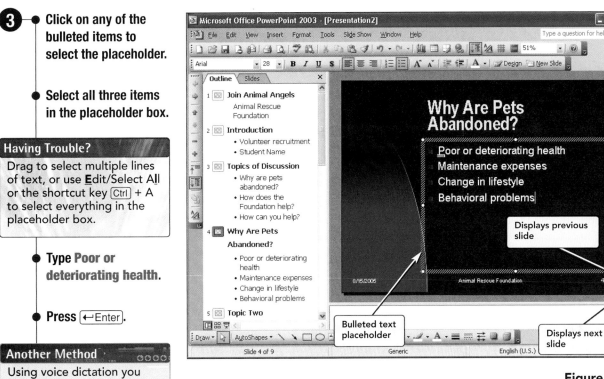

Figure 1.22

In the next slide you will enter information about how people can help the Animal Rescue Foundation. In addition to clicking on the slide in the Outline tab, the following features can be used to move to other slides in Normal view.

To Display	Action
Previous slide	Click [⬆]
	Click above scroll box
	Press [Page Up]
	Voice: Page up; Previous page
Next slide	Click [⬇]
	Click below scroll box
	Press [Page Down]
	Voice: Page down; Next page
Any slide	Drag scroll box until the ScreenTip displays the slide you want to view

You will enter a new slide title and text for the bulleted items.

4 ● Click [⬇] **Next Slide to display slide 5.**

Having Trouble?

The [⬆] Previous Slide and [⬇] Next Slide buttons are located at the bottom of the vertical scroll bar.

● **Replace the sample title text with How Can You Help?.**

● **Select all the text in the bulleted text placeholder.**

● **Type Donate your time and talent.**

● **Press [←Enter].**

Your screen should be similar to Figure 1.23

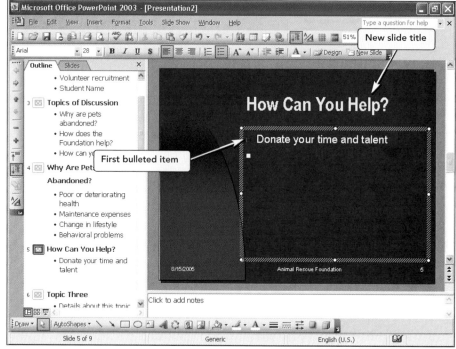

Figure 1.23

Demoting and Promoting Bulleted Items

You want the next bulleted item to be indented below the first bulleted item. Indenting a bulleted point to the right **demotes** it, or makes it a lower or subordinate topic in the outline hierarchy.

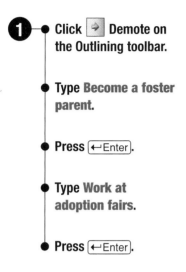

1 ● Click ⬛ **Demote** on the Outlining toolbar.

● Type **Become a foster parent.**

● Press ⬛Enter.

● Type **Work at adoption fairs.**

● Press ⬛Enter.

Your screen should be similar to Figure 1.24

Additional Information

You can also demote and promote bulleted items in the Outline tab using the same procedure. In addition, in the Outline tab you can drag a selected item to the left or right to promote or demote it.

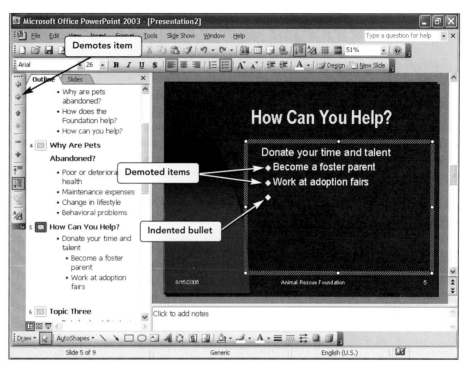

Figure 1.24

The bullet style of the demoted lines is ◆. When you demote a bulleted point, PowerPoint continues to indent to the same level until you cancel the indent. Before entering the next item, you want to remove the indentation, or **promote** the line. Promoting a line moves it to the left, or up a level in the outline hierarchy.

2 ● Click ⬍ Promote.

● Type **Donate new or used items.**

● Press ⏎Enter.

● **Enter the following two bulleted items:**

Crates and pads

Collars, leads, and other items

Your screen should be similar to Figure 1.25

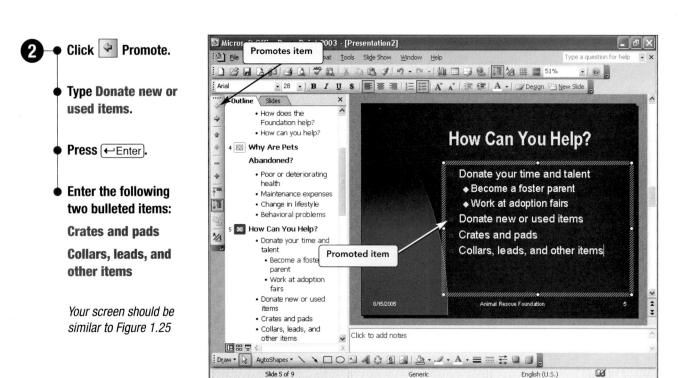

Figure 1.25

You can also promote or demote bulleted items after the text has been entered. The insertion point can be anywhere on the line to be promoted or demoted.

3 ● **Demote the items "Crates and pads" and "Collars, leads, and other items."**

Another Method

You can also press Tab⇆ or ⇧Shift + Tab⇆ to demote or promote an item. However, the insertion point must be at the beginning of the line. The ⬌ Increase Indent, and ⬌ Decrease Indent buttons on the Formatting toolbar can also promote and demote outline levels.

Your screen should be similar to Figure 1.26

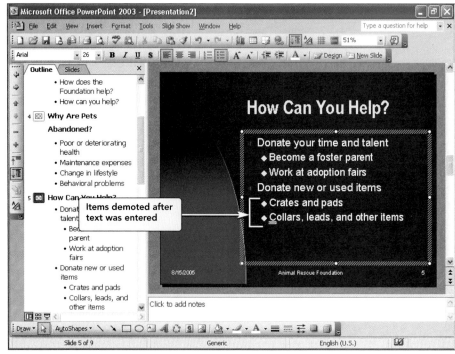

Figure 1.26

You still have three more bulleted items to add to this text placeholder. Notice, however, that the last item is near the bottom of the placeholder box. As you type the text the AutoFit feature will automatically reduce the line spacing and if needed the size of the text until the spillover text fits inside the placeholder.

④ ● Move to the end of "Collars, leads, and other items"

● Press ⏎Enter.

● Type **Provide financial support**

● Press ⏎Enter.

● Enter the following three bulleted items:

Send a donation

Sponsor a foster pet

Sponsor an adoption

● Promote the "Provide Financial Support" bullet.

Your screen should be similar to Figure 1.27

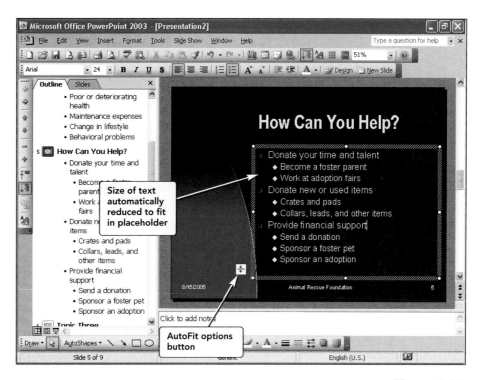

Figure 1.27

Additional Information

As you increase or decrease the size of the placeholder, the AutoFit feature will adjust the line spacing and text size appropriately.

As you continued entering more bulleted items, the text size reduced even more. Also notice that the ⬍ AutoFit Options button appears next to the placeholder. It contains options that allow you to control the AutoFit feature and to handle the over-spilling text.

Splitting Text Between Slides

Generally when creating slides, it is a good idea to limit the number of bulleted items on a slide to six. It is also recommended that the number of words on a line should not exceed five. In this case, because there are ten bulleted items on this slide, you want to split the slide content between two slides.

1 • Click the �338 **AutoFit Options button.**

• **Choose Split Text Between Two Slides.**

Your screen should be similar to Figure 1.28

2 • Click the title placeholder.

• Replace the title text with More Ways to Help!.

• Move to the end of the sixth bulleted item and press Delete.

• Edit the item to be "Sponsor a foster pet or adoption."

Your screen should be similar to Figure 1.29

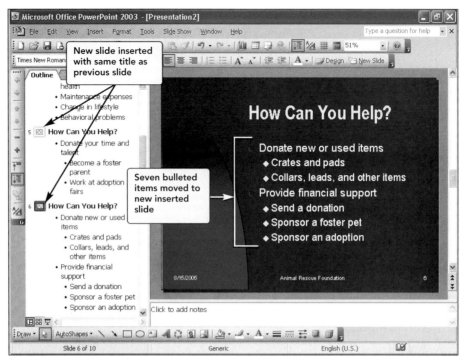

Figure 1.28

A new slide is inserted into the presentation containing the same title as the previous slide and the last two bulleted topic groups. Because the split occurs at a main topic, there are still seven bulleted items on the new slide. You will combine two items into one to reduce the number to six and change the title of the slide.

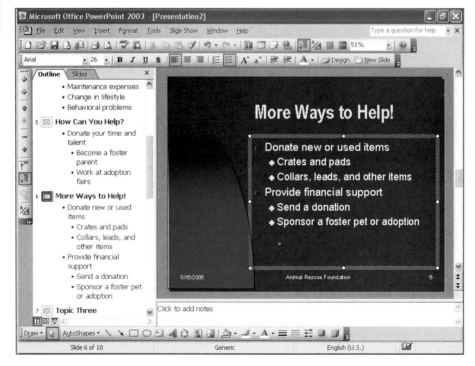

Figure 1.29

Saving, Closing, and Opening a Presentation

You have just been notified about an important meeting that is to begin in a few minutes. Before leaving for the meeting, you want to save the presentation. As you enter and edit text to create a new presentation, the changes you make are immediately displayed onscreen and are stored in your computer's memory. However, they are not permanently stored until you save your work to a file on a disk. After a presentation is saved as a file, it can be closed and opened again at a later time to be edited further.

As a backup against the accidental loss of work caused by a power failure or other mishap, Office 2003 includes an AutoRecover feature. When this feature is on, as you work you may see a pulsing disk icon briefly appear in the status bar. This icon indicates that the program is saving your work to a temporary recovery file. The time interval between automatic saving can be set to any period you specify; the default is every 10 minutes. When you start up again, the recovery file containing all changes you made up to the last time it was saved by AutoRecover is opened automatically. You then need to save the recovery file. If you do not save it, it is deleted when closed. While AutoRecover is a great feature for recovering lost work, it should not be used in place of regularly saving your work.

Saving the Presentation

You will save the work you have done so far on the presentation. The Save or Save As commands on the File menu are used to save files. The Save command or the 🖫 Save button will save the active file using the same file name by replacing the contents of the existing file with the document as it appears on your screen. The Save As command allows you to save a file with a new file name and/or to a new location. This action leaves the original file unchanged. When a presentation is saved for the first time, either command can be used. It is especially important to save a new presentation very soon after you create it because the AutoRecover feature does not work until a file name has been specified.

1 → Click 🖫 Save.

Another Method oooo

The voice command is
"Save."

*Your screen should be
similar to Figure 1.30*

Figure 1.30

Additional Information

Windows documents can
have up to 256 characters in
the file name. Names can
contain letters, numbers, and
spaces; the symbols
/,\,?,:,*,",", <, > cannot be
used.

The Save As dialog box is displayed in which you specify the location to
save the file and the file name. The Save In list box displays the default
location where files are stored. The File Name text box displays the title
from the first slide as the default file name. You will change the location to
the location where you save your files and the file name. Notice that the
default name is highlighted, indicating that it is selected and will be
replaced as you type the new name.

2 ● Type **Volunteer.**

Additional Information

The file name can be entered in either uppercase or lowercase letters and will appear exactly as you type it.

● **Open the Save In list box.**

Having Trouble?

Click the text box arrow to open the drop-down list.

● **Select the location where you will save your files from the Save In drop-down list.**

Having Trouble?

If you are saving to a floppy disk and an error message is displayed, check that your disk is properly inserted in the drive and click OK.

Your screen should be similar to Figure 1.31

Having Trouble?

If your dialog box does not display file extensions, your Windows program has this option deactivated.

Figure 1.31

The large list box displays the names of any PowerPoint files (if any) stored in that location. Only PowerPoint presentation files are listed, because the selected file type in the Save As Type list box is Presentation. Presentation files have a default file extension of .ppt.

You can also select the save location from the Places bar along the left side of the dialog box. The icons bring up a list of recently accessed files and folders, the contents of the My Documents and Favorites folders, the Windows desktop, and folders that reside on a network or Web through the My Network Places. Selecting a folder from one of these lists changes to that location. You can also click the button in the toolbar to return to folders that were previously opened during the current session.

3 • Click [Save].

Your screen should be similar to Figure 1.32

New file name

Closes document window

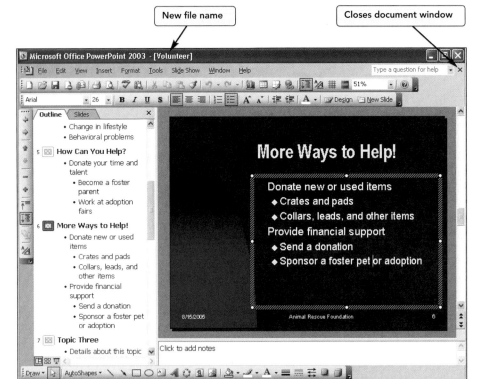

Figure 1.32

The new file name is displayed in the window title bar. The presentation is now saved in a new file named Volunteer. The view in use at the time the file is saved is also saved with the file.

Closing a Presentation

You are now ready to close the file.

● Click ☒ Close Window (in the menu bar).

Another Method

The menu equivalent is **F**ile/**C**lose and the voice command is "Close presentation."

Your screen should be similar to Figure 1.33

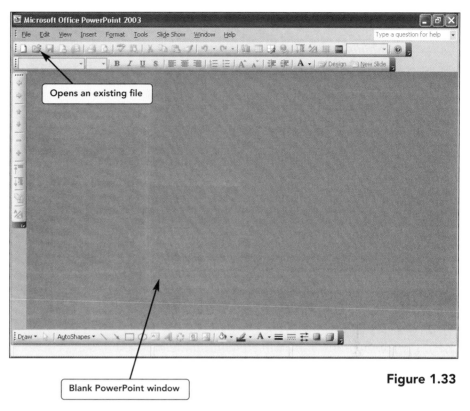

Opens an existing file

Blank PowerPoint window

Figure 1.33

The presentation is closed, and a blank PowerPoint window is displayed. Always save your slide presentation before closing a file or leaving the PowerPoint program. As a safeguard against losing your work if you forget to save the presentation, PowerPoint will remind you to save any unsaved presentation before closing the file or exiting the program.

Note: If you are ending your lab session now, choose **F**ile/E**x**it to exit the program.

Opening an Existing Presentation

After returning from your meeting, you hastily continued to enter the information for several more slides and saved the presentation using a new file name. You will open this file to see the information in the new slides and will continue working on the presentation.

1 ● Click 🖼 **Open.**

Another Method

The menu equivalent is **File/Open**, the keyboard shortcut is [Ctrl] + O, and the voice command is "Open."

● If necessary, select the location containing your data files from the Look In drop-down list box.

● **Select** pp01_Volunteer1.

Your screen should be similar to Figure 1.34

Having Trouble?
The files in your file list and the previewed file may be different than shown in Figure 1.34. If a preview is not displayed, click 🖼 Views and select Preview.

Additional Information
The **File/New** command or the 🗋 button opens a blank new presentation. You can also quickly open a recently used file by selecting it from the list of file names displayed at the bottom of the File menu and at the bottom of the Getting Started task pane.

Figure 1.34

In the Open dialog box you specify the location and name of the file you want to open. The Look In drop-down list box displays the last specified location, in this case the location where you saved the Volunteer presentation. The large list box displays the names of PowerPoint presentation files only, as specified by the setting in the Files of Type box. As in the Save As dialog box, the Places bar can be used to quickly access recently used files. A preview of the selected file is displayed in the right side of the dialog box.

You will open the selected file next.

Revised presentation outline

Spelling errors

File name of open file

2 • Click Open ▾.

Another Method

You could also double-click the file name to both select it and choose Open ▾.

• **If necessary, open the Outline tab.**

• **Edit slide 2 in the slide pane to display your name.**

• **Scroll the Outline pane to see the additional content that has been added to the presentation.**

Your screen should be similar to Figure 1.35

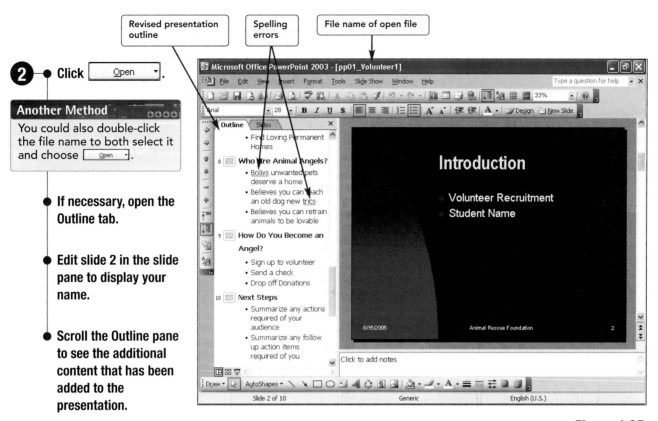

Figure 1.35

The presentation still contains ten slides, and all the sample text has been replaced with text for the volunteer recruitment presentation except for slide 10.

Checking Spelling

As you entered the information on the additional slides, you left several typing errors uncorrected. To correct the misspelled words and grammatical errors, you can use the shortcut menu to correct each individual word or error, as you learned earlier. However, in many cases you may find it more efficient to wait until you are finished writing before you correct any spelling or grammatical errors. Rather than continually breaking your train of thought to correct errors as you type, you can check the spelling on all slides of the presentation at once.

1 ● Click 🖰 Speling.

Another Method

The menu equivalent is **T**ools/**S**pelling and the keyboard shortcut is F7. You can also double-click the spelling indicator 📖 in the status bar to start the spelling checker. Using this method moves to the first potential spelling error and displays the shortcut menu.

Your screen should be similar to Figure 1.36

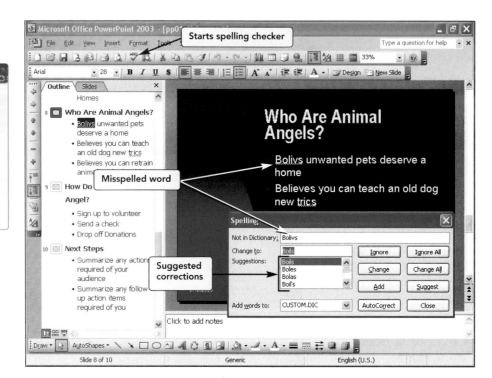

Figure 1.36

Additional Information

The spelling checker identifies many proper names and technical terms as misspelled. To stop this from occurring, use the Add Words To option to add those names to the custom dictionary.

The program jumps to slide 8, highlights the first located misspelled word, "Bolivs," in the Outline pane, and opens the Spelling dialog box. The Spelling dialog box displays the misspelled word in the Not in Dictionary text box. The Suggestions list box displays the words the spelling checker has located in the dictionary that most closely match the misspelled word. The first word is highlighted.

Although the list displays several additional suggestions, none of them is correct. Sometimes the spelling checker does not display any suggested replacements because it cannot locate any words in the dictionaries that are similar in spelling. If there are no suggestions, the Not in Dictionary text box simply displays the word that is highlighted in the text. When none of the suggestions is correct, you must edit the word yourself by typing the correction in the Change To text box.

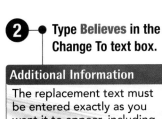

2 ● Type **Believes** in the Change To text box.

Additional Information

The replacement text must be entered exactly as you want it to appear, including capitalization.

● Click [Change].

Additional Information

You can also edit words directly in the presentation and then click [Resume] to continue checking spelling.

Your screen should be similar to Figure 1.37

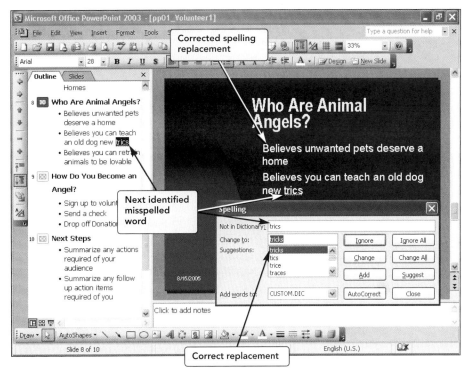

Figure 1.37

The corrected replacement is made in the slide. After the Spelling dialog box is open, the spelling checker continues to check the entire presentation for spelling errors. The next misspelled word, "trics," is identified. In this case, the suggested replacement is correct.

3 ● Click [Change].

Having Trouble?

If necessary, move the dialog box to see the located misspelled word.

● Correct any other located spelling errors as needed.

● Click [OK] in response to the message telling you that the spelling check is complete.

● Use **File/Save As** to save the revised presentation as Volunteer1 **to your solution file location.**

Your screen should be similar to Figure 1.38

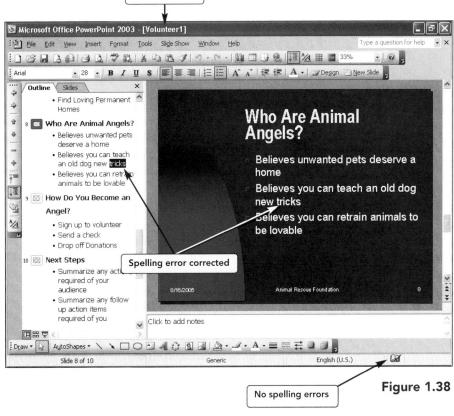

Figure 1.38

Working with Slides

To get a better overall picture of all slides in the presentation, you will switch to Slide Sorter view.

1 ● Click ⊞ **Slide Sorter view.**

Another Method

The menu equivalent is **V**iew/Sli**d**e Sorter.

● If necessary, move the Slide Sorter toolbar below the Standard toolbar.

Having Trouble?

If the Slide Sorter toolbar is not displayed, select it from the toolbar shortcut menu and display it below the Standard toolbar.

Your screen should be similar to Figure 1.39

Having Trouble?

Do not be concerned if your screen displays a different number of slides per row. This is a function of your monitor settings.

Figure 1.39

Viewing the slides side by side helps you see how your presentation flows. You can now see that slides 7 and 8 are out of order and do not follow the sequence of topics in the Topics for Discussion slide. You also see that you need to delete slide 10. As you continue to look at the slides, you also decide the second slide does not really add much to the presentation and you want to delete it.

This view also displays the Slide Sorter toolbar that is used to add enhancements to your presentation. The Formatting toolbar is not displayed because you cannot format slides in this view.

Deleting Slides

First you will delete slide 10 and then slide 2.

1 ● **Select slide 10.**

Having Trouble?

Clicking on a slide selects it.

● **Press** Delete .

● **In the same manner, select and delete slide 2.**

Another Method

The menu equivalent is **E**dit/**D**elete Slide.

Your screen should be similar to Figure 1.40

Figure 1.40

The slides have been deleted, and all remaining slides have been appropriately renumbered. An indicator line appears between slides 1 and 2 where the deleted slide once existed.

Moving Slides

Now you want to correct the organization of the slides by moving slide 6, How Does the Foundation Help?, and slide 7, Who Are Animal Angels?, before slide 4, How Can You Help?. To reorder a slide in Slide Sorter view, you drag it to its new location using drag and drop. As you drag the mouse, an indicator line appears to show you where the slide will appear in the presentation. When the indicator line is located where you want the slide to be placed, release the mouse button. You will select both slides and move them at the same time.

1 ● Select slide 6.

● Hold down [Ctrl] and click on slide 7.

● Point to either selected slide and drag the mouse until the indicator line is displayed before slide 4.

● Release the mouse button.

Your screen should be similar to Figure 1.41

Figure 1.41

The slides now appear in the order you want them.

Inserting Slides

During your discussion with the Foundation director, it was suggested that you add a slide showing the history of the organization. To include this information in the presentation, you will insert a new slide after slide 4.

1 Click in the space before slide 5.

Additional Information

The indicator line shows you where the new slide will be added.

• Click `New Slide`.

Another Method

The menu equivalent is Insert/**N**ew Slide, the keyboard shortcut is Ctrl + M and the voice command is "New slide."

Your screen should be similar to Figure 1.42

Figure 1.42

A blank new slide is inserted. It has the same design elements as the other slides in the presentation.

Selecting the Slide Layout

The Slide Layout task pane is automatically displayed so that you can select a slide layout for the new slide.

Concept 6
Layout

6   The **layout** controls the way items are arranged on a slide. A layout contains placeholders for the different items such as bulleted text, titles, charts, and so on. PowerPoint includes 27 predefined layouts that can be selected and applied to slides. For example, there are text layouts that include placeholders for a title and bulleted text, and content layouts that include placeholders for a table, diagram, chart, or clip art.

  You can change the layout of an existing slide by selecting a new layout. If the new layout does not include placeholders for objects that are already on your slide (for example, if you created a chart and the new layout does not include a chart placeholder), you do not lose the information. All objects remain on the slide and the selected layout is automatically adjusted by adding the appropriate type of placeholder for the object. Alternatively, as you add new objects to a slide, the layout automatically adjusts by adding the appropriate type of placeholder. You can also rearrange, size, and format placeholders on a slide any way you like to customize the slide's appearance.

  To make creating slides easy, use the predefined layouts. The layouts help you keep your presentation format consistent and, therefore, more professional.

The Slide Layout task pane displays examples of the 27 layout designs organized into four categories. Pointing to a layout displays the layout name in a ScreenTip. The default layout, Title and Text, is selected.

Because this slide will contain two columns of text about the history of the organization, you will use the two-column text layout.

1 ● Click ▦ Title and 2-Column Text.

● Close the Slide Layout task pane.

Having Trouble?

Click ☒ in the task pane title bar to close it.

● Double-click on slide 5 to switch to Normal view.

Your screen should be similar to Figure 1.43

Additional Information

The layout of an existing slide can be changed using Format/Slide Layout.

Figure 1.43

The slide displays the three placeholders created by the two-column text layout. Next, you will add text to the slide presenting a brief history of the Animal Rescue Foundation. First, you will enter the slide title and then the list of dates and events.

2 • Click in the title placeholder.

• Type **Animal Rescue Foundation History.**

• Click in the left text placeholder.

• Type **Year.**

• Press ⏎Enter.

• Continue entering the information shown below. Remember to press ⏎Enter to create a new line.

1990

1991

1997

2003

• In the same manner, enter the following text in the right text placeholder:

Event

Founded by Ed Wilton

Built first shelter

Began volunteer program

Expanded to 10 shelters

Your screen should be similar to Figure 1.44

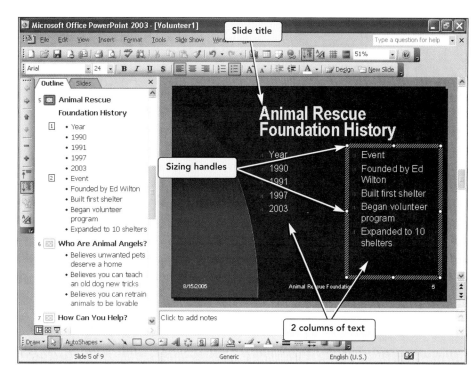

Figure 1.44

The left placeholder is too big for its contents, and the right placeholder is too small. To correct the size, you can adjust the size of the placeholders.

Sizing a Placeholder

The eight boxes in the selection rectangle are **sizing handles** that can be used to adjust the size of the placeholder. Dragging the corner sizing handles will adjust both the height and width at the same time, whereas the center handles adjust the side borders to which they are associated. When you point to the sizing handle, the mouse pointer appears as ↔ indicating the direction in which you can drag the border to adjust the size.

1 ● On the right text placeholder, drag the left-center sizing handle to the left until each item appears on a single line (see Figure 1.45).

● Select the left text placeholder and drag the right-center sizing handle to the left (see Figure 1.45).

Your screen should be similar to Figure 1.45

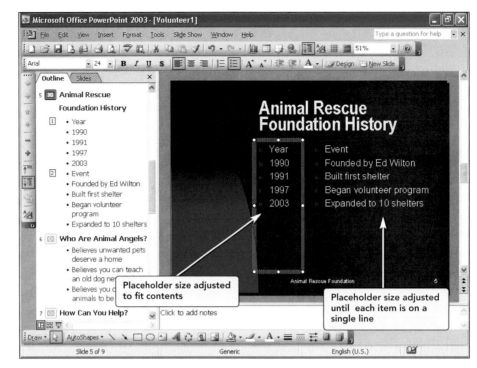

Figure 1.45

Moving a Placeholder

Next, you want to move the Year column placeholder closer to the Event column. Then you want to move both placeholders so they appear more centered in the space. An object can be moved anywhere on a slide by dragging the selection rectangle. The mouse pointer appears as ✛ when you can move a placeholder. You will select both placeholders and move them at the same time. As you drag the placeholder a dotted outline is displayed to show your new location.

1 • Point to the Year column selection rectangle (not a handle) and drag the selected placeholder to the right, closer to the Event column.

• With the left placeholder still selected, hold down Ctrl while clicking on the right placeholder to select both.

• Drag the selected placeholders to the left to their new location (see Figure 1.46).

• Save your changes to the presentation using the same file name.

Having Trouble?

Click ⊞ Save to quickly save the presentation.

Your screen should be similar to Figure 1.46

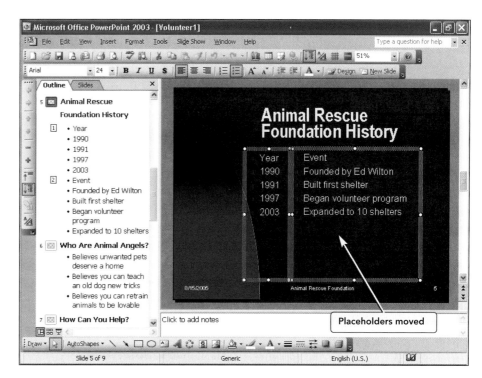

Figure 1.46

Rehearsing a Presentation

Now that the slides are in the order you want, you would like to see how the presentation would look when viewed by an audience. Rather than set up the presentation as you would to present it for an audience, a simple way to rehearse a presentation is to view it electronically on your screen as a slide show. A **slide show** displays each slide full screen and in order. While the slide show is running, you can plan what you want to say to supplement the information provided on the slides.

Using Slide Show View

When you view a slide show, each slide fills the screen, hiding the PowerPoint application window, so you can view the slides as your audience would. You will begin the slide show starting with the first slide.

- Select slide 1 in the Outline tab.

- Click 🖳 Slide Show.

Additional Information

Using 🖳 starts the slide show beginning with the currently selected slide.

Another Method

The menu equivalent is **V**iew/Slide Sho**w** and the voice command is "View show." Using these methods starts the slide show beginning with the first slide in the presentation.

Your screen should be similar to Figure 1.47

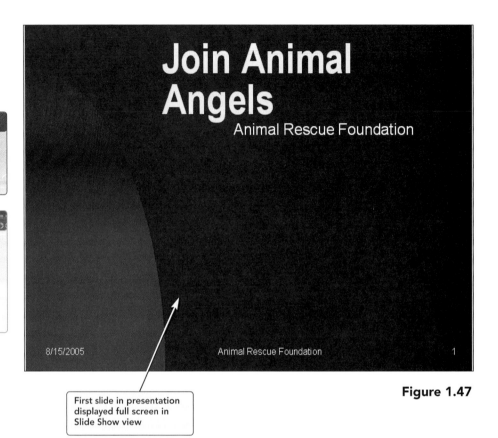

8/15/2005   Animal Rescue Foundation   1

First slide in presentation displayed full screen in Slide Show view

Figure 1.47

Additional Information

Pressing F1 while in Slide Show opens a Help window describing the actions you can use during the slide show.

The presentation title slide is displayed full screen, as it will appear when projected on a screen using computer projection equipment. The easiest way to see the next slide is to click the mouse button. You can also use the keys shown below to move to the next or previous slide.

Next Slide	Previous Slide
Spacebar	Backspace
←Enter	
→	←
↓	↑
Page Down	Page Up
N (for next)	P (for previous)

You can also select **N**ext, **P**revious, or Last **V**iewed from the shortcut menu. Additionally, moving the mouse pointer in Slide Show displays the Slide Show toolbar in the lower left corner of the window. Clicking ◀ or ▶ moves to the previous or next slide and ■ opens the shortcut menu.

Slide Show toolbar

2 ● Click to display the next slide.

● Using each of the methods described, slowly display the entire presentation.

● When the last slide displays a black window, click again to end the slide show.

Additional Information

You can press Esc or use **E**nd Show on the shortcut menu at any time to end the slide show.

Your screen should be similar to Figure 1.48

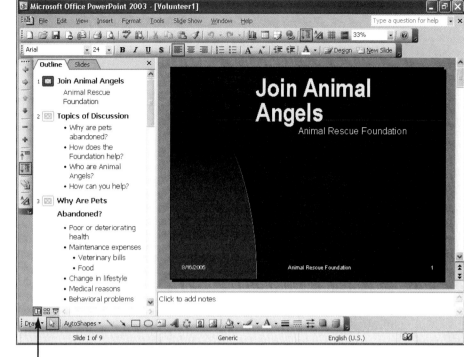

Program returns to normal view

Figure 1.48

After the last slide is displayed, the program returns to the view you were last using, in this case Normal view.

Formatting Slide Text

While looking at the slide show, you decide that the title slide needs to have more impact. You also want to remove the bullets from the items on the history slide. Enhancing the appearance of the slide to make it more readable or attractive is called **formatting**. The default design template already includes many basic formatting features.

Applying different formatting to characters and paragraphs can greatly enhance the appearance of the slide. **Character formatting** features affect the selected characters only. They include changing the character style and size, applying effects such as bold and italics, changing the character spacing, and adding animated text effects. **Paragraph formatting** features affect an entire paragraph. A paragraph is text that has a carriage return from pressing ←Enter at the end of it. Each item in a bulleted list, title, and subtitle is a paragraph. Paragraph formatting features include the position of the paragraph or its alignment between the margins, paragraph indentation, spacing above and below a paragraph, and line spacing within a paragraph.

Changing Fonts

First, you will improve the appearance of the presentation title by changing the font of the title text.

Concept 7
Font and Font Size

7 A **font**, also commonly referred to as a **typeface**, is a set of characters with a specific design. The designs have names such as Times New Roman and Courier. Using fonts as a design element can add interest to your presentation and give your audience visual cues to help them find information quickly.

There are two basic types of fonts: serif and sans serif. **Serif** fonts have a flair at the base of each letter that visually leads the reader to the next letter. Two common serif fonts are Roman and Times New Roman. Serif fonts generally are used for text in paragraphs. **Sans serif** fonts do not have a flair at the base of each letter. Arial and Helvetica are two common sans serif fonts. Because sans serif fonts have a clean look, they are often used for headings in documents. It is good practice to use only two or three different fonts in a presentation because too many can distract from your presentation content and can look unprofessional.

Each font has one or more sizes. Font size is the height and width of the character and is commonly measured in **points**, abbreviated pt. One point equals about 1/72 inch, and text in most documents is 10 pt or 12 pt.

Several common fonts in different sizes are shown in the following table.

Font Name	Font Type	Font Size
Arial	Sans serif	This is 10 pt. This is 16 pt.
Courier New	Serif	This is 10 pt. This is 16 pt.
Times New Roman	Serif	This is 10 pt. This is 16 pt.

To change the font before typing the text, use the command and then type. All text will appear in the specified setting until another font setting is selected. To change a font setting for existing text, select the text you want to change and then use the command. If you want to apply font formatting to a word, simply move the insertion point to the word and the formatting is automatically applied to the entire word.

1 ● Select the text "Join Animal Angels" in the slide pane.

Additional Information

The font used in the title is Arial Narrow, as displayed in the `Arial Narrow` button.

● Open the `Arial Narrow` **Font drop-down list.**

`Arial Narrow`
- ℡ Batang
- ℡ MS Mincho
- ℡ SimSun
- ℡ Agency FB
- ℡ ALGERIAN
- ℡ Allegro BT
- ℡ Arial
- ℡ Arial Black
- ℡ Arial Narrow

● **Scroll the list and choose Comic Sans MS.**

Another Method

The menu equivalent is Format/Font/Font.

Your screen should be similar to Figure 1.49

Additional Information

You can show or hide the text formatting in the Outline tab using 💠 Show Formatting.

Font of current selection displayed in Font button

Displays or hides formatting in Outline tab

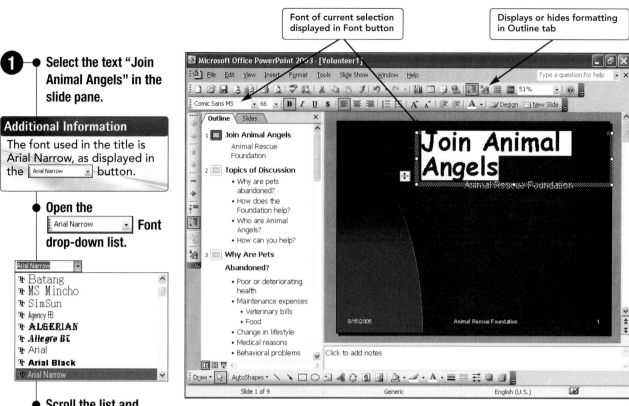

Figure 1.49

The text has changed to the new font style, and the Font button displays the font name used in the current selection. The formatting effects appear in the slide pane but are not displayed in the Outline tab.

Changing Font Size

The title text is also a little larger than you want it to be.

1 • Click Decrease Font Size 2 times.

• Size and move the title placeholder to display the title on one line above the red graphic line.

Additional Information

Use Increase Font Size to incrementally increase the point size of selected text.

Another Method

You could also specify the point size from the `18` Font Size drop-down list or use **F**ormat/**F**ont/**S**ize.

Your screen should be similar to Figure 1.50

Additional Information

If a selection includes text in several different sizes, the smallest size appears in the Font Size button followed by a + sign.

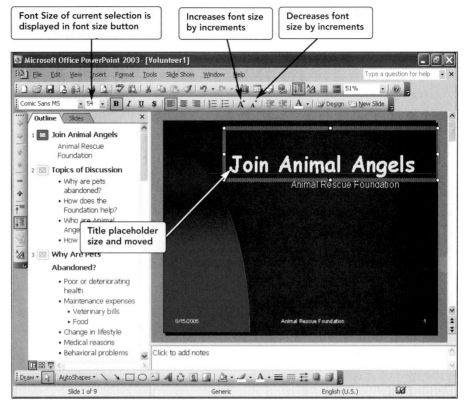

Figure 1.50

The Font Size button displays the point size of the current selection.

2 • Replace the subtitle text with your name.

• Reduce the size of the subtitle placeholder to fit the contents.

Having Trouble?

Drag the sizing handles to size the placeholder.

• Move the placeholder to the location shown in Figure 1.51.

Your screen should be similar to Figure 1.51

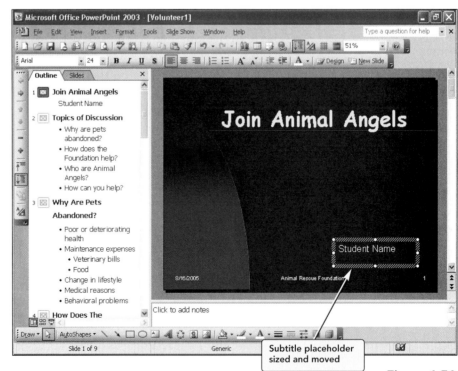

Figure 1.51

Adding and Removing Bullets

Next, you want to remove the bullets from the items on the history slide. You can quickly apply and remove bullets using ⊞ Bullets on the Formatting toolbar. This button applies the bullet style associated with the design template you are using. Because the placeholder items already include bullets, using this button will remove them.

1 ● **Select slide 5.**

   ● **Select both text placeholders.**

Having Trouble?

Hold down Ctrl while clicking on the placeholders to select both.

   ● **Click** ⊞ **Bullets.**

Another Method ○○○○

The menu equivalent is Format/**B**ullets and Numbering/Bulleted/None.

Your screen should be similar to Figure 1.52

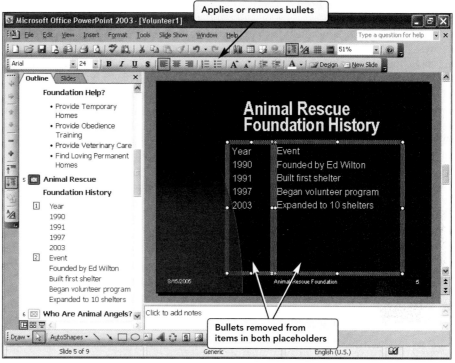

Figure 1.52

The bullets are removed from all the items in both placeholders. Now, however, you think it would look better to add bullets back to the four items under each column heading.

2 • Select the four years in the left column.

• Click ☰ Bullets.

• Apply bullets to the four events in the right column.

• Click outside the selected object to deselect it.

• Save the presentation again.

Your screen should be similar to Figure 1.53

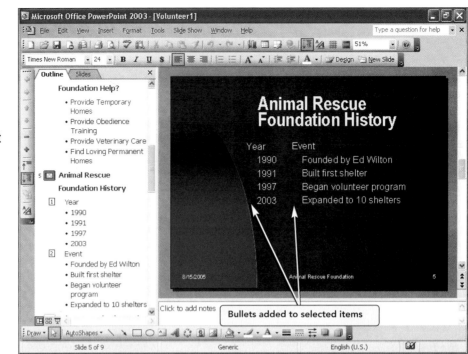

Figure 1.53

Bullets appear before the selected text items only.

Working with Graphics

Finally, you want to add a picture to the title slide. A picture is one of several different graphic objects that can be added to a slide.

Concept 8
Graphics

8 A **graphic** is a non-text element or object, such as a drawing or picture, that can be added to a slide. A graphic can be a simple **drawing object** consisting of shapes such as lines and boxes that can be created using features on the Drawing toolbar. A drawing object is part of your presentation document. A **picture** is an image such as a graphic illustration or a scanned photograph. Pictures are graphics that were created from another program and are inserted in a slide as embedded objects. An **embedded object** becomes part of the presentation file and can be opened and edited using the **source program**, the program in which it was created. Several examples of drawing objects and pictures are shown below.

Add graphics to your presentation to help the audience understand concepts, to add interest, and to make your presentation stand out from others.

Photograph

Clip Art

Drawing Object

Inserting a Graphic from the Clip Organizer

You want to add a graphic to the slide below the title line. Graphic files can be obtained from a variety of sources. Many simple drawings called **clip art** are available in the Clip Organizer that comes with Office 2003. The Clip Organizer's files, or clips, include art, sound, animation, and movies you can add to a presentation.

You can also create graphic files using a scanner to convert any printed document, including photographs, to an electronic format. Most images that are scanned and inserted into documents are stored as Windows bitmap files (.bmp). All types of graphics, including clip art, photographs, and other types of images, can be found on the Internet. These files are commonly stored as .jpg or .pcx files. Keep in mind that any images you locate on the Internet may be protected by copyright and should only be used with permission. You can also purchase CDs containing graphics for your use.

You decide to check the Clip Organizer to find a suitable graphic.

- Select slide 1.

- Click Insert Clip Art (in the Drawing toolbar).

Your screen should be similar to Figure 1.54

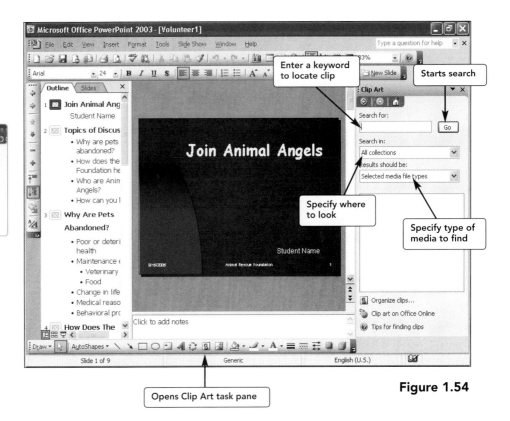

Figure 1.54

The Clip Art task pane appears in which you can enter a keyword, a word or phrase that is descriptive of the type of graphic you want to locate. The graphics in the Clip Organizer are organized by topic and are identified with several keywords that describe the graphic. You can also specify the locations to search and the type of media files, such as clip art, movies, photographs or sound, to display in the search results. You want to find clip art and photographs of animals.

2
- If necessary, select any existing text in the Search For text box.

- In the Search for text box, type **animal**.

- If All Collections is not displayed in the Search In text box, select Everywhere from the drop-down list.

- Open the Results Should Be drop-down list.

- Select Photographs and Clip Art and deselect Movies and Sounds.

Having Trouble?

Click the box next to an option to select or deselect (clear the checkmark).

- Click outside the drop-down list to close it.

- Click Go .

- Point to a thumbnail in the Results area.

Your screen should be similar to Figure 1.55

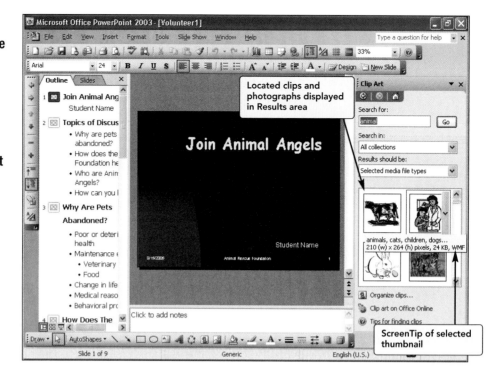

Figure 1.55

The program searches all locations on your computer and, if you have an Internet connection established, searches Microsoft's Clip Art and Media Web site for clip art and graphics that match your search term. The Results area displays thumbnails of all located graphics. Pointing to a thumbnail displays a ScreenTip containing the **keywords** associated with the picture and information about the picture properties. It also displays a drop-down list bar that accesses the item's shortcut menu.

3 ● Scroll the results list to the bottom to view all of the located clips and photographs.

Your screen should be similar to Figure 1.56

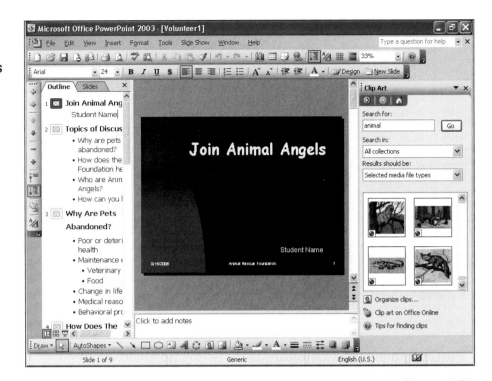

Figure 1.56

Additional Information

Entering keywords separated with a comma requires that either keyword be associated with the graphic and therefore expands the search.

Because so many pictures were located, you decide to narrow your search to display pictures of animals and healthcare only. Adding a second word to your search will narrow the number of graphics located. This is because it requires that both words must be associated with the graphic in order for it to appear in the results. Additionally, because the graphic is sometimes difficult to see, you can preview it in a larger size.

④ ● Add the word **healthcare** following the word "animal" in the Search For text box.

● Click **Go**.

● If necessary, scroll the results area to see the graphic of two people and a dog.

● Point to the graphic and click ⌄ to open the shortcut menu.

Additional Information

The shortcut menu commands are used to work with and manage the items in the Clip Organizer.

● Choose **Preview/Properties**.

Your screen should be similar to Figure 1.57

Having Trouble?

If this graphic is not available in the Clip Organizer, close the Clip Art task pane and choose **I**nsert/**P**icture/**F**rom File and insert pp01_Animalcare.bmp from your data file location. Skip to below Figure 1.58.

Because the search term is more specific, fewer results are displayed. The Preview/Properties dialog box displays the selected graphic larger so it is easier to see. It also displays more information about the properties associated with the graphic. You can now see that animals and healthcare are both keywords associated with this graphic. You think this looks like a good choice and will insert it into the document.

Figure 1.57

5 • Click [Close] to close the dialog box.

• Click on the graphic to insert it in the document.

Another Method
You could also choose Insert from the thumbnail's shortcut menu.

• Close the Clip Art task pane.

Your screen should be similar to Figure 1.58

Figure 1.58

The clip art graphic is inserted in the center of the slide. It is a selected object and can be sized and moved like any other selected object. The **Picture toolbar** is also automatically displayed and is used to modify the graphic.

Inserting a Graphic from a File

Although you think this graphic looks good, you want to see how a photograph you recently scanned of a puppy would look instead. The photograph has been saved as pp01_Puppy.jpg.

1 • Click 🖼 Insert Picture (on the Drawing toolbar).

Another Method
The menu equivalent is Insert/Picture/From File.

• Change the location to your data file location.

Your screen should be similar to Figure 1.59

Having Trouble?
Your screen may display additional picture files.

Figure 1.59

The Insert Picture dialog box is similar to the Open and Save dialog boxes, except that the only types of files listed are files with picture file extensions. A thumbnail preview of each picture is displayed above the file name.

2 ● Select pp01_Puppy.jpg.

● Click [Insert ▼].

● Move the picture to the right to see the underlying clip art.

Your screen should be similar to Figure 1.60

Figure 1.60

The second graphic is inserted on the slide on top of the clip art object. As objects are added to a slide, they automatically stack in individual layers.

Concept 9

Stacking Order

9 **Stacking order** is the order in which objects are inserted into different layers of the slide. As each object is added to the slide, it is added to the top layer. Adding objects to separate layers allows each object to be positioned precisely on the page, including in front of and behind other objects. As objects are stacked in layers, they may overlap. To change the stacking order, open the Draw menu on the Drawing toolbar and select Order.

Because the photograph was the last object added to the slide, it is on the top layer of the stack. Although the photograph looks good, you think the clip art introduces the topic of volunteering better.

3 ● Click Undo (2 times).

Your screen should be similar to Figure 1.61

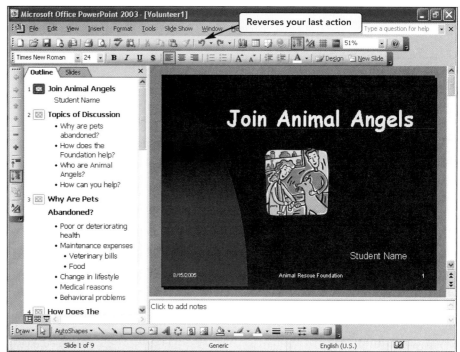

Figure 1.61

Using Undo reverses your last action. Notice that the Undo button includes a drop-down list button. Clicking this button displays a list of the most recent actions that can be reversed, with the most recent action at the top of the list. When you select an action from the drop-down list, you also undo all actions above it in the list.

Sizing and Moving a Graphic

Frequently, when a graphic is inserted, its size or placement will need to be adjusted. A graphic object is sized and moved just like a placeholder. You want to increase the graphic size slightly and position it in the space below the title.

1 ● **Click on the graphic to select it.**

● **Drag the bottom left corner sizing handle to increase its size to that shown in Figure 1.62.**

● **Drag the graphic to position it as shown in Figure 1.62.**

● **Click outside the graphic to deselect it.**

Your screen should be similar to Figure 1.62

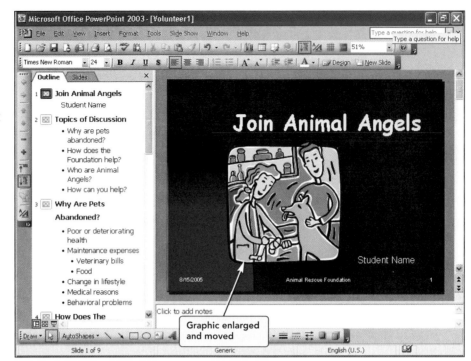

Figure 1.62

Now you think the title slide will make a much better impression. To see how the changes and enhancements you have made to the presentation will look full screen, you will run the slide show again.

2 ● **Save the presentation again.**

● **Run the slide show from the first slide.**

Previewing and Printing the Presentation

Although you still plan to make many changes to the presentation, you want to give a copy of the slides to the Foundation director to get feedback regarding the content and layout. Although your presentation looks good on your screen it may not look good when printed. Previewing the presentation allows you to see how it will look before you waste time and paper printing it out. Many times, you will want to change the print and layout settings to improve the appearance of the output.

Previewing the Presentation

Shading, patterns, and backgrounds that look good on the screen can make printed handouts unreadable, so you want to preview how the printout will look before making a copy for the director.

1 Click Print Preview.

Another Method

The menu equivalent is **F**ile/Print Pre**v**iew and the voice command is "Print preview."

Your screen should be similar to Figure 1.63

Having Trouble?

Your Print Preview may appear in color if you have a color printer.

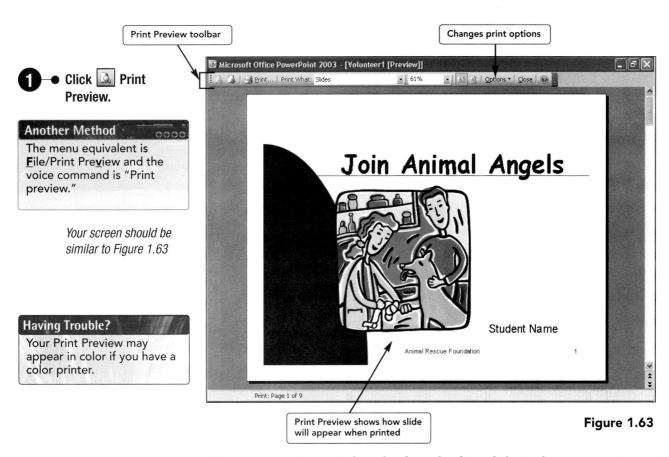

Print Preview shows how slide will appear when printed

Figure 1.63

The Print Preview window displays the first slide in the presentation as it will appear when printed using the selected printer. It is displayed in color if your selected printer is a color printer; otherwise, it appears in grayscale (shades of gray) as in Figure 1.63. Even if you have a color printer, you want to print the slides in grayscale. The Print Preview window also includes its own toolbar that lets you modify the default print settings.

2 If you need to change to grayscale, click Options ▾ .

● Choose **C**olor/Grayscale/**G**rayscale.

The default grayscale setting (shown in Figure 1.63) shows you how the slide would look with some of the background in white, with black text, and with patterns in grayscale.

Specifying Printed Output

The Preview window displays a single slide on the page as it will appear when printed. This is the default print setting. You can change the type of printed output using the Print What option. The output types are described in the table below. Only one type of output can be printed at a time.

Output Type	Description
Slides	Prints one slide per page.
Handouts	Prints multiple slides per page.
Outline View	Prints the slide content as it appears in Outline view.
Notes Pages	Prints the slide and the associated notes on a page.

Additional Information

You will learn about notes in Lab 2.

You want to change the print setting to Handouts to print several slides on a page.

- **Open the Print What drop-down menu.**

- **Choose Handouts (6 slides per page).**

Your screen should be similar to Figure 1.64

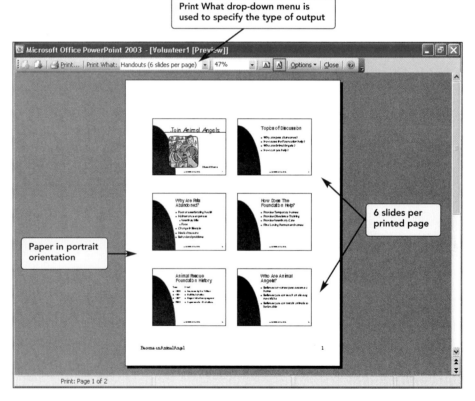

Figure 1.64

Changing Page Orientation

You also want to change the orientation or the direction the output is printed on a page. The default orientation for handouts is **portrait**. This setting prints across the width of the page. You will change the orientation to **landscape** so that the slides print across the length of the paper. Then you will preview the other pages.

1 ● Click [A] **Landscape.**

● Click [⬛] **Next Page to view page 2 of the handout.**

Your screen should be similar to Figure 1.65

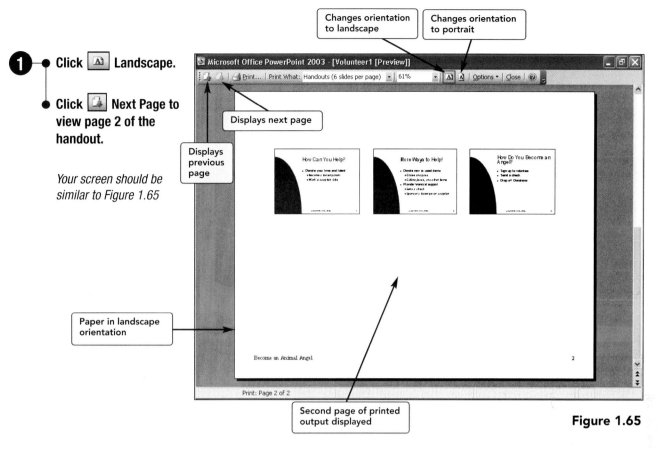

Changes orientation to landscape

Changes orientation to portrait

Displays next page

Displays previous page

Paper in landscape orientation

Second page of printed output displayed

Figure 1.65

The last three slides in the presentation are displayed on the second page in landscape orientation.

Printing the Presentation

Now, you are ready to print the handouts.

1 ● Click [🖨 Print...].

Another Method

The menu equivalent is **File/Print** and the keyboard shortcut is [Ctrl] + P. You can use [🖨] Print on the Standard toolbar if you do not need to make any changes to the default print settings.

Your screen should be similar to Figure 1.66

Selected printer name

Specifies number of copies

Specifies slides to print

Specifies type of output

Figure 1.66

Note: Please consult your instructor for printing procedures that may differ from the following directions.

The Name text box in the Printer section displays the name of the selected printer. You may need to specify the printer you will be using. (Your instructor will provide the printer to select.) The Print Range settings specify the slides to print. The default setting, All, prints all the slides, while Current Slide prints only the slide you are viewing. The Slides option is used to specify individual slides or a range of slides to print by entering the slide numbers in the text box. The Copies section is used to specify the number of copies of the specified print range. The default is to print one copy.

At the bottom of the dialog box, PowerPoint displays options that allow you to print color slides as black-and-white slides, to make the slide images fill the paper, and to add a frame around the slide. The grayscale and handout options you specified in the Print Preview window are already selected. The Frame Slides option is selected by default and displays a border around each slide.

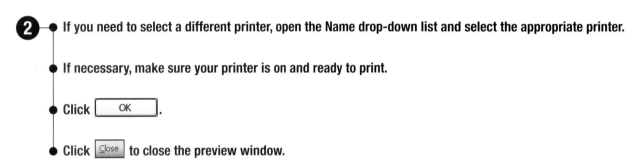

2 • If you need to select a different printer, open the Name drop-down list and select the appropriate printer.

• If necessary, make sure your printer is on and ready to print.

• Click OK .

• Click Close to close the preview window.

The 🖨 Printer icon appears in the status bar, indicating that the program is sending data to the Print Manager, and your handouts should be printing. Your printed output should be similar to that shown in the Case Study at the beginning of the lab.

Exiting PowerPoint

You have finished working on the presentation for now and will exit the PowerPoint program.

1 • Click ☒ Close in the title bar.

• If asked to save the file again, click Yes .

Another Method
The menu equivalent is **File/Exit** and the voice command is "File exit."

Focus on Careers

EXPLORE YOUR CAREER OPTIONS

Account Executive

Sales is an excellent entry point for a solid career in any company. Account Executive is just one of many titles that a sales professional may have; Field Sales and Sales Representative are two other titles. Account executives take care of customers by educating them on the company's latest products, designing solutions using the company's product line, and closing the deal to make the sale and earn their commission. These tasks require the use of effective PowerPoint presentations that educate and motivate potential customers. The salary range of account executives is limited only by his/her ambition; salaries range from $27,450 to more than $102,000. To learn more about this career visit http://www.bls.gov/oco/ocos119.htm, the Web site for the Bureau of Labor Statistics of the U.S. Department of Labor.

concept summary

Creating a Presentation

Template (PP1.7)

A template is a file containing predefined settings that can be used as a pattern to create many common types of presentations.

Presentation Style (PP1.10)

A PowerPoint presentation can be made using five different styles: onscreen presentations, Web presentations, black-and-white or color overheads, and 35mm slides.

Slide (PP1.11)

A slide is an individual "page" of your presentation.

AutoCorrect (PP1.19)

The AutoCorrect feature makes some basic assumptions about the text you are typing and, based on these assumptions, automatically identifies and/or corrects the entry.

Spelling Checker (PP1.20)

The spelling checker locates all misspelled words, duplicate words, and capitalization irregularities as you create and edit a presentation, and proposes possible corrections.

Layout (PP1.43)

The layout controls the way items are arranged on a slide.

Layout

Font and Font Size

Font and Font Size (PP1.50)

A font is a set of characters with a specific design. Each font has one or more sizes.

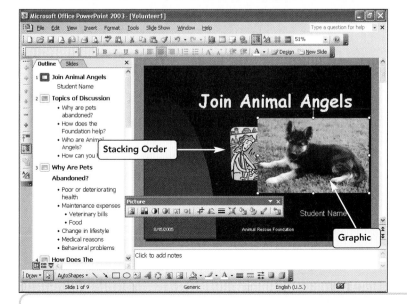

Graphics (PP1.54)

A graphic is a non-text element or object, such as a drawing or picture, that can be added to a slide.

Stacking Order (PP1.60)

Stacking order is the order in which objects are inserted in to different layers of the slide.

Concept Summary   **PP1.69**

key terms

AutoCorrect   PP1.19

character formatting   PP1.49

clip art   PP1.55

current slide   PP1.15

custom dictionary   PP1.20

default   PP1.7

demote   PP1.27

drawing object   PP1.54

Drawing toolbar   PP1.5

embedded object   PP1.54

font   PP1.50

font size   PP1.50

footer   PP1.11

format   PP1.49

graphic   PP1.54

keyword   PP1.56

landscape   PP1.64

layout   PP1.43

main dictionary   PP1.20

object   PP1.23

Outlining toolbar   PP1.5

pane   PP1.13

paragraph formatting   PP1.49

picture   PP1.54

Picture toolbar   PP1.59

placeholder   PP1.23

point   PP1.50

portrait   PP1.64

promote   PP1.27

sans serif   PP1.50

selection rectangle   PP1.24

serif   PP1.50

sizing handles   PP1.45

slide   PP1.11

slide show   PP1.47

source program   PP1.54

spelling checker   PP1.20

stacking order   PP1.60

template   PP1.7

thumbnail   PP1.13

typeface   PP1.50

view   PP1.12

wizard   PP1.8

workspace   PP1.6

microsoft office specialist skills

The Microsoft Office Specialist certification program is designed to measure your proficiency in performing basic tasks using the Office 2003 applications. Certification demonstrates that you have the skills and provides a valuable industry credential for employment. After completing this lab, you have learned the following Microsoft Office PowerPoint 2003 Specialist skills:

Skill Sets	Skill Standards	Page
Creating Content	Create new presentations from templates	PP1.7
	Insert and edit text-based content	PP1.16
	Insert pictures, shapes, and graphics	PP1.54
Formatting Content	Format text-based content	PP1.49
	Format pictures, shapes, and graphics	PP1.61
Managing and Delivering Presentations	Organize a presentation	PP1.12,1.40–1.45
	Deliver presentations	PP1.47
	Save and publish presentations	PP1.31
	Print slides, outlines, handouts, and speaker notes	PP1.62

command summary

Command	Shortcut Key	Button	Voice	Action
File/**N**ew	Ctrl + N			Creates new presentation
File/**O**pen	Ctrl + O		Open / File open / Open file	Opens existing presentation
File/**C**lose		✕	Close presentation	Closes presentation
File/**S**ave	Ctrl + S		Save	Saves presentation
File/Save **A**s				Saves presentation using new file name and/or location
File/Print Pre**v**iew			Print preview	Displays preview of file
File/**P**rint	Ctrl + P			Prints presentation
Edit/**U**ndo	Ctrl + Z		Undo	Reverses last action
Edit/Cu**t**	Ctrl + X	✂	Cut	Cuts selection to Clipboard
Edit/**P**aste	Ctrl + V		Paste	Pastes item from Clipboard
Edit/Select A**l**l	Ctrl + A			Selects all objects on a slide or all text in an object, or (in Outline pane) an entire outline
Edit/**D**elete Slide	Delete			Deletes selected slide
View/**N**ormal			Normal / Normal view	Switches to Normal view
View/Sli**d**e Sorter			Slide sorter	Switches to Slide Sorter view
View/Slide Sho**w**			View show / Begin slide show / Start slide show / Slide show view	Runs slide show

command summary (continued)

Command	Shortcut Key	Button	Voice	Action
Insert/New Slide	Ctrl + M	New Slide	New slide Insert new slide	Inserts new slide
Insert/Picture/Clip Art				Opens Clip Organizer and inserts selected clip art
Insert/Picture/From File				Inserts a picture from file on disk
Format/Font/Font		Arial		Changes font type
Format/Font/Size		18		Changes font size
Format/Bullets and Numbering/Bulleted				Adds and removes selected bullets
Format/Slide Layout				Changes the layout of an existing or new slide
Tools/Spelling	F7	ABC		Spell-checks presentation

lab exercises

1. In the following PowerPoint screen, several items are identified by letters. Enter the correct term for each item in the spaces that follow.

A. _____
B. _____
C. _____
D. _____
E. _____
F. _____
G. _____
H. _____

I. _____
J. _____
K. _____
L. _____
M. _____
N. _____
O. _____

Possible answers for the screen identification are:

Font	Placeholder
Normal view	Show formatting
Slide Sorter	Align left
Notes pane	Bullets
Design template	Spelling
Current slide	Misspelled word
Promotes item	Footer
Demotes item	Print Preview

lab exercises

matching

Match the numbered item with the correct lettered description.

1. formatting _____ **a.** allows text entry, deletion, selection, and formatting of an object when border appears hatched

2. title slide _____ **b.** use to view and rearrange all slides

3. slide show _____ **c.** demotes items in outline

4. [→] _____ **d.** controls the way items are arranged on a slide

5. .ppt _____ **e.** file of predefined settings used as a pattern to create common types of presentations

6. Slide Sorter view _____ **f.** displays each slide full screen and in order

7. workspace _____ **g.** boxes that contain specific types of items or objects

8. template _____ **h.** default file extension for PowerPoint documents

9. selection rectangle _____ **i.** first slide in a presentation

10. layout _____ **j.** large area of the screen where presentations are displayed

_____ **k.** enhancing the appearance of the slide to make it more readable or attractive

multiple choice

Circle the letter of the correct response.

1. If you want to provide copies of your presentation to the audience showing multiple slides on a page, you would print _____.
   a. slides
   b. handouts
   c. note pages
   d. outline area

2. If you only have access to an overhead projector, you should create _____.
   a. onscreen presentations
   b. Web presentations
   c. black-and-white or color transparencies
   d. all the above

3. The step in the development of a presentation that focuses on determining the length of your speech, the audience, the layout of the room, and the type of audiovisual equipment available is _____.
   a. planning
   b. creating
   c. editing
   d. enhancing

4. If you wanted to view the slides as your audience would, you would:
   a. print the notes pages
   b. run the slide show
   c. maximize the PowerPoint application window
   d. close the tabs pane

5. To make your presentation professional and easy to read, you would use a _____ font for the text and a _____ font for the headings.
   a. serif; sans serif
   b. large; small
   c. sans serif; serif
   d. red; black

6. If you want to work on all aspects of your presentation, switch to _____ view, which displays the slide pane, outline pane, and note pane.
   a. Slide Sorter
   b. Outline
   c. Slide
   d. Normal

7. When the spelling checker is used, you can create a _____ dictionary to hold words that you commonly use but are not included in the main dictionary.
   a. custom
   b. official
   c. personal
   d. common

8. Dragging the _____ sizing handles adjusts both the height and width of the placeholder at the same time.
   a. top
   b. bottom
   c. side
   d. corner

9. A(n)_____is an onscreen display of your presentation.
   a. outline
   b. handout
   c. slide show
   d. slide

10. Onscreen presentations can be designed specifically for the World Wide Web, where a(n) _____ serves as the presentation tool.
    a. overhead projector
    b. browser
    c. white board
    d. computer screen

true/false

Circle the correct answer to the following questions.

1.	A slide is a set of characters with a specific design.	True	False
2.	The suggested maximum number of bullets on a slide is six.	True	False
3.	All drawing objects are inserted into the same layer of the presentation.	True	False
4.	Practicing the delivery of your presentation is the final step in presentation development	True	False
5.	Sans serif fonts have a flair at the base of each letter that visually leads the reader to the next letter.	True	False
6.	The page orientation can be landscape or portrait.	True	False
7.	Graphics are objects, such as charts, drawings, pictures, and scanned photographs, that provide visual interest or clarify data.	True	False
8.	Character formatting features affect selected characters only, while paragraph formatting features affect an entire paragraph.	True	False
9.	A layout contains placeholders for the different items such as bulleted text, titles, charts, and so on.	True	False
10.	Font size is the width of the character and is commonly measured in points.	True	False

fill-in

Complete the following statements by filling in the blanks with the correct terms.

1. _____ order is the order objects are inserted in the different layers of the slide.

2. An embedded object is edited using the _____ program.

3. The _____ Wizard is a guided approach that helps you determine the content and organization of your presentation through a series of questions.

4. The size of a _____ can be changed by dragging its sizing handles.

5. Boxes that are designed to contain specific types of objects such as the slide title, bulleted text, charts, tables, and pictures are called _____.

6. The _____ toolbar contains buttons that are used to change the appearance or format of the presentation.

7. A _____ is text or graphics that appears at the bottom of each slide.

8. A _____ is an individual "page" of your presentation.

9. _____ is a PowerPoint feature that advises you of misspelled words as you add text to a slide and proposes possible corrections.

10. A _____ is a miniature of a slide.

step-by-step

Triple Crown Presentation ★

1. Logan Thomas works at Adventure Travel Tours. He is working on a presentation about lightweight hiking he will present to a group of interested clients. He has found some new information to add to the presentation. Logan also wants to rearrange several slides and make a few other changes to improve the appearance of the presentation. The handouts of the completed presentation are shown here.

a. Open the file pp01_Triple Crown. Enter your name in the subtitle on slide 1.

b. Run the slide show to see what Logan has done so far.

c. Spell-check the presentation, making the appropriate corrections.

d. Change the layout of slide 2 to Title, Text, and content. (Hint: Use F**o**rmat/Slide **L**ayout.) Increase the font size of the bulleted text on slide 2 from 28 to 32 points. Size and position the title, graphic, and text appropriately.

e. Appropriately size and position the graphic on slide 3.

f. Insert the picture pp01_Jump on slide 4. Size and position it appropriately.

g. Move slide 6 before slide 5.

h. Select slide 4. Open the Outline tab and click at the end of the last bullet under "Why go lightweight?" Press Enter and promote the new bullet twice. Enter the title **Less is More**.

i. Change the layout of the new slide to Title, Text, and Content. Insert the picture pp01_Stream in the content placeholder.

j. Change the layout of slide 7 to Title and Text layout. Add the following text in the text place-holder: **Contact Tracey Lynn at Adventure Travel Tours or visit us on the Web at www.AdventureTravel Tours.com/hiking**.

k. Run the slide show.

l. Save the presentation as Triple Crown Presentation. Print the slides as handouts (four per page).

Writing Effective Resumes ★ ★

2. You work for the career services center of a university and you are planning a presentation on how to write effective resumes and cover letters. A coworker has started such a presentation, but has not had time to edit or finalize it. You need to clean it up and enhance it a bit before presenting it. The handouts of the completed presentation are shown here.

a. Open the PowerPoint presentation pp01_Resume.

b. Run the Spelling Checker and correct any spelling errors.

c. In Normal view, change the font size of the title in the title slide to 44 pt. Increase the subtitle to 36 pt.

d. Replace "Student Name" in slide 2 with your name.

e. On slide 5, capitalize the first word of each bulleted item.

f. Since there is too much text on slide 6, split the slide content into two slides.

g. Reorganize the bulleted items on slide 10 so that "Types of cover letters" is the first item. To match the slide order with the way the topics are now introduced, move slide 13 before slide 11.

h. Break each bulleted item on slide 13 into two or three bullets

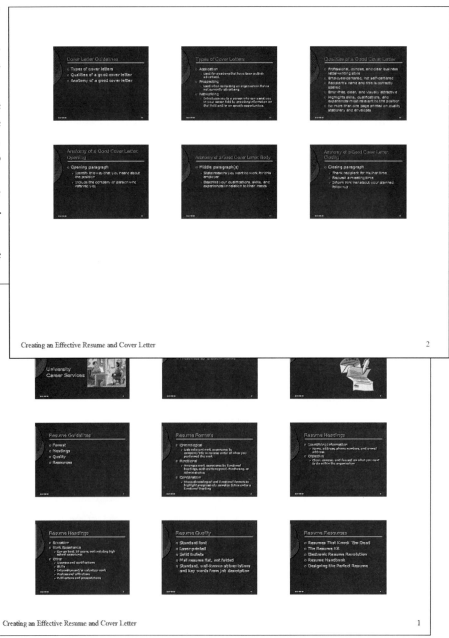

each as appropriate. Capitalize the first word of each bulleted item. Remove commas and periods at the end of the items. Split the slide content into three slides. Add an appropriate slide title to the slides.

i. On the title slide, insert the pp01_Success clip art. Resize and position it as shown in the example.

j. On slide 3, insert the pp01_Cover Letter clip art below the bulleted list. Position it in the lower right corner of the slide.

k. Save the presentation as Resume1.

l. Run the slide show.

m. Print the slides as handouts (nine per page in landscape orientation) and close the presentation.

Massage Therapy ★ ★

3. Lifestyle Fitness Club is opening a new spa offering personal services that include therapeutic massage. Prior to opening, the club wants to promote the services to the community. The spa manager has asked you create a presentation that can be used as a sales tool with local groups and organizations. You have organized the topics to be presented and located several clip art graphics that will complement the talk. Now you are ready to begin creating the presentation. The handouts of the completed presentation are shown here.

a. Start PowerPoint 2003. Open the New Presentation task pane.

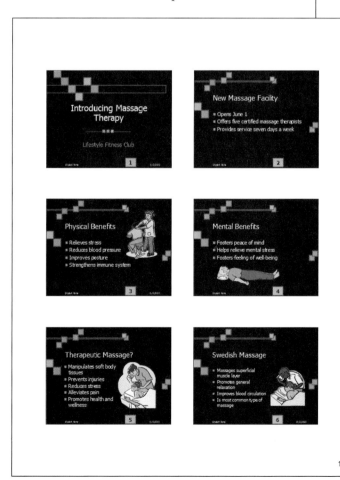

b. Using the AutoContent wizard, select Recommending a Strategy as the type of presentation, and select On-screen as the style of output for the presentation. Enter **Introducing Massage Therapy** in the Presentation Title text box. Enter your name in the footer text box. Keep the other footer options as they are.

c. Replace the owner name, your first name, on the title slide with **Lifestyle Fitness Club**.

d. Delete slide 2.

e. Replace the title and sample bullets on slide 2 with:

Title: **New Massage Facility**

Bullet 1: **Opens May 1**

Bullet 2: **Offers five certified massage therapists**

Bullet 3: **Provides service seven days a week**

Bullet 4: **Call now for an appointment**

f. Replace the title and sample bulleted text on slide 3 with:

Title: **Therapeutic Massage**

Bullet 1: **Manipulates soft body tissues**

Bullet 2: **Prevents injuries**

Bullet 3: **Alleviates pain**

Bullet 4: **Reduces stress**

Bullet 5: **Promotes health and wellness**

g. Change the title of slide 4 to **Reflexology** and replace the sample bullet text with the following bulleted items:

Bullet 1: **Massage points on hands and feet**

Bullet 2: **Points correspond to areas of the body**

Bullet 3: **Entire body affected**

h. Change the title of slide 5 to **Sports Massage Therapy** and include the following bulleted items:

Bullet 1: **Maintenance Massage**

Demoted Bullet 2: **Regular program of massage**

Demoted Bullet 3: **Helps athletes reach optimal performance**

Bullet 4: **Event Massage**

Demoted Bullet 5: **Readies athlete for top performance**

Demoted Bullet 6: **Stimulates circulation**

Bullet 7: **Rehabilitation Massage**

Demoted Bullet 8: **Speeds healing**

Demoted Bullet 9: **Reduces discomfort**

i. Change bullet 1 on slide 2 to **Opens June 1**. Delete bullet 4.

j. Insert a new slide after slide 2 using the Title and Text layout. Add the title **Benefits** and the following bulleted items:

Bullet 1: **Physical**

Demoted Bullet 2: **Relieves stress**

Demoted Bullet 3: **Reduces blood pressure**

Demoted Bullet 4: **Improves posture**

Demoted Bullet 5: **Strengthens immune system**

Bullet 6: **Mental**

Demoted Bullet 7: **Fosters peace of mind**

Demoted Bullet 8: **Helps relieve mental stress**

Demoted Bullet 9: **Fosters a feeling of well-being**

Change the order of bullets 3 and 4 on slide 4.

k. Insert a new slide after slide 5 using the Title and Text layout. Add the title **Shiatsu and Accupressure** and the following bulleted items:

Bullet 1: **Uses system of finger-pressure massage**

Bullet 2: **Based on Asian healing concepts**

Bullet 3: **Treats invisible channels of energy flow**

l. Change the title of slide 8 to **Swedish Massage** and include the following bulleted items:

Bullet 1: **Massages superficial muscle layer**

Bullet 2: **Promotes general relaxation**

Bullet 3: **Improves blood circulation**

Bullet 4: **Is most common type of massage**

m. Split the text on slide 3 between two slides. Title the first slide **Physical Benefits** and the second slide **Mental Benefits**. Delete the first bullet on both slides and promote the remaining bullets.

n. Change the font of the title on the title slide to 48 pt and the subtitle to 32 pt.

o. Insert the graphic pp01_Relaxation on slide 4. Size and position it appropriately.

p. Move slide 9 before slide 6.

q. Insert graphics of your choice to slides 3, 5, and 6. Size and position them appropriately.

r. Spell-check the presentation, making the appropriate changes.

s. Run the slide show.

t. Save the presentation as Massage Therapy.

u. Print the slides as handouts (six per page).

Coffee Product Knowledge ★ ★ ★

4. As the manager of the Downtown Internet Café, you want to make a presentation to the other employees about the various blends of coffee that the cafe offers. The purpose of this presentation is to enable employees to answer the many questions that are asked by customers when looking at the Blend of the Day board or choosing the type of coffee beans they want to purchase. The handouts of the completed presentation are shown here.

a. Start PowerPoint 2003. Open the new Presentation task pane.

b. Using the AutoContent wizard, select Training as the type of presentation and select Color Overheads as the presentation style. Enter **Coffee Talk** in the Presentation Title text box. Enter your name in the footer text box and keep the other footer settings as they are.

c. Replace your name in the title slide with **Downtown Internet Cafe**.

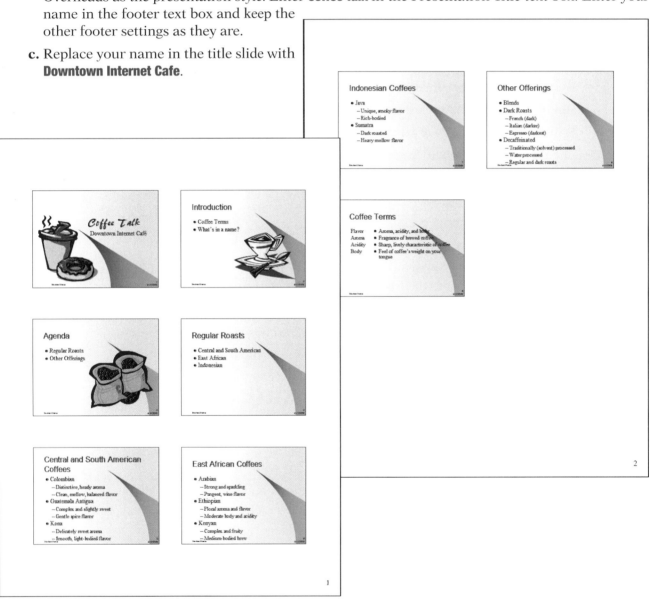

d. Replace the sample bulleted text on slide 2 with the following:

    Bullet 1: **What's in a name?**

e. Replace the sample bulleted text on slide 3 with the following:

    Bullet 1: **Regular Roasts**

    Bullet 2: **Other Offerings**

f. Move slide 4 to the end of the presentation after slide 9.

g. In Normal view, change the title of slide 4 to **Regular Roasts** and replace the sample bulleted text with the following:

    Bullet 1: **Central and South American**

    Bullet 2: **East African**

    Bullet 3: **Indonesian**

h. Change the title of slide 5 to **Central and South American Coffees** and replace the sample bulleted text with the following:

    Bullet 1: **Colombian**

        Demoted Bullet 2: **Distinctive, heady aroma**

        Demoted Bullet 3: **Clean, mellow, balanced flavor**

    Bullet 4: **Guatemala Antigua**

        Demoted Bullet 5: **Complex and slightly sweet**

        Demoted Bullet 6: **Gentle spice flavors**

    Bullet 7: **Kona**

        Demoted Bullet 8: **Delicately sweet aroma**

        Demoted Bullet 9: **Smooth, light-bodied flavor**

i. Change the title of slide 6 to **East African Coffees** and replace the sample bulleted text with the following:

    Bullet 1: **Arabian**

        Demoted Bullet 2: **Strong and sparkling**

        Demoted Bullet 3: **Pungent, wine flavor**

    Bullet 4: **Ethiopian**

        Demoted Bullet 5: **Floral aroma and flavor**

        Demoted Bullet 6: **Moderate body and acidity**

    Bullet 7: **Kenyan**

        Demoted Bullet 8: **Medium-bodied brew**

        Demoted Bullet 9: **Complex and fruity**

j. Change the title of slide 7 to **Indonesian Coffees** and replace the sample bulleted text with the following:

    Bullet 1: **Java**

        Demoted Bullet 2: **Unique, smoky flavor**

        Demoted Bullet 3: **Rich-bodied**

Bullet 4: **Sumatra**

  Demoted Bullet 5: **Dark roasted**

  Demoted Bullet 6: **Heavy mellow flavor**

k. Change the title of slide 8 to **Other Offerings** and replace the sample bulleted text and graphic with the following:

  Bullet 1: **Blends**

  Bullet 2: **Dark Roasts**

    Demoted Bullet 3: **French (dark)**

    Demoted Bullet 4: **Italian (darker)**

    Demoted Bullet 5: **Espresso (darkest)**

  Bullet 6: **Decaffeinated**

    Demoted Bullet 7: **Traditionally (solvent) processed**

    Demoted Bullet 8: **Water processed**

    Demoted Bullet 9: **Regular and dark roasts**

l. Change the order of the last two demoted bulleted items in slide 6.

m. Add a second bullet to slide 2 with the text **Coffee Terms**.

n. Change the title of slide 9 to **Coffee Terms**. Change the layout to Title and 2-Column Text. (Hint: Use F<u>o</u>rmat/Slide <u>L</u>ayout.) Select and delete the graphic. Replace the sample bulleted text with the following in the columns indicated:

Left Column	Right Column
Bullet 1: **Flavor**	**Aroma, acidity, and body**
Bullet 2: **Aroma**	**Fragrance of brewed coffee**
Bullet 3: **Acidity**	**Sharp, lively characteristic of coffee**
Bullet 4: **Body**	**Feel of coffee's weight on your tongue**

o. On slide 9, remove the bullets from the left column. Size and position the column placeholders to align the information in both columns as shown in the example.

p. On the title slide, position the subtitle directly under the title. Change the font and size of the title to improve its appearance.

q. On the title slide, insert the clip art pp01_Logo. Resize and position it in the lower left corner. Move the title and subtitle to the right of the logo.

r. Insert the clip art pp01_Cuppa on slide 2. Appropriately size and position the bulleted items and clip art on the slide.

s. Insert the clip art pp01_Beans on slide 3. Appropriately size and position the clip art on the slide.

t. Run the Spelling Checker and correct any spelling errors.

u. Save the presentation as Coffee.

v. Run the slide show.

w. Print the slides as handouts (six per page).

Job Fair Presentation ★ ★

5. Jane is preparing for her talk on "Job Fairs" for her Career Club meeting. She has organized the topic to be presented and located several clip art graphics that will complement the talk. She is now ready to begin creating the presentation in PowerPoint. The handouts of the completed presentation are shown here.

a. Start PowerPoint 2003 and open the new Presentation task pane. Using the AutoContent wizard, select Recommending a Strategy as the type of presentation, and select Color Overheads as the style of output for the presentation. Enter **Making a Job Fair Work for You** in the Presentation Title text box. Enter your name in the footer text box. Keep the other footer options as they are.

b. Change the font of the title to 48 pts. Replace your name on the title slide with **University Career Club**.

c. Delete slide 2.

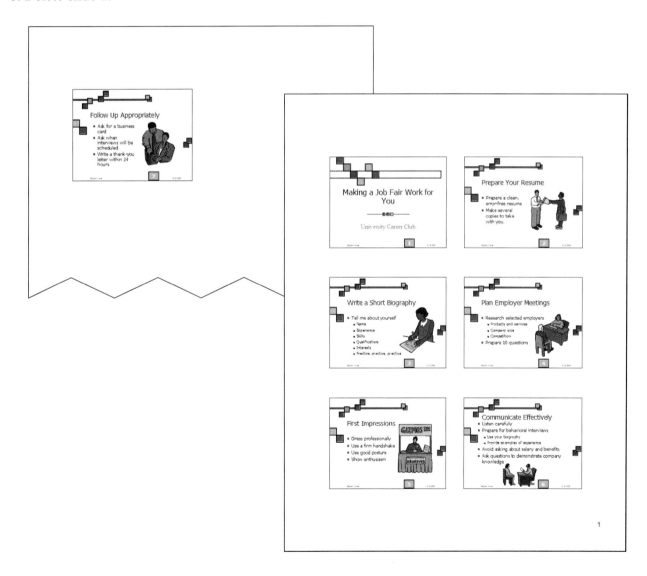

d. Replace the title and sample bulleted text on the new slide 2 with:

    Title: **Prepare Your Resume**

    Bullet 1: **Prepare a clean, error-free resume**

    Bullet 2: **Make several copies to take with you**

e. Replace the title and sample bulleted text in slide 3 with:

    Title: **Write a Short Biography**

    Bullet 1: **Tell me about yourself**

        Demoted Bullet 2: **Name**

        Demoted Bullet 3: **Experience**

        Demoted Bullet 4: **Skills**

        Demoted Bullet 5: **Qualifications**

        Demoted Bullet 6: **Interests**

        Demoted Bullet 7: **Practice, practice, practice**

f. Replace the title and sample bulleted text in slide 4 with:

    Title: **Plan Employer Meetings**

    Bullet 1: **Research selected employers**

        Demoted Bullet 2: **Products and services**

        Demoted Bullet 3: **Company size**

        Demoted Bullet 4: **Competition**

    Bullet 5: **Prepare 10 questions**

g. Change the title of slide 5 to **Communicate Effectively** and include the following bulleted items:

    Bullet 1: **Listen carefully**

    Bullet 2: **Prepare for behavioral interviews**

        Demoted Bullet 2: **Use your biography**

        Demoted Bullet 3: **Provide examples of experience**

    Bullet 3: **Avoid asking about salary and benefits**

    Bullet 4: **Ask questions to demonstrate company knowledge**

h. Change the title of slide 6 to **First Impressions** and include the following bulleted items:

    Bullet 1: **Dress professionally**

    Bullet 2: **Use a firm handshake**

    Bullet 3: **Use good posture**

    Bullet 4: **Show enthusiasm**

i. Insert a new title and text slide after slide 6. Change the title to **Follow Up Appropriately** and include the following bulleted items:

    Bullet 1: **Ask for a business card**

    Bullet 2: **Ask when interviews will be scheduled**

    Bullet 3: **Write a thank-you letter within 24 hours**

j. In Slide Sorter view, move slide 6 before slide 5.

k. Change the font of the subtitle on the title slide to Times New Roman and the size to 36 pt.

l. Insert the following graphics in the slides indicated. Adjust the slide layout as needed. Size and position the graphics appropriately.

Slide 2: pp01_Resume

Slide 3: pp01_Biography

Slide 4: pp01_Meeting

Slide 5: pp01_Booth

Slide 6: pp01_Interview

Slide 7: pp01_Follow Up

m. Run the slide show.

n. Save the presentation as Job Fairs.

o. Print the slides as handouts (six per page).

on your own

Internet Policy Presentation ★

1. You are working in the information technology department at Global Center Corporation. Your manager has asked you to give a presentation on the corporation's Internet policy to the new hire orientation class. Create your presentation in PowerPoint, using the information in the file pp01_InternetPolicy as a resource. Use the AutoContent wizard and the Generic template. Include your name in the footer. When you are done, run the spelling checker, then save your presentation as Internet Policy and print it.

Telephone Training Course ★ ★

2. You are a trainer with Super Software, Inc. You received a memo from your manager alerting you that many of the support personnel are not using proper telephone protocol or obtaining the proper information from the customers who call in. Your manager has asked you to conduct a training class that covers these topics. Using the pp01_Memo data file as a resource, prepare the slides for your class. Use the AutoContent wizard and select an appropriate presentation type. Include your name in the footer. When you are done, save the presentation as Phone Etiquette and print the handouts.

Pet Activities Presentation ★ ★

3. The director of Animal Rescue Foundation has asked you to prepare a presentation that introduces activities people can do with their new adopted pet. Using the pp01_Animals data file as a resource, create an onscreen presentation using the AutoContent wizard. Select an appropriate presentation type. Add clip art, where applicable. Include your name in the footer. When you are done, save the presentation as Pet Activities and print the handouts.

Job Placement Services ★ ★ ★

4. You work at a job placement agency, and you have been asked to do a presentation for new clients that describes the services your company offers and the categories used to list available jobs. Visit a local placement agency or search the Web to gather information about job placement agency services and job listings. Using the AutoContent wizard, select an appropriate presentation type to create a short presentation. Include your name in the footer. When you are done, save the presentation as Placement Services and print the handouts.

Careers with Animals ★ ★ ★

5. You have been volunteering at the Animal Rescue Foundation. The director has asked you to prepare a presentation on careers with animals to present to local schools in hopes that some students will be inspired to volunteer at the foundation. Using the pp01_AnimalCareers data file as a resource, create an onscreen presentation using the AutoContent wizard. Select an appropriate presentation type. Add some clip art where appropriate. Include your name in the footer. When you are done, save the presentation as Careers with Animals and print the handouts.

Modifying and Refining a Presentation

LAB **2**

Objectives

After completing this lab, you will know how to:

① Find and replace text.

② Create and enhance a table.

③ Modify graphic objects and create a text box.

④ Create and enhance AutoShapes.

⑤ Change the presentation's design and color scheme.

⑥ Change slide and title masters.

⑦ Hide the title slide footer.

⑧ Duplicate and hide slides.

⑨ Add animation, sound, transition, and build effects.

⑩ Control and annotate a slide show.

⑪ Add speaker notes.

⑫ Check style consistency.

⑬ Document a file.

⑭ Customize print settings.

Case Study

Animal Rescue Foundation

The Animal Rescue Foundation director was very impressed with your first draft of the presentation to recruit volunteers, and asked to see the presentation onscreen. While viewing it together, you explained that you plan to make many more changes to improve the appearance of the presentation. For example, you plan to use a different design background and to include more art and other graphic features to enhance the appearance of the slides. You also explained that you will add more action to the slides using the special effects included with PowerPoint to keep the audience's attention.

The director suggested that you include more information on ways that volunteers can help. Additionally, because the organization has such an excellent adoption rate, the director wants you to include a table to illustrate the success of the adoption program.

Office PowerPoint 2003 gives you the design and production capabilities to create a first-class onscreen presentation. These features include artist-designed layouts and color schemes that give your presentation a professional appearance. In addition, you can add your own personal touches by modifying text attributes, incorporating art or graphics, and including animation to add impact, interest, and excitement to your presentation.

© Ryan McVay/Getty Images

Slide designs and color schemes quickly enhance the look of a presentation.

Displaying information in tables makes data easy to understand.

Slide transitions, builds, and special effects add action to a slide show.

Replacing Text

You have updated the content to include the additional information on ways that volunteers can help the Animal Rescue Foundation. You want to see the revised presentation.

①

- **Start Office PowerPoint 2003.**

- **Open the file** pp02_Volunteer2.

- **If necessary, switch to Normal view and close the task pane.**

- **Replace Student Name in slide 1 with your name.**

- **Scroll the Outline tab to view the content of the revised presentation.**

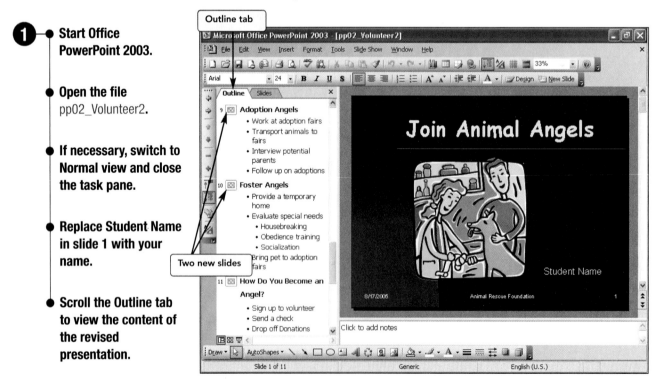

Your screen should be similar to Figure 2.1

Figure 2.1

You added two new slides, 9 and 10, with more information about the Animal Angels volunteer organization, making the total number of slides in the presentation 11. As you reread the content of the presentation, you decide to edit the text by replacing the word "pet" in many locations with the word "animal."

Concept 1
Find and Replace

1 To make editing easier, you can use the **Find and Replace** feature to find text in a presentation and re-place it with other text. For example, suppose you created a lengthy document describing the type of clothing and equipment needed to set up a world-class home gym, and then you decided to change "sneakers" to "athletic shoes." Instead of deleting every occurrence of "sneakers" and typing "athletic shoes," you can use the Find and Replace feature to perform the task automatically.

This feature is fast and accurate; however, use care when replacing so that you do not replace unintended matches.

Using Find and Replace

You want to replace selected occurrences of the word "pet" with "animal" throughout the presentation.

1 • If necessary, display slide 1.

• Choose **Edit/Replace**.

Another Method
The keyboard shortcut is Ctrl + H.

Additional Information
The **Edit/Find** command locates specified text only.

Your screen should be similar to Figure 2.2

Figure 2.2

In the Find What text box, you enter the text you want to locate. The text you want to replace is entered in the Replace With text box. The replacement text must be entered exactly as you want it to appear in your presentation. The two options described in the following table allow you to refine the procedure that is used to conduct the search.

Option	Effect on Text
Match Case	Distinguishes between uppercase and lowercase characters. When selected, finds only those instances in which the capitalization matches the text you typed in the Find What box.
Find Whole Words Only	Distinguishes between whole and partial words. When selected, locates matches that are whole words and not part of a larger word. For example, finds "cat" only and not "catastrophe" too.

You want to find all occurrences of the complete word "pet" and replace them with the word "animal." You will not use either option because you want to locate all words regardless of case and because you want to find "pet" as well as "pets" in the presentation. You will enter the text to find and replace and begin the search.

2
- Type **pet** in the Find What text box.

- Pres **Tab** or click in the Replace with text box.

Additional Information
After entering the text to find, do not press **←Enter** or this will choose **Find Next** and the search will begin.

- Type **animal** in the Replace With text box.

- Click **Find Next**.

- If necessary, move the dialog box so you can see the located text.

Your screen should be similar to Figure 2.3

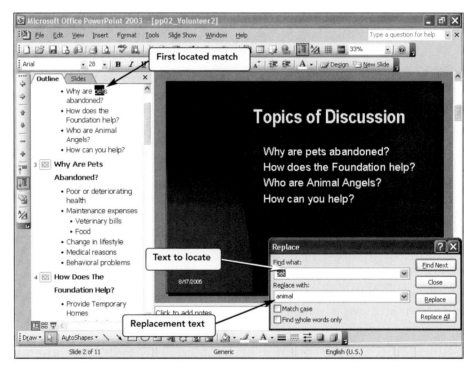

Figure 2.3

Additional Information
Find and Replace will highlight located text in whichever pane is current when the procedure started.

Immediately, the first occurrence of text in the presentation that matches the entry in the Find What text box is located and highlighted in the Outline tab. You will replace the located word in slide 2 with the replacement text.

3 ● Click [Replace].

Having Trouble?

If the next occurrence is not located automatically, click [Find Next] to continue.

Your screen should be similar to Figure 2.4

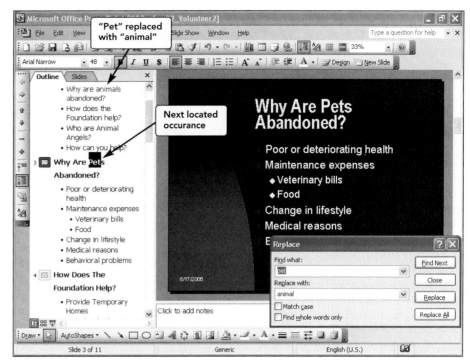

Figure 2.4

The highlighted text is replaced, and the next occurrence of the Find text is located in slide 3. Again, you want to replace this occurrence. As you do, notice the replacement is entered in lowercase even though it is replacing a word that begins with an uppercase character. You will correct this when you have finished using find and replace. If you do not want to replace a word, you can use [Find Next] to skip to the next occurrence without replacing it. You will continue to respond to the located occurrences.

4 Click **Replace**.

Having Trouble?
If the next occurrence is not located automatically, click **Find Next** to continue.

● Click **Find Next** to skip the third located text in slide 6.

● Replace the fourth located text in slide 8.

● Replace the located text in slide 10.

● Click **Find Next** to confirm that you want to skip the text in slide 6 again.

● Click **OK** in response to the finished searching dialog box.

● Click **Close** to close the Replace dialog box.

● Edit the word "animals" to "Animals" in the title of slide 3.

● Save the presentation as Volunteer2.

Your screen should be similar to Figure 2.5

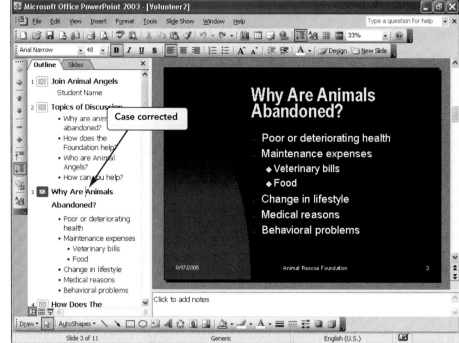

Figure 2.5

As you noticed, when you skip an occurrence, the program rechecks the presentation and asks you to reconfirm your choice before finishing. If you plan to change all occurrences, it is much faster to use the Replace All command button. Exercise care when using Replace All, however, because the search text you specify might be part of another word and you may accidentally replace text you want to keep.

In a similar manner you can find and replace fonts throughout a presentation using **F**ormat/**R**eplace Fonts. When using this feature, however, all text throughout the presentation that is in the specified font to find is automatically changed to the selected replacement font.

Creating a Simple Table

During your discussion with the director, he suggested that you add a slide containing data showing the success of the adoption program. The information in this slide will be presented using a table layout.

Concept 2
Table

2 A **table** is used to organize information into an easy-to-read format of horizontal rows and vertical columns. The intersection of a row and column creates a **cell** in which you can enter data or other information. Cells in a table are identified by a letter and number, called a **table reference**. Columns are identified from left to right beginning with the letter A, and rows are numbered from top to bottom beginning with the number 1. The table reference of the top leftmost cell is A1 because it is in the first column (A) and first row (1) of the table. The third cell in column 2 is cell B3. The fourth cell in column 3 is C4.

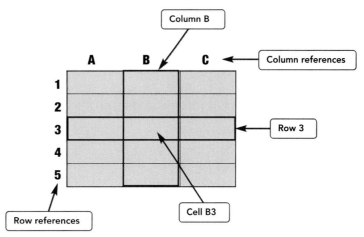

Tables are a very effective method for presenting information. The table layout organizes the information for readers and greatly reduces the number of words they have to read to interpret the data. Use tables whenever you can to make the information in your presentation easier to read.

The table you will create will display columns for the year, and for the number of rescues and adoptions. The rows will display the data for the past four years. Your completed table will be similar to the one shown here.

Year	Rescues	Adoptions
2000	1759	1495
2001	1847	1784
2002	1982	1833
2003	2025	2002

Using the Table Layout

To include this information in the presentation, you will insert a new slide after slide 5. Because this slide will contain a table showing the adoption data, you want to use the table slide layout.

1 ● Display slide 5.

● Click [🗐 New Slide].

● Under the Other Layouts group, click [▦] Title and Table.

● Close the Slide Layout task pane.

Your screen should be similar to Figure 2.6

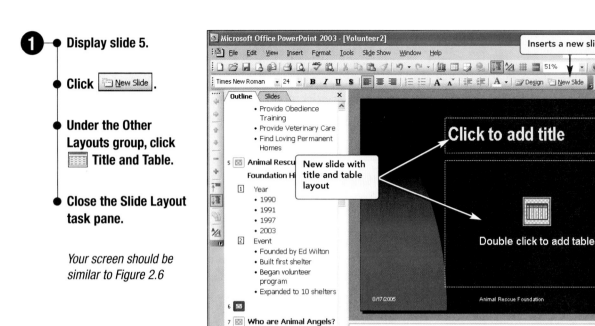

Figure 2.6

A new slide 6 with title and table placeholders is inserted.

Inserting the Table

Next, you want to add a slide title and then create the table to display the number of adoptions and rescues.

1 ● Enter the title **Success Rate** in the title placeholder.

● Double-click the table placeholder.

Your screen should be similar to Figure 2.7

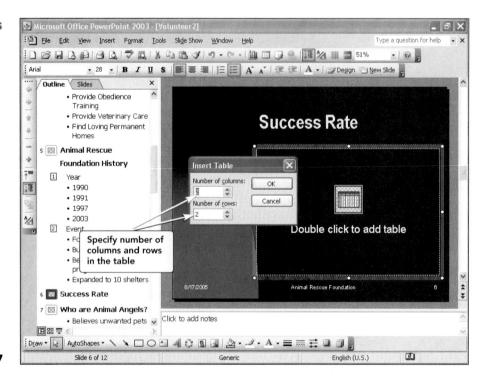

Figure 2.7

In the Insert Table dialog box, you specify the number of rows and columns for the table.

2 Specify 3 columns and 5 rows.

Having Trouble?
You can type in the number or use the scroll buttons to increase or decrease the number.

● Click [OK].

● If necessary, move the Tables and Borders toolbar out of the way or dock it below the Formatting toolbar.

Your screen should be similar to Figure 2.8

Having Trouble?
If the Tables and Borders toolbar is not displayed automatically, open it from the Toolbar shortcut menu.

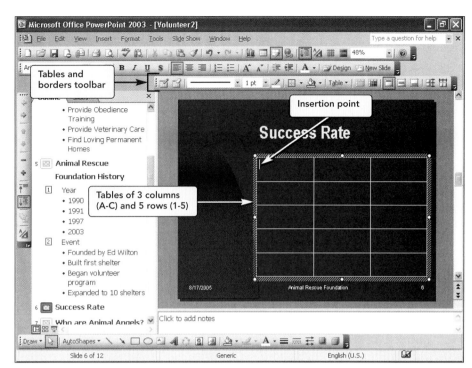

Figure 2.8

A basic table consisting of three columns and five rows is displayed as a selected object. The Tables and Borders toolbar buttons (identified below) are used to modify features associated with tables.

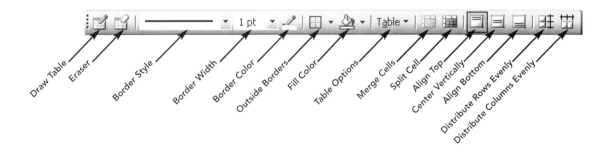

Entering Data in a Table

Now, you can enter the information into the table. The insertion point appears in the top left corner cell, cell A1, ready for you to enter text. To move in a table, click on the cell or use [Tab ⇆] to move to the next cell to the right and [⇧ Shift] + [Tab ⇆] to move to the cell to the left. If you are in the last cell of a row, pressing [Tab ⇆] takes you to the first cell of the next row. You can also use the [↑] and [↓] directional keys to move up or down a row. When you enter a large amount of text in a table, using [Tab ⇆] to move rather than the mouse is easier because your hands are already on the keyboard.

1 • Type Year.

• Press `Tab ⇥` or click on the next cell to the right.

Having Trouble?

Do not press `↵Enter` to move to the next cell as this adds a new line to the current cell. If this happens, press `Backspace` to remove it.

• Add the rest of the information shown below to the table.

Figure 2.9

	Col. A	Col. B	Col. C
Row 1	Year	Rescues	Adoptions
Row 2	2000	1759	1495
Row 3	2001	1847	1784
Row 4	2002	1982	1833
Row 5	2003	2025	2002

Your screen should be similar to Figure 2.9

Notice that text that is attached to an object, in this case a table, is not displayed in the outline pane.

Applying Text Formats

Additional Information

Many of the Formatting toolbar buttons are toggle buttons, which means that you can click the button to turn on the feature for the selection, and then click it again to remove it from the selection.

Next, you want to improve the table's appearance by formatting the table text. Fonts and font size are two basic text attributes that you have used already. The table below describes some additional text formats and their uses. The Formatting toolbar contains buttons for many of the formatting effects.

Format	Example	Use
Bold, italic	**Bold** *Italic*	Adds emphasis
Underline	<u>Underline</u>	Adds emphasis
Superscript	"To be or not to be."[1]	Used in footnotes and formulas
Subscript	H_2O	Used in formulas
Shadow	Shadow	Adds distinction to titles and headings
Color	Color Color Color	Adds interest

You will increase the font size of the table text and add bold and color.

1 ● Drag to select row 1 containing the column headings and increase the font size to 36 pt.

● Click **B** Bold to bold the selection.

Another Method ○○○○○

The menu equivalent is Format/Font/Font Style/Bold and the voice command is "On bold" to apply it and "Off bold" to remove it.

Figure 2.10

● Click 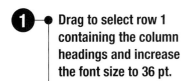 Font Color (in the Formatting or Drawing toolbar).

● Click on the blue color.

Another Method ○○○○

The menu equivalent is Format/Font/Color.

● Select rows 2 through 5 and increase the font size to 28.

Your screen should be similar to Figure 2.10

Sizing the Table Columns

Because you increased the font size of the headings, two of the headings are too large to display on a single line in the cell space. To correct this problem, you will adjust the size of the columns to fit their contents. To adjust the column width or row height, drag the row and column boundaries. The mouse pointer appears as a ↔ when you can size the column and ↕ when you can size the row.

1 ● **Decrease the width of the Year column and then adjust the width of the other two columns as in Figure 2.11.**

Your screen should be similar to Figure 2.11

Figure 2.11

Now the column headings easily fit within the cell space.

Aligning Text in Cells

Now that the columns are more appropriately sized, you want to center the text and data in the cells. To do this, you can change the alignment of the text entries.

Concept 3

Alignment

3

Alignment controls the position of text entries within a space. You can change the horizontal placement of an entry in a placeholder or a table cell by using one of the four horizontal alignment settings: left, center, right, and justified. You can also align text vertically in a table cell with the top, middle, or bottom of the cell space.

Horizontal Alignment	Effect on Text	Vertical Alignment	Effect on Text
Left	Aligns text against the left edge of the placeholder or cell, leaving the right edge of text, which wraps to another line, ragged.	Top **Text**	Aligns text at the top of the cell space.
Center	Centers each line of text between the left and right edges of the placeholder or cell.	Middle **Text**	Aligns text in the middle of the cell space.
Right	Aligns text against the right edge of the placeholder or cell, leaving the left edge of multiple lines ragged.	Bottom **Text**	Aligns text at the bottom of the cell space.
Justified	Aligns text evenly with both the right and left edges of the placeholder or cell.		

The commands to change horizontal alignment are options under the F**o**rmat/**A**lignment menu. However, using the shortcuts shown below is much quicker.

Alignment	Keyboard Shortcut	Button	Voice
Left	Ctrl + L	☰	Left justify
Center	Ctrl + E	☰	Centered
Right	Ctrl + R	☰	Right justify
Justified	Ctrl + J	☰	

You will center the cell entries both horizontally and vertically in their cell spaces.

1 • Select the entire contents of the table.

• Click ▤ Center (on the Formatting toolbar).

• Click ▣ Center Vertically (on the Tables and Borders toolbar).

Your screen should be similar to Figure 2.12

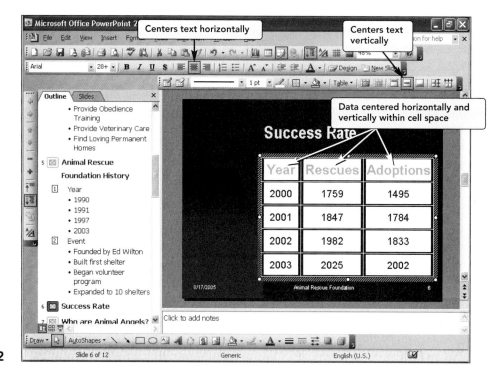

Figure 2.12

Changing the Border Size and Color

Next, you will add a color to the outside border and increase the thickness or weight of the border line. The Tables and Borders toolbar is used to make these enhancements.

1 • Open the 1 pt ▾ Border Width drop-down menu (on the Tables and Borders toolbar).

• Choose 4½ pt.

• Click 🖉 Border Color.

• Choose the dark red color.

Another Method ⦿⦿⦿⦿
You can also use the **T**able command on the F**o**rmat menu to modify borders.

• Point to the outside top border.

Your screen should be similar to Figure 2.13

Figure 2.13

The mouse pointer is a ✐ indicating that the Draw Table feature has been turned on. When on, this feature allows you to add row and column lines to an existing table. It is also used to modify the settings associated with the existing lines. You will drag the mouse pointer over the existing outside border to modify it to the new settings you have selected. As you drag, a dotted line identifies the section of the border that will be modified.

2 • Drag along the top border to apply the new settings.

Having Trouble?
You will need to look carefully to see the dotted line as you drag, as it is difficult to see in the cross-hatch border.

• In the same manner, apply the new border formats to the remaining three sides of the table.

• Click ▦ Draw Table to turn off the Draw Table feature.

• Click outside the table to deselect it.

Your screen should be similar to Figure 2.14

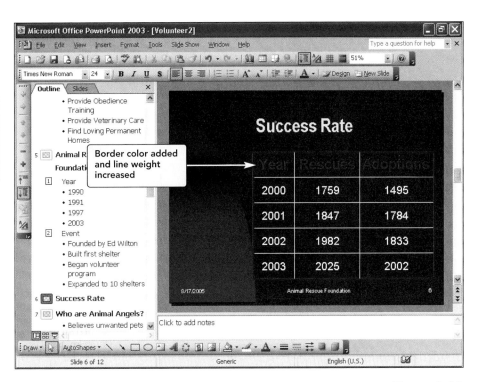

Figure 2.14

The increased weight and color have been applied to the outside border of the table.

Adding Background Fill Color

Finally, you will add a background fill color to the table.

1 ● Select the entire table.

● Click [ ] ▾ Fill Color.

Additional Information

You can use the [ ] ▾ Fill Color button on either the Drawing toolbar or the Tables and Borders toolbar.

● Choose <u>M</u>ore Fill Colors.

● If necessary, open the Standard tab.

Your screen should be similar to Figure 2.15

Figure 2.15

From the Standard tab of the Colors dialog box, you can select from a wider range of colors. The current fill color, gray, is selected. The sample box will show the new color you select in the upper half and the current color in the lower half. Because you have not yet selected a new color, only one color is displayed. You want to use a gold color for the table background.

2 ● Click on a gold color.

● Click [OK].

● Click outside the table to deselect it.

Your screen should be similar to Figure 2.16

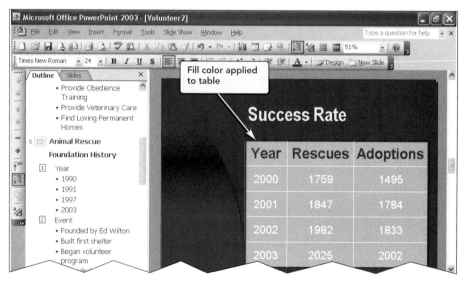

Figure 2.16

The new background color makes the data and row and column lines difficult to see. To correct this problem, you will change the color of the lines and data. You will change the interior line color to the same as the outside border color. Because there are many interior table lines, you will use the Format Table dialog box to make this change quickly.

3 ● **Change the font color of the years to the same blue as the column headings.**

● **Change the font color of the numeric data to a dark color of your choice.**

● **Select the entire table.**

● **Choose Borders and Fill from the table shortcut menu.**

● **Select the red color from the Color drop-down palette.**

● **Click on the two interior table border lines in the diagram.**

● **Click [Preview].**

● **If necessary, move the Format table dialog box to see the table.**

Your screen should be similar to Figure 2.17

Figure 2.17

All interior table lines in the table in the slide have changed to the selected color. This was faster than changing each interior line color using the Draw Table feature.

4 ● Click [OK] to apply the settings and close the dialog box.

● Choose <u>V</u>iew/<u>R</u>uler to display the ruler.

Additional Information

Use the ruler as a guide for placement of objects on the slide.

● Center the table horizontally on the slide as in Figure 2-18.

Having Trouble?

Drag the table placeholder border when the mouse pointer is ⁺✥ to move the table.

Having Trouble?

Align the center sizing handle of the table placeholder with the 0 position on the horizontal ruler.

● Click outside the table to deselect it.

● Save the presentation.

Your screen should be similar to Figure 2.18

Figure 2.18

The enhancements you added to the table greatly improve its appearance.

Modifying and Creating Graphic Objects

Now you are ready to enhance the presentation by adding several graphics. As you have seen, you can add many ready-made graphics to slides. Many of these can be customized to your needs by changing colors and adding and deleting elements. You can also create your own graphics using the AutoShapes feature.

Changing the Slide Layout

First, you want to add a graphic to slide 2. Before adding the graphic, you will change the slide layout from the bulleted list style to a style that is designed to accommodate text as well as other types of content such as graphics.

1 Display slide 2.

• From the slide shortcut menu, choose Slide **L**ayout.

Another Method ○○○○
The menu equivalent is F**o**rmat/Slide **L**ayout.

• Click Title, Text, and Content (from the Text and Content Layouts category).

Your screen should be similar to Figure 2.19

Figure 2.19

A content placeholder was added on the right side of the slide, and the bulleted text placeholder was resized and moved to the left side of the slide. Inside the content placeholder are six icons representing the different types of content that can be inserted. Clicking an icon opens the appropriate feature to add the specified type of content. You will add a clip art graphic of a question mark and then size the placeholder.

2

- Close the Slide Layout task pane.

- Click Insert Picture in the content placeholder.

- If necessary, change the Look In location to the location containing your data files.

- Locate and select the pp02_Question Mark clip art.

- Click 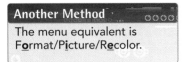.

- Increase the size of the graphic and position it as in Figure 2.20.

Your screen should be similar to Figure 2.20

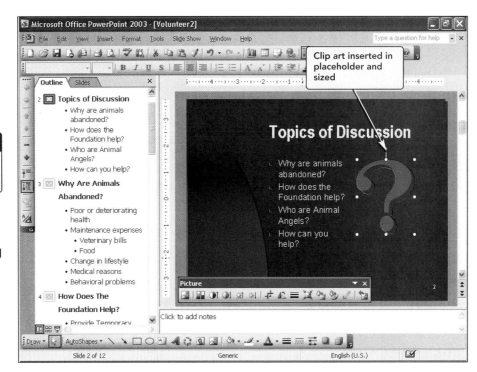

Figure 2.20

Recoloring a Picture

Now you want to change the color of the graphic to a bright gold color.

1

- If necessary, display the Picture toolbar.

- Click 🔲 Recolor Picture.

Your screen should be similar to Figure 2.21

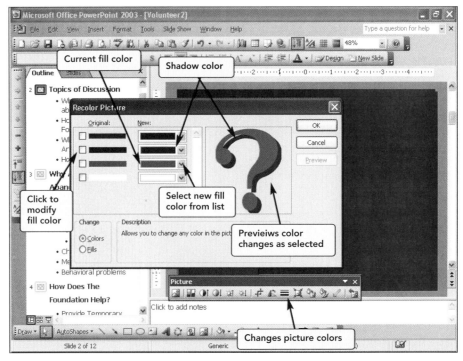

Figure 2.21

The original colors for each component of the picture are listed. Selecting the check box for a component allows you to change the color to a new color. You want to change the light blue color to gold. The preview area reflects your color changes as they are made.

2 ● Select the Original light blue color check box.

● Open the New color drop-down menu for the selected component and select gold.

Additional Information

To restore the original color, clear its check box.

● Click [OK].

● Deselect the clip art and, if necessary, turn off the Picture toolbar.

Your screen should be similar to Figure 2.22

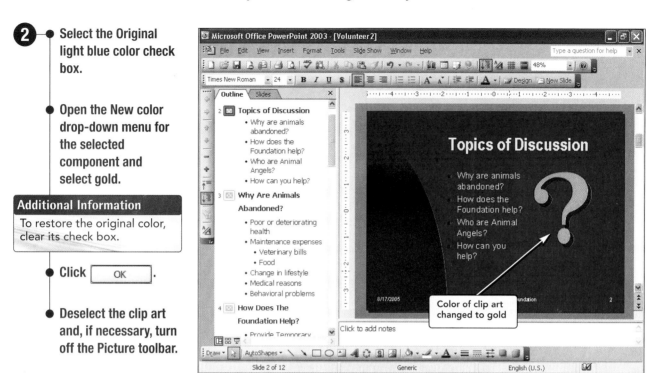

Figure 2.22

The graphic now adds much more color to the slide.

Duplicating a Slide

At the end of the presentation, you want to add a concluding slide. This slide needs to be powerful, because it is your last chance to convince your audience to join Animal Angels. To create the concluding slide, you will duplicate slide 1 and then create a graphic to complement the slide.

Duplicating a slide creates a copy of the selected slide and places it directly after the selected slide. You can duplicate a slide in any view, but in this case you will use the Outline tab in Slide view to duplicate slide 1 and move it to the end of the presentation.

1 ● Click slide 1 in the Outline tab.

● Choose **I**nsert/**D**uplicate Slide.

● Drag slide 2 in the Outline tab to the end of the list of slides.

Another Method ○○○○○
You can also duplicate a slide using the **C**opy and **P**aste commands on the **E**dit menu.

Your screen should be similar to Figure 2.23

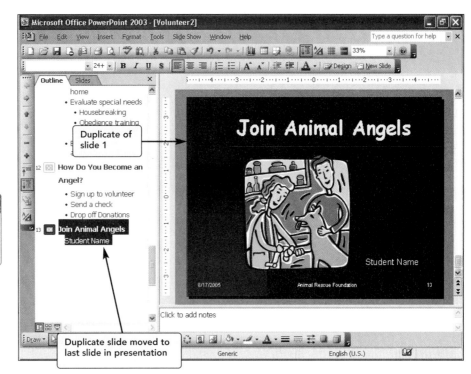

Figure 2.23

Duplicating the slide saved you time because you do not need to redo the changes to the title and subtitle.

Inserting an AutoShape

Additional Information
Most shapes can also be inserted from the Clip Organizer as well.

You want to replace the graphic with another of a heart. To quickly add a shape, you will use one of the ready-made shapes supplied with PowerPoint called **AutoShapes**. These include such basic shapes as rectangles and circles, a variety of lines, block arrows, flowchart symbols, stars and banners, and callouts.

1 ● Select the graphic and press Delete.

● Click AutoShapes ▾ (in the Drawing toolbar).

● Select **B**asic Shapes.

● Click ♡ Heart.

● In the space on the left side of the slide, click and drag downward and to the right to create the heart.

Another Method

The menu equivalent is **I**nsert/**P**icture/**A**utoShapes.

● If necessary, size and position the heart as in Figure 2.24.

Additional Information

An AutoShape can be sized and moved just like any other object.

Another Method

To maintain the height and width proportions of the AutoShape, hold down ⇧Shift while you drag.

Your screen should be similar to Figure 2.24

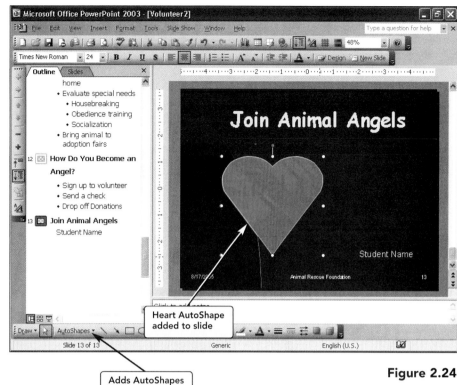

Figure 2.24

Enhancing the AutoShape

Next, you will enhance its appearance by changing the fill color of the heart and adding a shadow behind the heart. Then you will change the color of the shadow. Generally, a darker shade of the object's color for a shadow is very effective.

1 ● Click Fill Color and select a bright yellow from the Standard Colors palette.

● Click ⬚ Shadow Style (on the Drawing toolbar).

● Select any shadow style from the pop-up menu.

● Click ⬚ Shadow Style and choose Shadow Settings.

● Click ⬚ ▾ Shadow Color from the Shadow Settings toolbar and select gold.

● Close the Shadow Settings toolbar.

Your screen should be similar to Figure 2.25

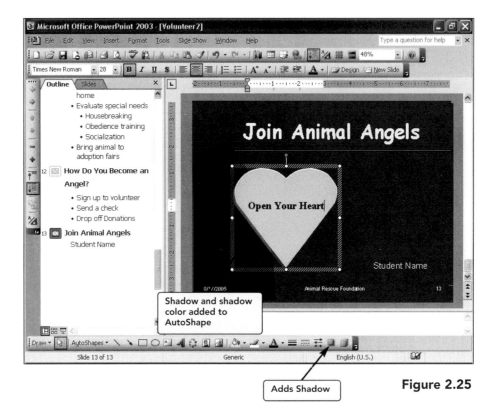

Figure 2.25

The addition of fill color and Shadow effect greatly improves the appearance of the heart.

Adding Text to an AutoShape

Next, you will add text to the heart object. Text can be added to all shapes and becomes part of the shape; when the shape is moved, the text moves with it.

1 • Right-click on the AutoShape object to open the shortcut menu, and choose Add Te**x**t.

• Click **B** Bold.

• Increase the font size to 28 points.

• Change the font color to blue.

• Type Open Your Heart.

• If necessary, adjust the size of the heart to display the text on a single line.

Your screen should be similar to Figure 2.26

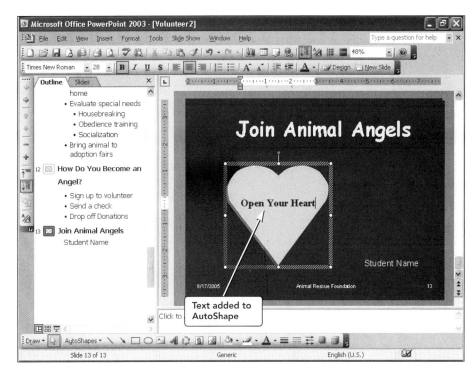

Figure 2.26

Additional Information

Holding down ⇧Shift while using the rotate handle rotates the object in 15-degree increments.

Rotating the Object

Finally, you want to change the angle of the heart. You can rotate an object 90 degrees left or right, or to any other angle. You will change the angle of the heart to the right using the ⬆ **rotate handle** for the selected object, which allows you to rotate the object to any degree in any direction.

1 ●── Hold down ⇧Shift while you drag the rotate handle to the left one increment.

Additional Information

The mouse pointer appears as 🔄 when positioned on the rotate handle.

Your screen should be similar to Figure 2.27

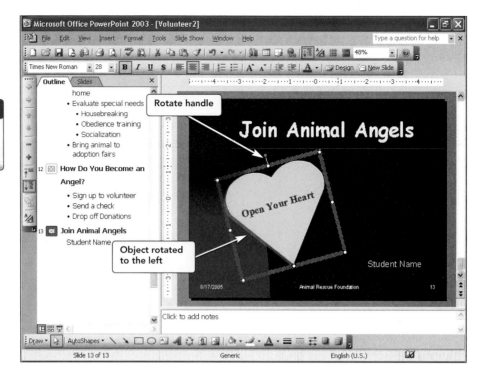

Figure 2.27

The graphic is a nice addition to the final slide of the presentation.

Working with Text Boxes

On slide 12, you want to add the organization's name and address. To make it stand out on the slide, you will put it into a text box. A **text box** is a container for text or graphics. The text box can be moved, resized, and enhanced in other ways to make it stand out from the other text on the slide.

Creating a Text Box

First you create the text box, and then you add the content.

1 Display slide 12.

● Click 🔲 Text Box (on the Drawing toolbar).

Another Method

The menu equivalent is Insert/Text Box.

● Point to a blank area below the bullets and click to create a default size text box.

Additional Information

Do not drag to create the text box. If you do, it will not resize appropriately when you enter text in the next step.

Your screen should be similar to Figure 2.28

Creates text box

Figure 2.28

The text box is a selected object and is surrounded with a hatched border, indicating you can enter, delete, select, and format the text inside the box.

Adding Text to a Text Box

Additional Information

You could also copy text from another location and paste it into the text box.

The text box displays an insertion point, indicating that it is waiting for you to enter the text. As you type the text in the text box, it will resize automatically as needed to display the entire entry.

1 Type the organization's name and address shown below in the text box. (Press ⏎Enter at the end of a line.)

Animal Rescue Foundation

1166 Oak Street

Lakeside, NH 03112

(603) 555-1313

Your screen should be similar to Figure 2.29

Figure 2.29

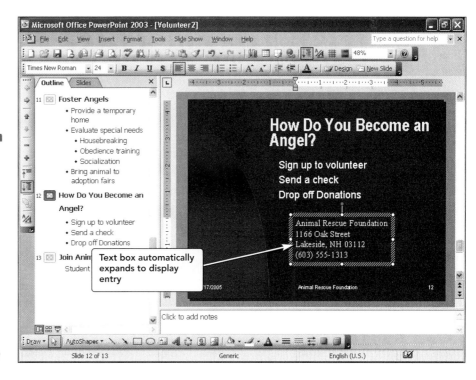

Again, because a text box is an object, the content is not displayed in the outline pane.

Enhancing the Text Box

Like any other object, the text box can be sized and moved anywhere on the slide. It can also be enhanced by adding a border, fill color, shadow effect, or a three-dimensional effect to the box. You want to add a border around the box to define the space and add a fill color behind the text.

1 ● Click ▤ Line Style (on the Drawing toolbar) and select a style of your choice from the menu.

● Click ⬥ ▾ Fill Color and select a color of your choice from the color palette.

● If the text does not look good with the fill color you selected, change the text color to a color of your choice.

● Position the text box as in Figure 2.30.

● Deselect the text box.

● Save the presentation.

Your screen should be similar to Figure 2.30

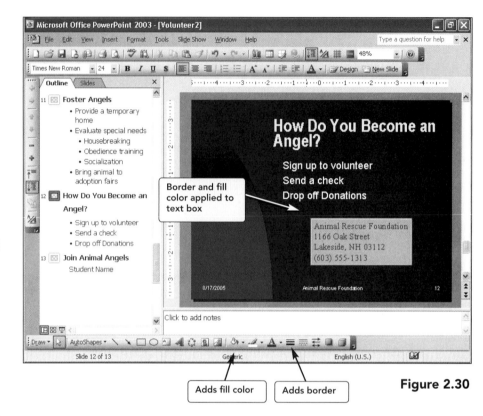

Figure 2.30

The information in the text box now stands out from the other information on the slide.

Changing the Presentation Design

Now you are satisfied with the presentation's basic content and organization. Next you want to change its style and appearance by applying a different design template.

Concept 4

Design Template

4   A **design template** is a professionally created slide design that is stored as a file and can be applied to your presentation. Design templates include features that control the slide color scheme, the type and size of bullets and fonts, placeholder sizes and positions, background designs and fills, and other layout and design elements. PowerPoint provides more than 100 design templates that can be used to quickly give your presentations a professional appearance. Additional design templates are available at the Microsoft Office Template Gallery Web site, or you can create your own custom design templates.

A design template can be applied to all slides or selected slides in a presentation. You can also use more than one type of design template in a single presentation. Use a design template to ensure that your presentation has a professional, consistent look throughout.

Applying a Design Template

A design template can be applied to the entire presentation or to selected slides. You want to change the design template for the entire presentation.

● **Display slide 1.**

● **Click** [Design] **on the Formatting toolbar.**

Another Method

The menu equivalent is F**o**rmat/Slide **D**esign.

● **Point to the first design preview in the task pane.**

Having Trouble?

If your task pane displays large preview images, open any preview's menu and clear the Show Large Previews option.

Your screen should be similar to Figure 2.31

Additional Information

Design templates are stored in a file with a .pot file extension.

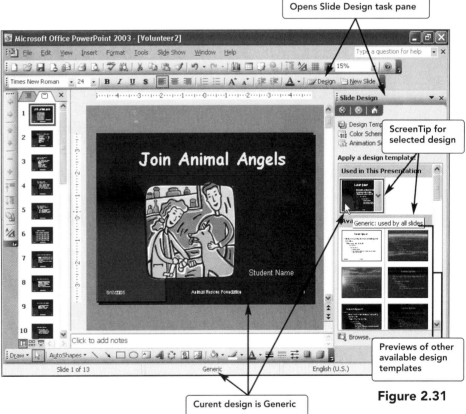

Opens Slide Design task pane

ScreenTip for selected design

Previews of other available design templates

Curent design is Generic

Figure 2.31

The Slide Design task pane displays previews of the design templates. The first design preview is the design that is currently used in the presentation. This is the Generic design as identified in the status bar and in the ScreenTip. If other designs were recently used, they appear in the Recently Used section. Previews of other available design templates are displayed in the Available For Use section of the pane.

2 ● Click ▨ **Balance in the Available For Use section to see how this design would look.**

Your screen should be similar to Figure 2.32

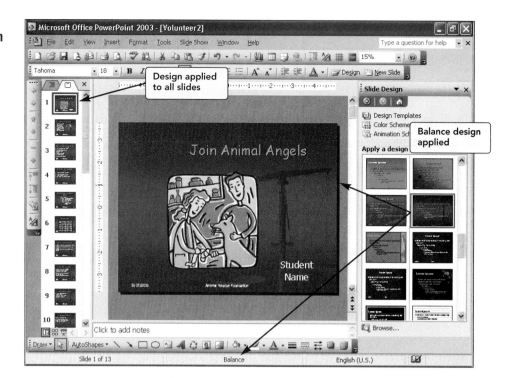

Figure 2.32

The Balance design template is applied to all slides in the presentation and the status bar displays the name of the current design. As different designs are selected, the previously used designs appear in the Recently Used section.

You will preview several other design templates, and then use the Beam template for the presentation.

3 ● **Preview several other design templates.**

● **Choose the Beam template design.**

Your screen should be similar to Figure 2.33

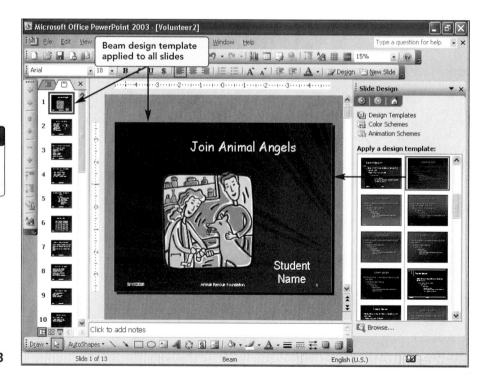

Figure 2.33

The Beam design template has been applied to all slides in the presentation. When a new template design is applied, the text styles, graphics, and colors that are included in the template replace the previous template settings. Consequently, the layout may need to be adjusted. For example, your name may appear on two lines because the font size of the subtitle using this design template is 36 points.

However, if you had made changes to a slide, such as changing the font of the title, these changes are not updated to the new design. In this case, the title is still the Comic Sans MS font you selected, however, its font size has been reduced and it is now too small. You will correct that shortly.

4 ● On the title slide, reduce the subtitle font size to 24 points and, if necessary, size the placeholder to display your name on a single line.

● Use the Slide tab to select each slide and check the layout.

● Make the adjustments shown in the table below to the indicated slide.

Your screen should be similar to Figure 2.34

Figure 2.34

Slide	Adjustment
2	Increase the text placeholder width to display each bulleted item on a single line. Move the question mark graphic to the lower right side of the slide.
5	Increase the width of the Event column to display each item on a single line. Center the Year and Event columns on the slide.
6	Adjust the size of the table columns and center the table below the title. If necessary, change the table text colors to coordinate with the new design.

Having Trouble?
If you selected a different design template, you may need to make different adjustments than indicated in the table at left.

Changing the Color Scheme

To make the presentation livelier, you decide to try a different color scheme. Each design template has several alternative color schemes from which you can choose.

1 • Display slide 1.

• **Click Color Schemes in the Slide Design task pane.**

Your screen should be similar to Figure 2.35

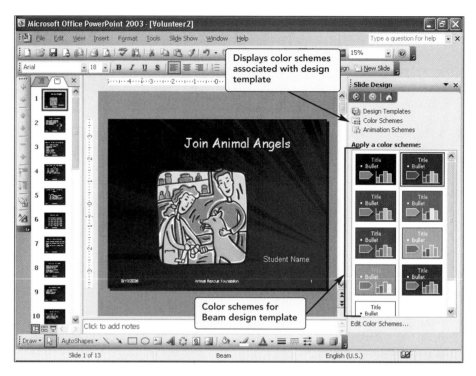

Figure 2.35

The nine color schemes for the Beam design template are displayed in the Slide Design pane. The color scheme with the medium blue background is selected. Each color scheme consists of eight coordinated colors that are applied to different slide elements. Using predefined color schemes gives your presentation a professional and consistent look. You want to see how the dark blue color scheme would look.

2 • Select the dark blue color scheme (first column, first row).

Your screen should be similar to Figure 2.36

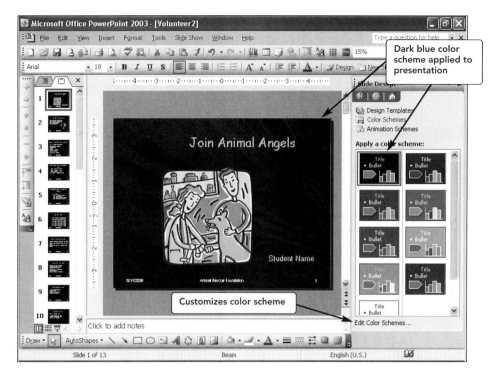

Figure 2.36

The slides display in the selected color scheme. Although you like this color scheme, you think it is a little dark. You can customize color schemes by changing colors associated with the different elements. You will change the background, shadow, and title text colors.

3 • Click Edit Color Schemes at the bottom of the Slide Design task pane.

• Open the Custom tab, if necessary.

Your screen should be similar to Figure 2.37

Figure 2.37

The Scheme Colors area of the dialog box shows you the eight colors that are applied to different elements of the template design. The sample box shows where the selected colors are used in a slide. The option to change the background color is selected by default. You will change the color of the background and title first.

4 • If necessary, select Background.

• Click Change Color...

• From the Standard tab select the blue color to the left of the current blue.

• Click OK.

• Select Title Text.

• Click Change Color...

• From the Standard tab select a gold color.

• Click OK.

• Click Preview.

• Move the Edit Color Scheme dialog box to see more of the slide.

Your screen should be similar to Figure 2.38

Figure 2.38

The background and title color has changed on all slides in the presentation. Changing the colors has made the slides much brighter. However, you do not like the dark blue used in the shadow color of the beams and will change it to a lighter blue. Because the shadow color is not a standard color found on the Standard color tab, the Custom tab will open automatically. Colors are selected from this tab by dragging the cross-hair to select a color and dragging the slider on the color bar to adjust the brightness.

Custom Color tab

5 • **Select Shadows and click** Change Color... .

• **Drag the** ◄ **slider up the color bar to increase the brightness.**

Additional Information

The degrees of red, green, and blue change as you drag the bar. The figures use Red 57, Green 0, and Blue 238.

• **Click** OK .

• **Click** Preview .

• **Click** Apply **when you are satisfied with your shadow color selection.**

• **Close the Slide Design pane.**

• **Save the presentation.**

Your screen should be similar to Figure 2.39

Figure 2.39

The new colors give the presentation much more impact. In addition, a new custom color scheme template is added to the available color schemes list in the task pane. This makes it easy to reapply your custom settings in the future.

Working with Master Slides

While viewing the slides, you think the slide appearance could be further improved by changing the bullet design on all slides. Although you can change each slide individually as you did in Lab 1, you can make the change much faster to all the slides by changing the slide master.

Concept 5

5 A **master** is a special slide or page that stores information about the formatting for all slides or pages in a presentation. There are four key components of a presentation—slides, title slides, speaker notes, and handouts—and each has a master associated with it. The four masters are described below.

Master	Function
Slide Master	Defines the format and placement of title, body, and footer text; bullet styles; background design; and color scheme of each slide in the presentation.
Title Master	Defines the format and placement of titles and text for slides that use the Title Slide layout.
Handout Master	Defines the format and placement of the slide image, text, headers, footers, and other elements that will appear on every handout.
Notes Master	Defines the format and placement of the slide image, note text, headers, footers, and other elements that will appear on all speaker notes.

Any changes you make to a master affect all slides or pages associated with that master. Each design template comes with its own slide master and title master. When you apply a new design template to a presentation, all slides and masters are updated to those of the new design template. Using the master to modify or add elements to a presentation ensures consistency and saves time.

You can create slides that differ from the master by changing the format and placement of elements in the individual slide rather than on the master. For example, when you changed the font settings of the title on the title slide, the slide master was not affected. Only the individual slide changed, making it unique. If you have created a unique slide, the elements you changed on that slide retain their uniqueness even if you later make changes to the slide master. That is the reason that the title font did not change when you changed the design template.

Modifying the Slide Master

You will change the bullet style in the slide master so that all slides in the presentation will be changed.

1 • Choose **V**iew/**M**aster/**S**lide Master.

• If necessary, dock the Slide Master View toolbar below the Formatting toolbar.

Your screen should be similar to Figure 2.40

Figure 2.40

The view has changed to Master view, and the Slide Master View toolbar is displayed. Thumbnails for both the title master and slide master for the Beam design template appear in the left pane of this view. The second thumbnail for the title master is selected, and the slide pane displays the master for it. The status bar identifies the master you are viewing. You want to make changes to the slide master first.

2 • Point to the slide master thumbnail to see the ScreenTip.

• Click on the first master thumbnail to select it.

Your screen should be similar to Figure 2.41

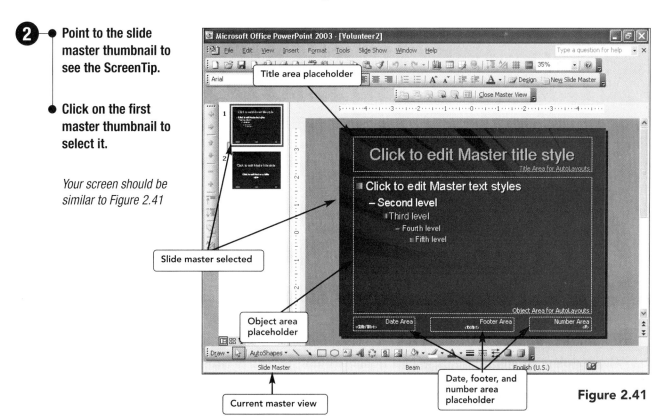

Figure 2.41

The slide master consists of five area placeholders that control the appearance of all slides except a title slide. Each placeholder displays sample text to show you how changes you make in these areas will appear. You make changes to the master slide in the same way that you change any other slide. You will modify the object area placeholder by changing the graphic that is used for the bullet style.

3 • **Click the object area to select it.**

Having Trouble?
Do not select an individual item within the object area or the changes will be applied to the item only.

• **Choose Format/Bullets and Numbering.**

• **Click** Picture... .

Your screen should be similar to Figure 2.42

Figure 2.42

From the Picture Bullet dialog box, you select the bullet design you want to use from the bullet styles listed. You will use the square, yellow bullet design.

4 ● Double-click ▣ (first bullet, third row).

Having Trouble?
If this bullet style is not available, select another of your choice.

Your screen should be similar to Figure 2.43

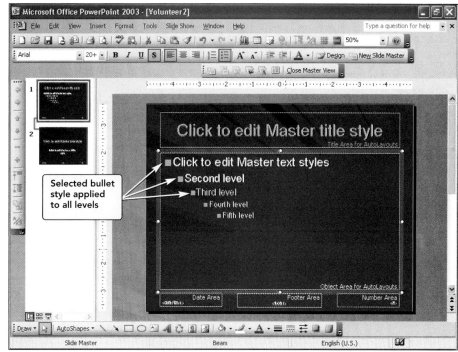

Figure 2.43

Additional Information
You can apply different bullet styles to each level by selecting each level individually.

The selected bullet style has been applied to all levels of items in the object area. Additionally, you decide to delete the date from the footer by deleting the Date Area placeholder.

5 ● Select the Date Area placeholder.

● Press ⟨Delete⟩.

Additional Information
You can restore deleted placeholders or add new placeholders to the slide master using F**o**rmat/**M**aster Layout and selecting the type of placeholder you want to add.

Your screen should be similar to Figure 2.44

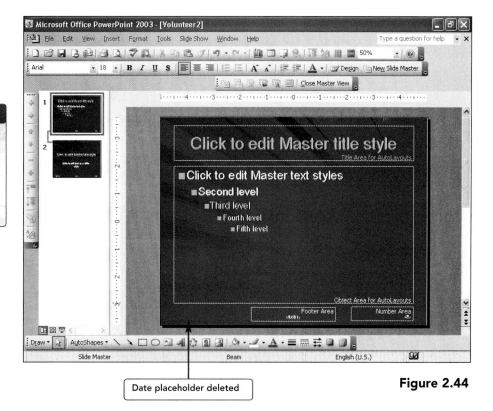

Date placeholder deleted

Figure 2.44

Now, you want to see how the changes you have made to the slide master have affected the slides.

6 Click ⊞ Slide Sorter view.

Your screen should be similar to Figure 2.45

Bullet style updated to picture bullet

Date footer removed

Figure 2.45

You can now see that the change you made to the bullet style in the slide master is reflected in all slides in the presentation. Additionally, none of the slides, except the title slides, displays the date in the footer. Using the slide master allows you to quickly make global changes to your presentation.

Modifying the Title Master

Next you want to enhance the appearance of the two slides that use the title slide layout by changing the title and subtitle.

1 Display slide 1 in Normal view.

Your screen should be similar to Figure 2.46

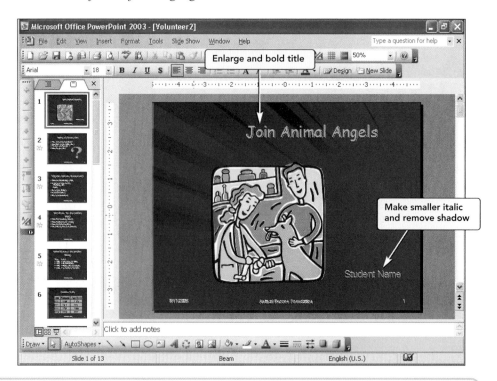

Figure 2.46

Earlier, you changed the font, size, and placement of the title and the placement and font size of the subtitle. Although you still like these changes, you want the title to be larger and the subtitle text smaller and italicized. You also want to remove the shadow from the subtitle.

2 ● **Display the Slide Master view.**

● **Display the title master.**

● **Click the master title text placeholder.**

Your screen should be similar to Figure 2.47

Figure 2.47

Notice that the title master has a slightly different appearance from the title slide in your presentation. This is because you modified the title slide by moving placeholders and changing the font, size, and color, making it a unique slide. The unique changes you made to that slide were not changed when the title master of the Beam design template was applied. The title master attributes reflect the attributes associated with the Beam template, such as the title font of Arial, 48 pt as shown in the toolbar buttons.

3 ● **Change the font style to Comic Sans MS.**

● **Increase the font size to 54.**

● **Click** **B** **Bold.**

● **Move the title placeholder toward the top of the slide as in Figure 2.48.**

● **Select the subtitle area placeholder.**

Another Method ○○○○

The menu equivalent is F**o**rmat/**F**ont/F**o**nt Style/Italic and the voice command is "Italic."

● **Click** **S** **Shadow to remove the shadow.**

● **Reduce the font size to 28.**

● **Click** **I** **Italic.**

● **Decrease the size of the placeholder and move it to the location shown in Figure 2.48.**

Your screen should be similar to Figure 2.48

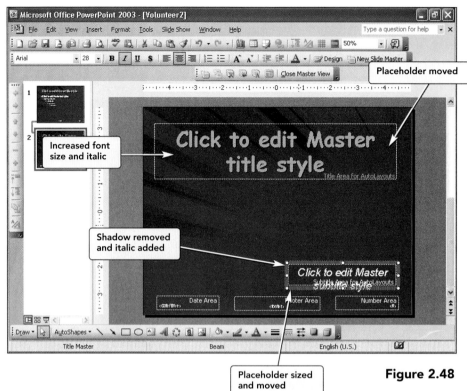

Figure 2.48

You want to see how the title slide looks with the changes you have made.

4 ● Switch to Normal view.

● Click on the title placeholder.

Your screen should be similar to Figure 2.49

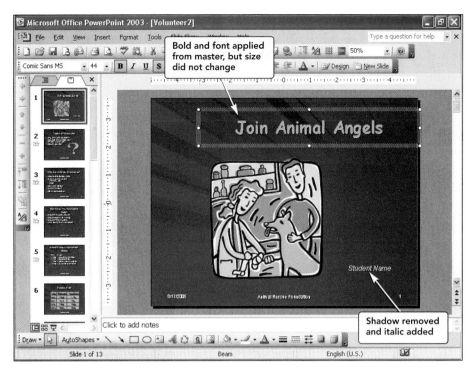

Figure 2.49

Some of the changes you made to the title master were applied to the title slide automatically; however, others were not. This is because the earlier changes you made, such as the font size, made the slide unique. Changes made to an individual slide override the master slide.

Reapplying a Slide Layout

You decide to apply all the settings on the master title slide to the title slides in the presentation. To do this you reapply the slide layout.

1 ● Choose Format/Slide Layout.

● Point to the Title Slide layout in the Slide Layout task pane.

● Click to open the drop-down menu for the Title Slide layout.

● Choose Reapply Layout.

Your screen should be similar to Figure 2.50

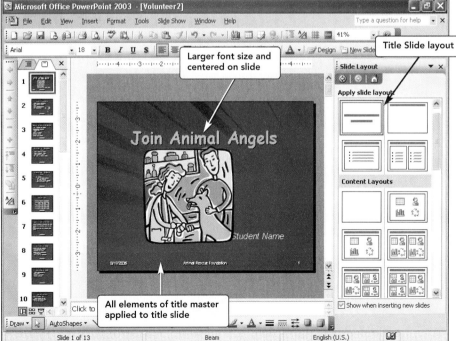

Figure 2.50

All elements of the title master slide have been applied to the title slide. The only adjustment you want to make to slide 1 is to reposition the graphic. Then you will reapply the slide layout to the concluding slide.

2 ● Move the graphic so it does not overlap the subtitle.

● Display slide 13 and reapply the Title Slide layout.

● Choose View/Ruler to hide the ruler.

● Close the Slide Layout task pane.

Your screen should be similar to Figure 2.51

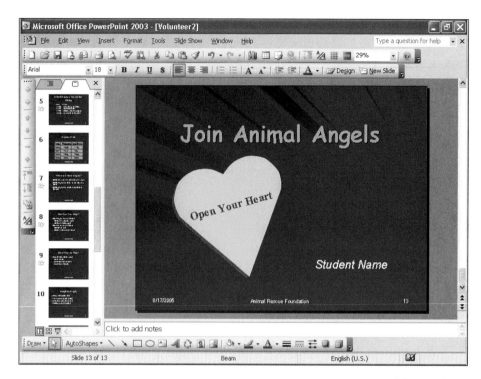

Figure 2.51

The layout settings have been applied and the concluding slide should not need any adjustments.

Changing and Hiding Footer Text

You would also like to hide the display of the footer information on the title slides and change the information displayed in the other slides. When you created the presentation using the AutoContent Wizard, you specified the information to appear in the footer area for all slides in the presentation. The slide and title masters control the placement and display of the footer information, but they do not control the information that appears in those areas. As you have seen, one way to stop the footer information from appearing, is to delete the footer placeholder from the master. Alternatively, you can change or turn off the display of selected footer information or hide the footer in title slides only.

1 • Choose <u>V</u>iew/<u>H</u>eader and Footer.

• Open the Slide tab, if necessary.

Your screen should be similar to Figure 2.52

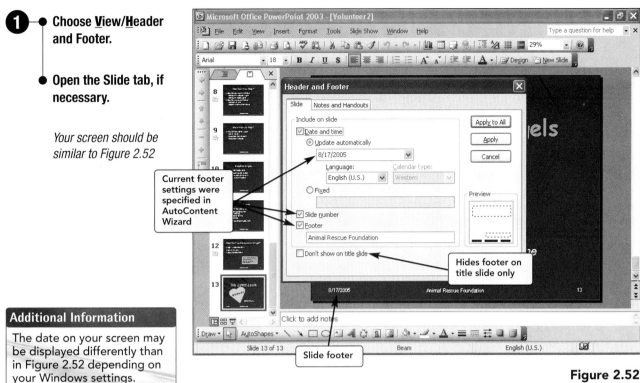

Current footer settings were specified in AutoContent Wizard

Hides footer on title slide only

Slide footer

Figure 2.52

The Date and Time option is selected, and the date is set to update automatically using the current system date whenever the presentation is opened. However, because you deleted the Date area placeholder from the slide master, this information is not displayed on all (except title slides). You can also change this option to enter a fixed date that will not change.

Because the slide number option is selected, the slide number is displayed in the Number area placeholder on each slide. The text you entered, "Animal Rescue Foundation," appears in the footer text box and is displayed in the Footer area placeholder. You want to turn off the display of the slide number. Also, you do not want to display any footer information on the title slides, and will select the option to hide it.

2 Click Slide **N**umber to deselect this option.

● Select Don't show on title **S**lide.

● Click `Apply to All`.

● Save the presentation.

Your screen should be similar to Figure 2.53

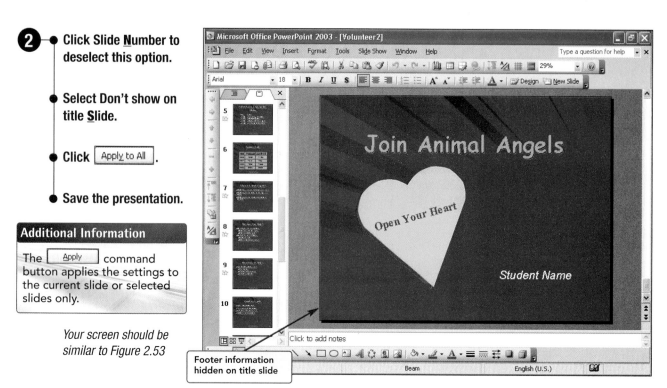

Footer information hidden on title slide

Figure 2.53

No footer information is displayed on the concluding slide which uses the title slide layout. As you run the slide show next, you will also see that the footer does not display on the first slide. Additionally, the only footer information that appears on all other slides is the name of the organization because you deleted the Date area placeholder and deselected the slide number footer option.

3 ● Run the slide show beginning with slide 1.

● Click on each slide to advance through the presentation.

You think the presentation looks quite good, but you have several changes in mind to make it more interesting.

Note: If you are ending your session now, save the presentation and exit PowerPoint. When you begin again, open this file.

Using Special Effects

You decide to use some of PowerPoint's special effects to enhance the onscreen presentation.

Concept 6

Special Effects

6   **Special effects** such as animation, sound, slide transitions, and builds are used to enhance an onscreen presentation.

Animation adds action to text and graphics so they move around on the screen. You can assign sounds to further enhance the effect.

Transitions control the way that the display changes as you move from one slide to the next during a presentation. You can select from many different transition choices. You may choose Dissolve for your title slide to give it an added flair. After that you could use Wipe Right for all the slides until the next to the last, and then use Dissolve again to end the show. As with any special effect, use slide transitions carefully.

Builds are used to display each bullet point, text, paragraph, or graphic independently of the other text or objects on the slide. You set up the way you want each element to appear (to fly in from the left, for instance) and whether you want the other elements already on the slide to dim or shimmer when a new element is added. For example, because your audience is used to reading from left to right, you could design your build slides so the bullet points fly in from the left. Then, when you want to emphasize a point, bring a bullet point in from the right. That change grabs the audience's attention.

When you present a slide show, the content of your presentation should take center stage. You want the special effects you use, such as animation, builds, and transitions, to help emphasize the main points in your presentation—not draw the audience's attention to the special effects.

Animating an Object and Adding Sound Effects

You will begin by adding animation and sound to the AutoShape object on the final slide.

1 • Display slide 13.

• From the heart AutoShape's shortcut menu select Custom Animation.

Another Method

The menu equivalent is Slide Show/Cust**o**m Animation.

Your screen should be similar to Figure 2.54

Figure 2.54

The Custom Animation task pane is used to assign animations and sound to objects on the slide. As you add animated items to a slide, each item is numbered. The number determines the order in which they display. A non-printing numbered tag appears on the slide near each animated item that correlates to the effects in the list.

You will animate the AutoShape object only. As you make selections, the Custom Animation list box will display the selected settings for the object and the effect will be demonstrated in the slide.

2
- **If necessary, select the AutoPreview option.**

- **Click** **select Entrance, and choose 5, Fly In.**

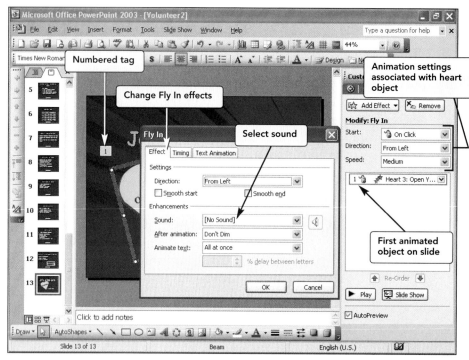

Having Trouble?

If Fly In is not available on the drop-down menu, select **M**ore Effects and select it from the dialog box.

- **From the Direction drop-down menu, select From Left.**

- **From the Speed drop-down menu, select Medium.**

- **Display the**
  `1  Heart 3: Open Y...`
  drop-down menu and select Effect Options.

Your screen should be similar to Figure 2.55

Figure 2.55

The list box in the task pane displays information about the first animated object on the slide. The numbered tag near the AutoShape identifies the animated object. The tag does not display when the slide show is run.

The Fly In dialog box includes the setting you already specified for the direction of the effect. You want to include a sound with the fly-in effect.

3 • From the Sound drop-down menu, choose Chime.

• Click [OK].

Additional Information

You must have a speaker and a sound card to hear the sound.

Your screen should be similar to Figure 2.56

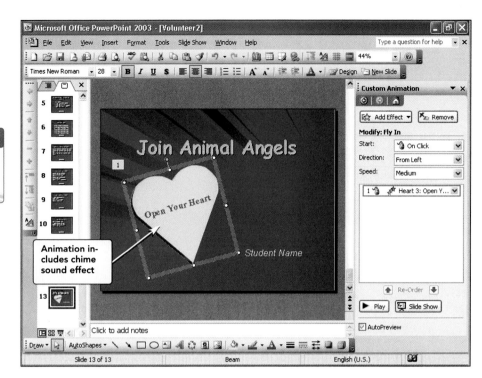

Figure 2.56

The heart appeared using the fly-in effect, and the chime sound played as it will when the slide show is run.

Adding Transition Effects

Next, you want to add a transition effect to all the slides. Although you can add transitions in Normal view, you will use Slide Sorter view because it has its own toolbar that makes it easy to perform many different tasks in this view.

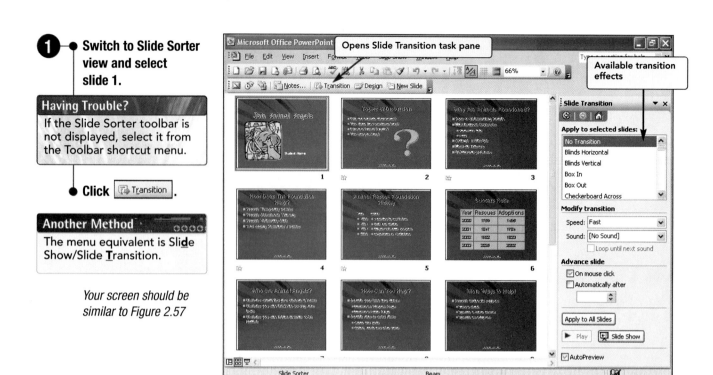

Figure 2.57

In the Slide Transition task pane, the list box displays the names of the transition effects that can be used on the slides. Currently, No Transition is selected, because the current slide does not include a transition effect. Because the AutoPreview option is selected, as you select a transition effect, the effect is displayed in the current slide. You can also replay the transition effect by clicking [Play].

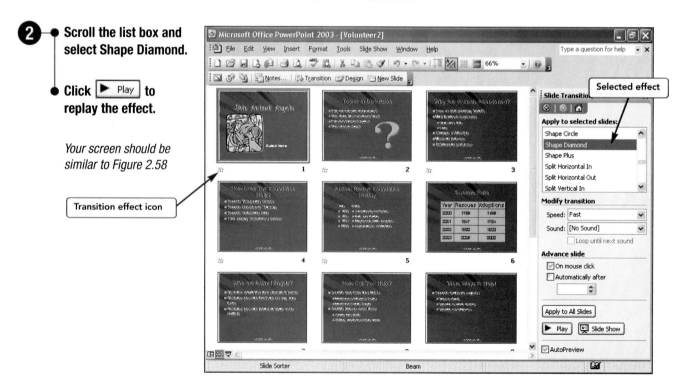

Figure 2.58

A preview of the selected transition effect is displayed on the current slide, and a ⌨ transition icon is displayed below slide 1. This indicates that a transition effect has been applied to the slide. Several other slides in the presentation also display a transition effect icon. This is because the AutoContent Wizard automatically used the Cut transition effect on all slides, except the title slide, that were added when the presentation was created originally.

You like the way the transition effects work and decide to use the Random Transition effect, which will randomly select different transition effects, on all the slides. You will select and change all the slides at once.

3 ● Choose Random Transition (last option in list).

● Click Apply to All Slides.

● Close the Slide Transition pane.

Your screen should be similar to Figure 2.59

Random transition effect applied to all slides

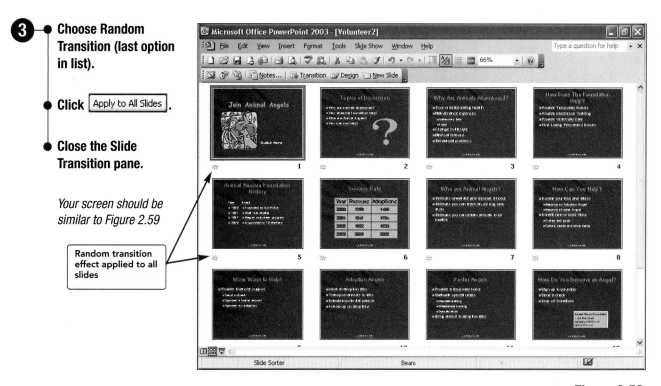

Figure 2.59

The transition icon appears below each slide, indicating that a transition effect has been applied to all slides.

4 ● Save the presentation.

● Run the slide show from the beginning to see the different transition effects.

Adding Build Effects

The next effect you want to add to the slides is a build effect that will display progressively each bullet on a slide. When a build is applied to a slide, the slide initially shows only the title. The bulleted text appears as the presentation proceeds. A build slide can also include different build transition effects, which are similar to slide transition effects. The effect is applied to the bulleted text as it is displayed on the slide.

1 • Click `Design`.

• Click **Animation Schemes** from the Slide Design task pane.

Your screen should be similar to Figure 2.60

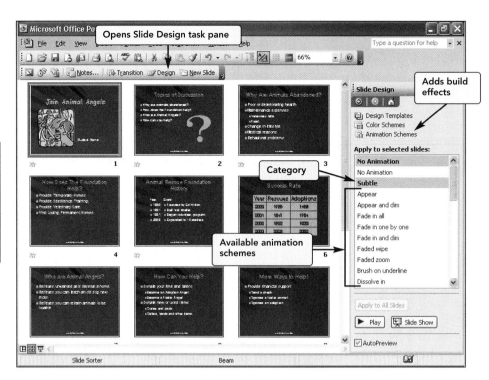

Figure 2.60

The Slide Design task pane displays a list of animation schemes. **Animation schemes** are preset visual effects that can be added to slide text. Each scheme usually includes an effect for the title as well as for the bulleted items. Some schemes include a slide transition effect as well. The schemes are divided into three categories: Subtle, Moderate, and Exciting.

You will use two different build effects in the presentation. The two title slides will use one build effect and all other slides except slides 5 and 6 will use another effect. You do not want slides 5 and 6 to have any build effects because they are tables and the content is not conducive to this type of animation.

2 If necessary, select AutoPreview to turn on this feature.

Make slide 2 the current slide and select a few animation schemes to see how they look.

Select Wipe from the Subtle category.

Click Apply to All Slides.

Select slides 5 and 6.

Having Trouble?
You can select and deselect multiple slides by holding down Ctrl while making your selection.

Select No Animation from the No Animation category.

Select slides 1 and 13.

Select the Big Title effect from the Exciting category.

Select slide 1 and click ☐ to start Slide Show.

Click on the slide to display the subtitle.

Your screen should be similar to Figure 2.61

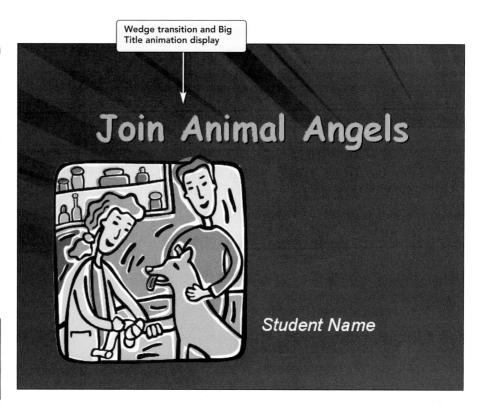

Wedge transition and Big Title animation display

Figure 2.61

The first slide is displayed using the Wedge transition effect and Big Title animation, but the subtitle did not display until you clicked on the slide. When a build is applied to a slide, the body items are displayed only when you click or use any of the procedures to advance to the next slide. This allows the presenter to focus the audience's attention and to control the pace of the presentation.

Controlling the Slide Show

As much as you would like to control a presentation completely, the presence of an audience usually causes the presentation to change course. PowerPoint has several ways to control a slide show during the presentation. Before presenting a slide show, you should rehearse the presentation. To help with this aspect of the presentation, PowerPoint includes a Rehearse Timings option on the Slide Show menu that records the time you spend on each slide as you practice your narration. If your computer is set up with a microphone, you could even record your narration with the Record Narration option.

Navigating in a Slide Show

Running the slide show and practicing how to control the slide show help you to have a smooth presentation. For example, if someone has a question about a previous slide, you can go backward and redisplay it. You will try out some of the features you can use while running the slide show.

1 ● Continue to click or press Spacebar until slide 6, Success Rate, appears.

● Press Backspace (2 times).

Additional Information
You can return to the first slide in the presentation by holding down both mouse buttons for two seconds.

You returned the onscreen presentation to slide 4, but now, because the audience has already viewed slides 5 and 6, you want to advance to slide 7. To go to a specific slide number, you type the slide number and press ←Enter.

2 ● Press 7.

● Press ←Enter.

Another Method
You also can choose **G**o to Slide from the shortcut menu and select a slide to display.

● Click 3 times to display the three bulleted items.

Additional Information
You can also white out the screen by pressing W or using S**c**reen/**W**hite Screen on the shortcut menu.

Slide 7, Who are Animal Angels?, is displayed. Sometimes a question from an audience member can interrupt the flow of the presentation. If this happens to you, you can black out the screen to focus attention onto your response.

3 ● Press B.

Another Method
The menu equivalent is S**c**reen/**B**lack Screen on the shortcut menu.

The screen goes to black while you address the topic. When you are ready to resume the presentation, you can bring the slide back.

4 ● Click, or press B.

Adding Freehand Annotations

During your presentation, you may want to point to an important word, underline an important point, or draw checkmarks next to items that you have covered. To do this, you can use the mouse pointer during the presentation. When you move the mouse, the mouse pointer appears and the Slide Show toolbar is displayed in the lower left corner of the screen.

1 Move the mouse on your desktop.

Your screen should be similar to Figure 2.62

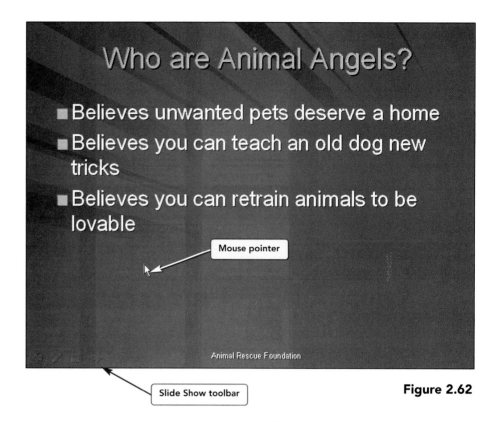

Figure 2.62

The mouse pointer in its current shape ⇲ can be used to point to items on the slide. You can also use it to draw on the screen by changing the mouse pointer to a ballpoint pen, felt tip pen, or highlighter, which activates the associated freehand annotation feature.

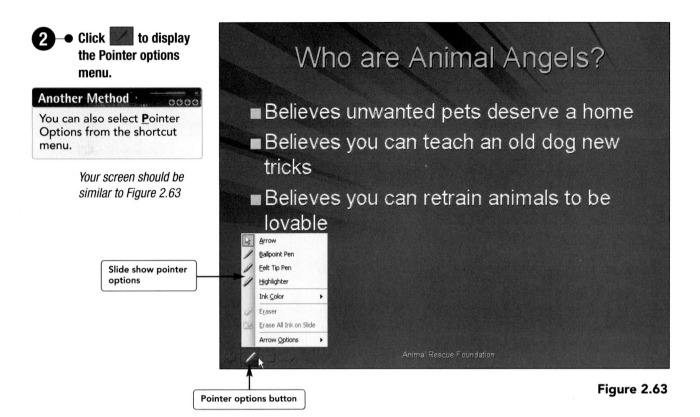

②—● Click [ ] to display the Pointer options menu.

Another Method
You can also select **P**ointer Options from the shortcut menu.

Your screen should be similar to Figure 2.63

Slide show pointer options

Arrow
Ballpoint Pen
Felt Tip Pen
Highlighter
Ink Color ▶
Eraser
Erase All Ink on Slide
Arrow Options ▶

Pointer options button

Figure 2.63

The mouse pointer and arrow options are described in the following table.

Pointer Options	Effect
Arrow	Displays the mouse pointer as an arrow.
Ballpoint Pen	Changes the mouse pointer to a diamond shape and turns on ballpoint pen annotation.
Felt Tip Pen	Changes the mouse pointer to a circle shape and turns on felt tip pen annotation.
Highlighter	Changes the mouse pointer to a bar shape and turns on highlighter.
Ink **C**olor	Displays a color palette to select a color for the annotation tool.
E**r**aser	Erases selected annotations.
Erase All Ink on Slide	Removes all annotations from the slide.
Arrow Options	**(These options apply only if A**rrow **is selected.)**
Au**t**omatic	Hides the mouse pointer if it is not moved for 15 seconds. It reappears when you move the mouse. This is the default setting.
Visible	Displays the mouse pointer as an arrow and does not hide it.
Hidden	Hides the mouse pointer until another pointer option is selected.

You will try out several of the freehand annotation features to see how they work. To draw, you select the pen style and then drag the pen pointer in the direction you want to draw.

3 ● Choose **F**elt Tip Pen.

Additional Information

The mouse pointer changes shape depending upon the selected annotation tool.

● Drag the dot pointer until a circle is drawn around the word "teach."

● Choose **H**ighlighter from the Pointer options menu and highlight the word "retrain."

● Choose **B**allpoint Pen from the Pointer options menu.

Another Method

You can also use Ctrl + P to display the Ballpoint pen.

● Choose Ink **C**olor from the Pointer options menu and select gold.

Additional Information

The Automatic ink color setting determines the default color to use for annotations based upon the slide design colors.

● In the first bulleted item, draw a caret after the word "a" and write the word "good" above the line.

Your screen should be similar to Figure 2.64

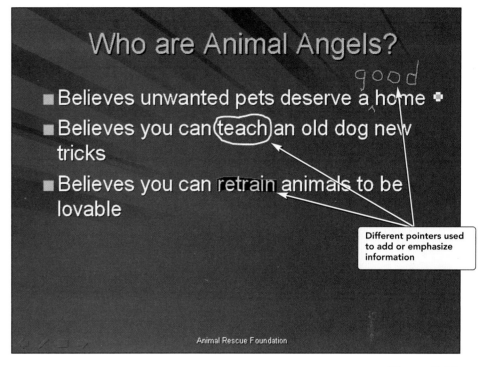

Figure 2.64

4 Practice using the freehand annotator to draw any shapes you want on the slide.

● To erase the annotations, select **E**rase All Ink on Slide from the Pointer options menu.

Another Method

The keyboard shortcut is E.

● To turn off freehand annotation, select **A**rrow from the Pointer options menu.

Another Method

You can also use Ctrl + A to display the arrow.

● Press Esc to end the slide show.

● Close the task pane.

If you do not erase annotations before ending the presentation, you are prompted to keep or discard the annotations when you end the slide show. If you keep the annotations they are saved to the slides and will appear as part of the slide during a presentation.

Hiding Slides

As you reconsider the presentation, you decide to show the Success Rate slide only if someone asks about this information. To do this, you will hide the slide.

1 Select slide 6.

● Click 🔲 Hide Slide.

Additional Information

The menu equivalent is Sli**d**e Show/**H**ide Slide.

Your screen should be similar to Figure 2.65

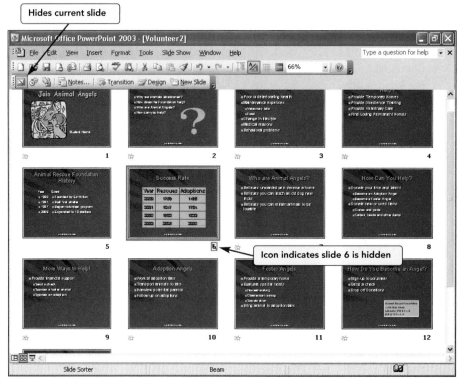

Figure 2.65

Notice that the slide number for slide 6 is surrounded by a box with a slash drawn through it which indicates that the slide is hidden. Next, you will run the slide show to see how hidden slides work. You will begin the show at the slide before the hidden slide.

2 ● Select slide 5.

● Click 🖳 to run the slide show from the current slide.

● Click to display the next slide, which should be Who Are Animal Angels?

Your screen should be similar to Figure 2.66

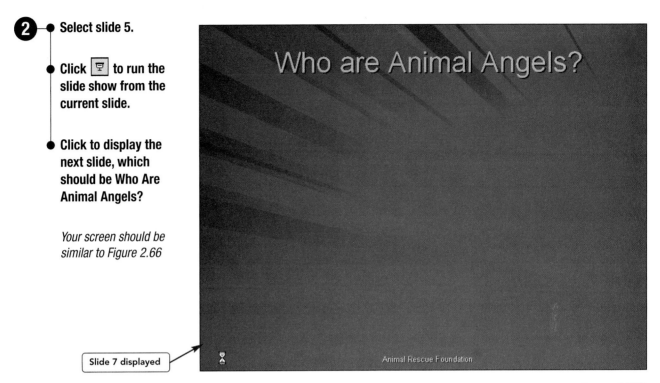

Slide 7 displayed

Figure 2.66

Slide 6 was not displayed because it is hidden. To show how to display a hidden slide, you will return to slide 5 and then display slide 6.

3

- Press [Page Up] twice to display slide 5 again.

- Press H to see slide 6.

Your screen should be similar to Figure 2.67

Success Rate

Year	Rescues	Adoptions
2000	1759	1495
2001	1847	1784
2002	1982	1833
2003	2025	2002

Animal Rescue Foundation

Hidden slide is displayed

Figure 2.67

Adding Speaker Notes

When making your presentation, there are some critical points you want to be sure to discuss. To help you remember the important points, you can add notes to a slide and then print the **notes pages**. These pages display the notes below a small version of the slide they accompany. You can create notes pages for some or all of the slides in a presentation. You decide to add speaker notes on slide 5 to remind you about the hidden slide.

1 • Press [Esc] to end the slide show.

• Display slide 5 in Normal view.

• Click in the notes pane.

• Type **Show the next hidden slide if someone asks about adoption rates.**.

Additional Information

You can enlarge the notes area by dragging the pane divider line.

Your screen should be similar to Figure 2.68

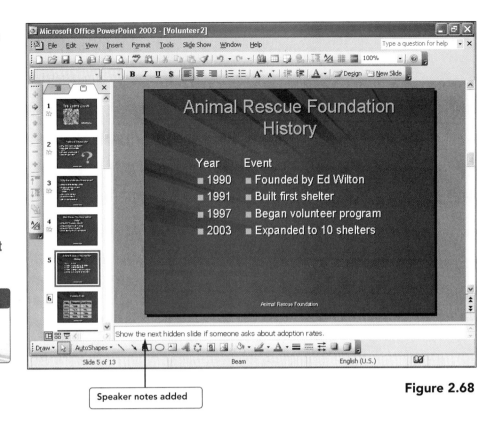

Speaker notes added

Figure 2.68

You want to preview the notes page to check its appearance before it is printed.

2 • Choose **View/Notes Page**.

Your screen should be similar to Figure 2.69

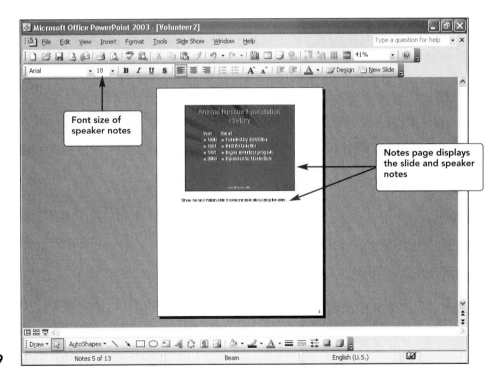

Font size of speaker notes

Notes page displays the slide and speaker notes

Figure 2.69

The notes pages display the notes you added below the slide that the note accompanies.

To make the speaker notes easy to read in a dimly lit room while you are making the presentation, you will increase the font size of the notes text.

3 • **Click on the note text to select the placeholder.**

• **Select the note text.**

• **Increase the font size to 24.**

Your screen should be similar to Figure 2.70

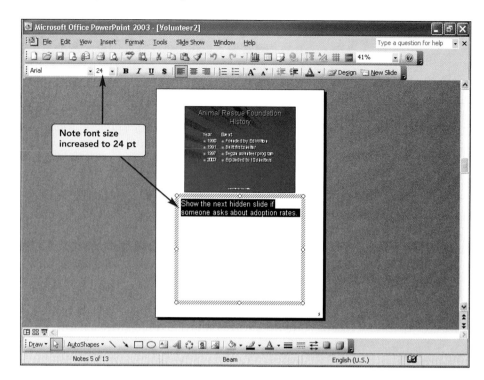

Figure 2.70

Checking Style

Having Trouble?

If your school has disabled the Office Assistant, you will not be able to complete this section.

You want to make a final check of the presentation for consistency and style. To help with this, you can use the **style check** feature which checks for consistency in punctuation and capitalization as well as for visual elements such as the maximum number of bulleted items in a list. To use this feature, you need to turn it on and set the options to check. Additionally, the Office Assistant feature must be on, otherwise you will not be notified about located style inconsistencies.

1 • Display slide 1 in Normal view.

• Choose **T**ools/**O**ptions.

• Open the Spelling and Style tab and select **C**heck Style.

• If prompted, click Enable Assistant to turn on the Office Assistant.

• Click Style Options... .

Your screen should be similar to Figure 2.71

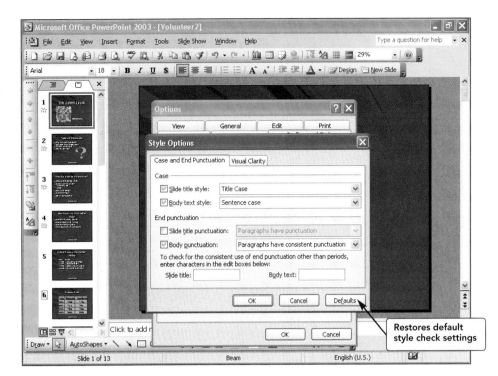

Figure 2.71

Additional Information

You can turn on/off options and change the default settings by selecting from the option's drop-down menu.

The Case and End Punctuation tab provides options that allow you to control the kind of style check used for capitalization and punctuation. The default style rule is to use title case (first letter of most words is capitalized) for slide titles and sentence case (only the first word is capitalized) for body text. Additionally, style checking looks for consistent use of end punctuation in body text.

You want to use the default settings for the style check.

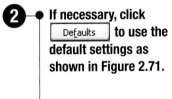

2 • If necessary, click Defaults to use the default settings as shown in Figure 2.71.

• Open the Visual Clarity tab.

• If necessary, select all the options.

Your screen should be similar to Figure 2.72

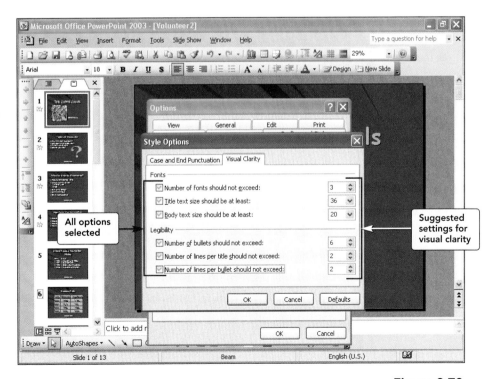

Figure 2.72

When a style check is made, each slide is examined for visual clarity. The default settings use guidelines for proper slide design: the font size is large, the number of fonts used is small, and the amount of text on a slide is limited. For example, the maximum number of bullets per slide is six and number of lines per bullet is two. All these settings help you adhere to good slide design.

The style check feature is active only when the Office Assistant is displayed. As you display each slide in Normal view, the style is evaluated. It displays a 💡 next to the placeholder area in any slides in which it detects a potential problem.

3 ● Click OK 2 times.

● Click on the slide pane of slide 1 to activate the pane.

● Because no problems were identified in slide 1, click in the scroll bar to display slide 2.

Having Trouble?
If you advance to the next slide using the Slides tab, you must click on the slide pane each time to activate it and evaluate the style.

● Click on the 💡.

● Move the Assistant character to the right side of the screen.

Your screen should be similar to Figure 2.73

Having Trouble?
Your Assistant character may be different from the character shown here.

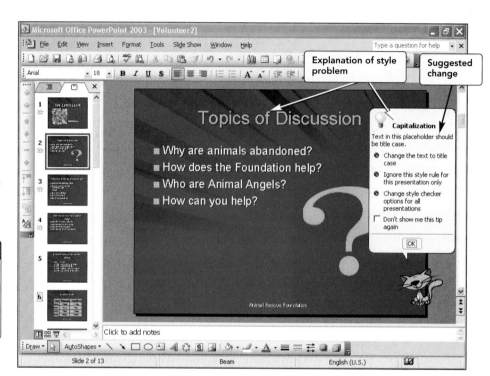

Figure 2.73

The Assistant displays an explanation of the problem it has located. In this case, because each word in the title is not capitalized, the title case rule has been violated. You will use the suggestion to correct the title case. As soon as you respond to the style checker, the correction is made and the next located potential problem is identified.

4 • Choose "Change the text to title case."

  • Click on the 💡 next to the object area placeholder.

Your screen should be similar to Figure 2.74

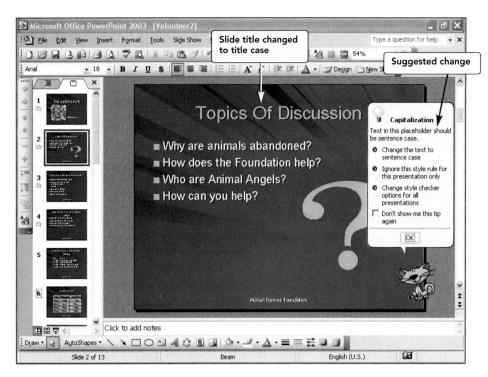

Figure 2.74

The title case is corrected and a second lightbulb appears indicating that another style problem has been identified. The suggested style change is to change the bulleted items to sentence case for body text.

5 • Choose "Change the text to sentence case."

Your screen should be similar to Figure 2.75

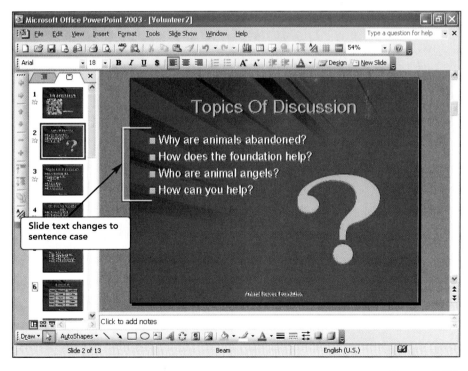

Figure 2.75

Making this change, however, changed proper names, such as the name of the volunteer organization, to lowercase. In this case, you do not want to keep this change. You will undo the change and skip the style check suggestion to clear it. Then you will continue checking the rest of the presentation.

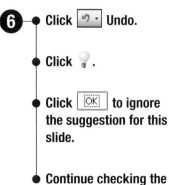

- Click <u>⟲ ▾</u> Undo.

- Click 💡 .

- Click ⟦OK⟧ to ignore the suggestion for this slide.

- Continue checking the style on the remaining slides in the presentation, making the changes shown in the table below Figure 2.76.

Your screen should be similar to Figure 2.76

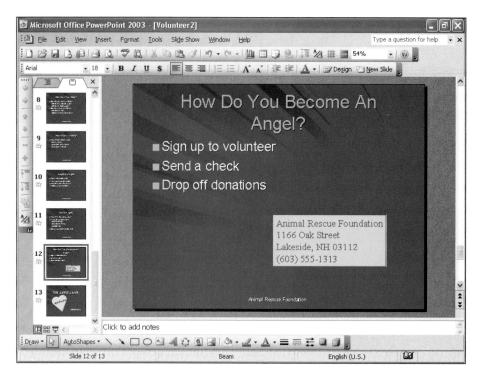

Figure 2.76

Slide	Adjustment
4	Change the text to sentence case.
5	Click ⟦OK⟧ to ignore changes for this slide.
7	Change the text to title case.
8	Click ⟦OK⟧ to ignore change for this slide.
9	Change the text to title case.
12	Change the text to title case. Change the text to sentence case.

Now that you have checked the presentation, you will turn off this feature.

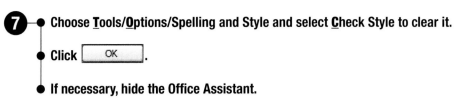

7 • Choose **T**ools/**O**ptions/Spelling and Style and select **C**heck Style to clear it.

• Click **OK** .

• If necessary, hide the Office Assistant.

Documenting a File

Before saving the completed presentation, you want to include file documentation with the file when it is saved.

1 • Display slide 1.

• Choose **F**ile/Proper**t**ies.

• Open the Summary tab if necessary.

Your screen should be similar to Figure 2.77

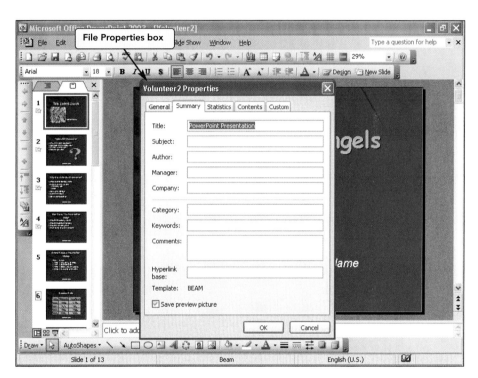

Figure 2.77

The Summary tab text boxes are used for the following:

Option	Action
Title	Enter the presentation title. This title can be longer and more descriptive than the presentation file name.
Subject	Enter a description of the presentation's content.
Author	Enter the name of the presentation's author. By default this is the name entered when PowerPoint was installed.
Manager	Enter the name of your manager.
Company	Enter the name of your company.
Category	Enter the name of a higher-level category under which you can group similar types of presentations.
Keywords	Enter words that you associate with the presentation so the Find File command can be used.
Comments	Enter any comments you feel are appropriate for the presentation.
Hyperlink base	Enter the path or URL that you want to use for all hyperlinks in the document.
Template	Identifies the template that is attached to the file.
Save Preview Picture	Saves a picture of the first slide with the file to display in the Open dialog box.

2 ● In the title text box, enter **Animal Angels**.

● In the subject text box, enter **Volunteer recruitment**.

● In the Author text box, enter **your name**.

● If necessary, select "Save preview picture."

Your screen should be similar to Figure 2.78

Figure 2.78

3 • Click [OK].

• Save the presentation.

Customizing Print Settings

You have created both slides and notes pages for the presentation. Now you want to print the notes page and some of the slides. Customizing the print settings by selecting specific slides to print and scaling the size of the slides to fill the page are a few of the ways to make your printed output look more professional.

Printing Selected Slides

First you will print the notes page for the slide on which you entered note text.

1 • Choose **File/Print**.

• If necessary, select the printer.

• From the Print Range section, select Slides.

• Type **5** in the Slides text box.

• From the Print **What** drop-down list box, select Notes Pages.

• If necessary, select Grayscale from the Color/**G**rayscale drop-down list box.

• Click [Pre**v**iew].

Your screen should be similar to Figure 2.79

Preview of notes page →

Animal Rescue Foundation History

Year	Event
1990	Founded by Ed Wilton
1991	Built first shelter
1997	Began volunteer program
2003	Expanded to 10 shelters

Show the next hidden slide if someone asks about adoption rates.

Page number in footer

Figure 2.79

The notes page is displayed in portrait orientation as it will appear when printed.

Adding Headers and Footers to Notes and Handouts

Currently, the only information that appears in the footer of the notes page is the page number. You want to include the date and your name in the header of the notes and handouts.

 Click Options ▼ and select Header and Footer.

Your screen should be similar to Figure 2.80

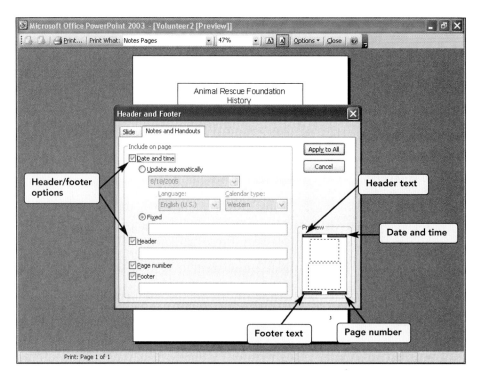

Figure 2.80

As in slides, you can display date and time information and footer text. In addition, on notes and handouts, you can include header text and a page number. The preview area identifies the four areas where this information will appear and identifies the currently selected areas in bold. The header option is selected, but because it does not include text, nothing is displayed.

2 • Click **Date and time** to turn on this option and, if necessary, select **Update** automatically.

• Enter **your name** in the Header text box.

• Click 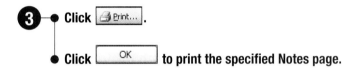.

Your screen should be similar to Figure 2.81

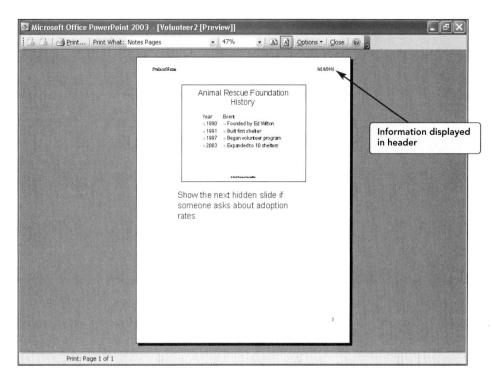

Figure 2.81

The information is displayed in the header as specified.

3 • Click 🖨 **Print...** .

• Click ⟦ OK ⟧ to print the specified Notes page.

Scaling Slides

Next you will print a few selected slides to be used as handouts. You will change the orientation to landscape and scale the slides to fit the paper size.

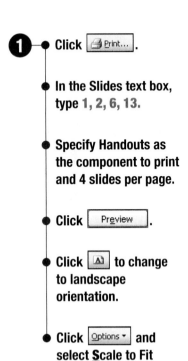

1 • Click [🖨 Print...].

• In the Slides text box, type **1, 2, 6, 13.**

• Specify Handouts as the component to print and 4 slides per page.

• Click [Preview].

• Click [🔳] to change to landscape orientation.

• Click [Options ▾] and select **S**cale to Fit Paper.

Your screen should be similar to Figure 2.82

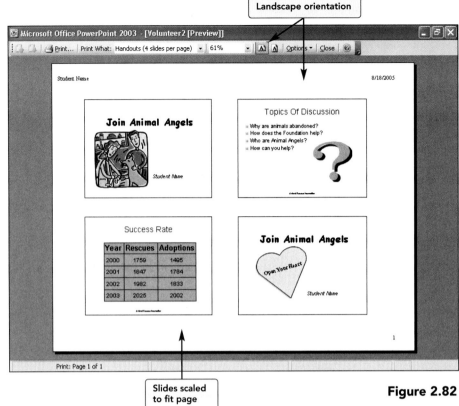

Figure 2.82

The four selected slides are displayed in landscape orientation and the slide images were sized as large as possible to fill the page.

2 • Print the handout.

• Close the Print Preview window.

• Save the completed presentation.

• Exit PowerPoint.

The view you are in when you save the file is the view that will be displayed when the file is opened. The print settings are also saved with the file.

Focus on Careers

EXPLORE YOUR CAREER OPTIONS

Marketing Communications Specialist

Are you interested in technology? Could you explain it in words and pictures? Marketing Communications Specialists assist sales and marketing management with communications media and advertising materials that represent the company's products and services to customers. In high-tech industries, you will take information from scientists and engineers and use PowerPoint to transform the data into eye-catching presentations that communicate effectively. You may also create brochures, develop Web sites, create videos, and write speeches. If you thrive in a fast-paced and high-energy environment and work well under the pressure of deadlines, then this job may be for you. Typically a bachelor's degree in journalism, advertising, or communications is desirable. The salary can range from $35,000 to $85,000, depending on the industry.

Find and Replace   (PP2.5)

To make editing easier, you can use the Find and Replace feature to find text in a presentation and replace it with other text as directed.

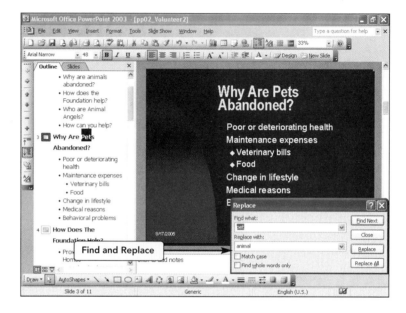

Table   (PP2.9)

A table is used to organize information into an easy-to-read format of horizontal rows and vertical columns.

Alignment   (PP2.15)

Alignment controls how text entries are positioned within a space.

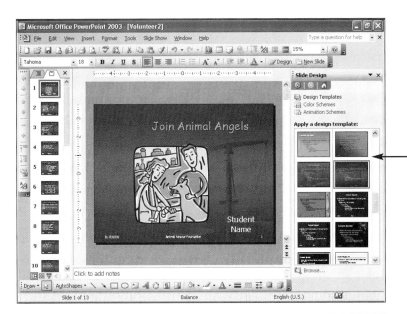

Design Template (PP2.31)

A design template is a professionally created slide design that is stored as a file and can be applied to a presentation.

Design template

Master (PP2.38)

A master is a special slide or page that stores information about the formatting for all slides in a presentation.

Master

Special Effects (PP2.49)

Special effects such as animation, sound, slide transitions, and builds are used to enhance the onscreen presentation.

Special effects

LAB 2
Modifying and Refining a Presentation

key terms

alignment PP2.15	cell PP2.9	rotate handle PP2.27
animation PP2.49	design template PP2.31	table PP2.9
animation scheme PP2.54	Find and Replace PP2.5	table reference PP2.9
AutoShape PP2.24	master PP2.38	text box PP2.28
build PP2.49	notes page PP2.62	transition PP2.49

microsoft office specialist skills

The Microsoft Office Specialist certification program is designed to measure your proficiency in performing basic tasks using the Office 2003 applications. Certification demonstrates that you have the skills and provides a valuable industry credential for employment. After completing this lab, you have learned the following Microsoft Office PowerPoint 2003 Specialist skills:

Skill Sets	Skill Standards	Page
Creating Content	Insert and edit text-based content	PP2.5
	Insert tables, charts, and diagrams	PP2.9
	Insert pictures, shapes, and graphics	PP2.22, 2.24
Formatting Content	Format text-based content	PP2.13, 2.15
	Format pictures, shapes, and graphics	PP2.22, 2.25
	Format slides	PP2.31, 2.33, 2.72
	Apply animation schemes	PP2.54
	Apply slide transitions	PP2.51
	Work with masters	PP2.38
Managing and Delivering Presentations	Organize a presentation	PP2.23, 2.63
	Set up slide shows for delivery	PP2.60
	Deliver presentations	PP2.56
	Save and publish presentations	PP2.8
	Print slides, outlines, handouts, and speaker notes	PP2.71

command summary

Command	Shortcut Key	Button	Voice	Action
File/Proper**t**ies				Displays statistics and stores information about presentation
Edit/**F**ind	Ctrl + F	🔍		Finds specified text
Edit/**R**eplace	Ctrl + H	🔍		Replaces located text with specified replacement text
View/Notes **P**age				Displays notes page view
View/**M**aster/**S**lide Master	⇧Shift + 🔲			Displays slide master for presentation
View/**R**uler				Displays or hides ruler
View/**H**eader and Footer				Specifies information that appears as headers and footers on slides, notes, outlines, and handout pages
Insert/**D**uplicate Slide				Inserts duplicate of current slide
Insert/**P**icture/**A**utoShapes		A⃰		Inserts selected AutoShape object
Insert/Te**x**t Box		🄰		Adds a text box
F**o**rmat/**F**ont/F**o**nt Style/Bold	Ctrl + B	**B**	On bold	Adds bold effect to selection
F**o**rmat/**F**ont/F**o**nt Style/Italic	Ctrl + I	*I*	Italic	Adds italic effect to selection
F**o**rmat/**F**ont/**C**olor		A ▾		Adds color to selection
F**o**rmat/**A**lignment	Ctrl + L	≣	Left justify	Aligns text in a cell or placeholder to left, center, right, or justified
	Ctrl + E	≣	Centered	
	Ctrl + R	≣	Right justify	
	Ctrl + J	≣		

Command	Shortcut Key	Button	Voice	Action
F**o**rmat/Slide **D**esign		Design		Changes appearance of slide by applying a different design template
F**o**rmat/**R**eplace Fonts				Finds specified font and replaces it with another
F**o**rmat/**P**icture/**R**ecolor				Changes color of a picture
F**o**rmat/**M**aster Layout				Selects placeholder to be added
F**o**rmat/**T**able				Changes table border and fill color
Tools/**O**ptions/Spelling and Style				Sets spelling and style options
Sli**d**e Show/Custo**m** Animation				Applies custom animation
Sli**d**e Show/Slide **T**ransition		Transition		Adds transition effects
Sli**d**e Show/**H**ide Slide				Hides selected slide
Slide Show Pointer Options Menu				
Arrow	Ctrl + A			Changes pointer to arrow and turns off freehand annotation
Ballpoint Pen	Ctrl + P			Changes pointer to ballpoint pen and turns on freehand annotation
Felt Tip Pen				Changes pointer to felt tip pen and turns on freehand annotation
Highlighter				Changes pointer to a highlighter
Ink **C**olor				Shows color palette for annotation tool
E**r**aser	Ctrl + E			Changes pointer to eraser
Erase all Ink on Slide	E			Removes all annotations from slide
Slide Show Screen Options Menu				
Go to Slide				Displays specified slide
S**c**reen/**B**lack Screen	B			Blacks out screen
S**c**reen/**W**hite Screen	W			Whites out screen

lab exercises

matching

Match the numbered item with the correct lettered description.

1. transition   _____   **a.** indicates a transition effect has been applied to the slide

2. [▧]   _____   **b.** ready-made shapes, such as block arrows, stars and banners, and callouts

3. design template   _____   **c.** special slide that controls format for the title slide only

4. slide master   _____   **d.** indicates the slide is hidden

5. build   _____   **e.** printed output that displays a slide and its related notes

6. [☆]   _____   **f.** controls the way one slide appears on the screen and the next appears

7. table   _____   **g.** defines the background design, text format, and placeholder placement for each slide

8. [Esc]   _____   **h.** professionally created slide design that can be applied to a presentation

9. AutoShapes   _____   **i.** ends the slide show and displays the slide last viewed as the current slide

10. notes pages   _____   **j.** special effect that controls how bulleted points appear during the slide show

    _____   **k.** displays information in a row and column format

multiple choice

Circle the letter of the correct response.

1. If you wanted to display a black slide during a presentation, you would press _____.
    a. H
    b. U
    c. B
    d. E

2. If you wanted to add a company logo on each slide in your presentation, you would place it on the _____.
    a. handout
    b. notes page
    c. outline slide
    d. master

lab exercises

3. To substitute one word for another in a presentation, you would use the _____ command on the Edit menu.
   a. Find
   b. Locate
   c. Replace
   d. Duplicate

4. To proportionally size an AutoShape, graphic, or picture, hold down _____ while you drag.
   a. Ctrl
   b. Alt
   c. ⇧ Shift
   d. Ctrl + Alt

5. To display bullets on a slide one at a time, you would apply a(n) _____ .
   a. build
   b. transition
   c. animation
   d. motion

6. To ensure that your presentation has a professional, consistent look throughout, use a(n) _____.
   a. slide layout
   b. design template
   c. animation scheme
   d. transition

7. Using a _____ to modify or add elements to a presentation ensures consistency and saves time.
   a. design template
   b. slide layout
   c. table
   d. master

8. Slide transitions and build slides are _____ that are used to enhance the onscreen presentation.
   a. animations
   b. slide masters
   c. graphics
   d. special effects

9. If you want to display information in columns and rows, you would create a(n) _____.
   a. table
   b. text box
   c. slide layout
   d. AutoShape

10. To help you remember the important points during a presentation, you can add comments to slides and print _____.
    a. notes pages
    b. slide handouts
    c. preview handouts
    d. handouts

true/false

Circle the correct answer to the following questions.

1. Builds control the way that the display changes as you move from one slide to another during a presentation. True False
2. Style checking looks for consistency in punctuation and capitalization. True False
3. Alignment controls the position of text entries in a placeholder. True False
4. Masters are professionally created slide designs that can be applied to your presentation. True False
5. An AutoShape is an object that can be enhanced using drawing tools and menu commands. True False
6. A handout master defines the format and placement of the slide image, text, headers, footers, and other elements that are to appear on every slide in the presentation. True False
7. A title master defines the format and placement of titles and text for slides that use the title layout. True False
8. Transitions are used to display each bullet point, text, paragraph, or graphic independently of the other text or objects on the slide. True False
9. An AutoShape is a container for text or graphics. True False
10. A master is a special slide or page on which the formatting for all slides or pages in your presentation is defined. True False

fill-in

Complete the following statements by filling in the blanks with the correct terms.

1. The _____ master controls format, placement, and all elements that are to appear on every audience handout.

2. The _____ feature checks the presentation for consistency in punctuation and capitalization.

3. _____ add action to text and graphics so they move on the screen.

4. A _____ is made up of rows and columns of cells that you can fill with text and graphics.

5. A _____ is a container for text or graphics.

6. Alignment controls the position of text entries within a _____ or _____.

7. _____ are used to define where text and graphics appear on a slide.

8. _____ display each bullet point, text, paragraph, or graphic independently of the other text or objects on the slide.

9. _____ are professionally created slide designs that can be applied to your presentation.

10. The _____ slide is a special slide on which the formatting for all slides in your presentation is defined.

step-by-step

Enhancing a College Recruiting Presentation ★

1. Bonnie is the Assistant Director of New Admissions at Arizona State University. Part of her job is to make recruiting presentations at community colleges and local high schools about the University. She has already created the introductory portion of the presentation and needs to reorganize the topics and make the presentation more visually appealing. Several slides of the modified presentation are shown here:

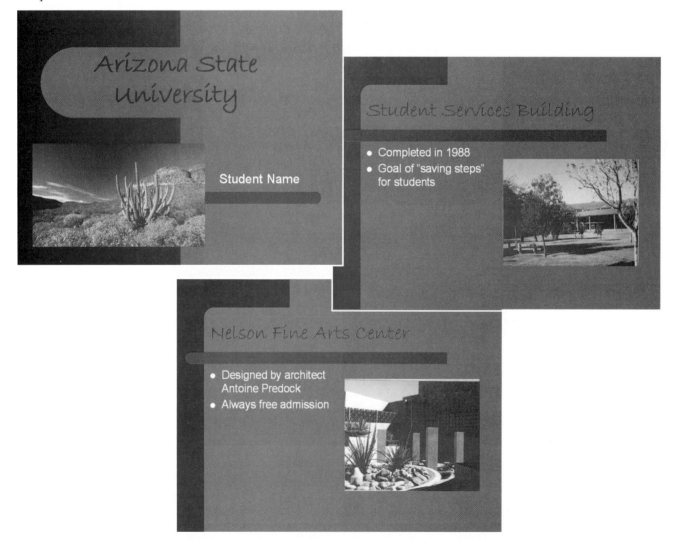

a. Open the file pp02_ASU Presentation.

b. Run the slide show to see what Bonnie has done so far.

c. Spell-check the presentation, making the appropriate corrections.

d. Move slide 5 before slide 3.

e. Move slide 5 before slide 4.

f. Use the Find and Replace command to locate all the occurrences of "Arizona State University" and replace them with **ASU** on all slides except the first and second slides.

g. Enter your name as the subtitle in slide 1. Insert the picture pp02_Arizona on the title slide. Size the picture and position the placeholders on the slide appropriately.

h. Demote all the bulleted items on slides 8 and 9 except the first item.

i. Apply a new presentation design of your choice to the presentation. Apply a new slide color scheme. Modify the font of the titles using the title and slide masters.

j. Duplicate slide 1 and move the duplicate to the end of the presentation. Delete the graphic. Replace your name with **Apply Now!**. Apply the Change Font Size custom animation Emphasis effect at a slow speed. Increase the font to a larger size.

k. Bonnie would like to add some pictures of the buildings at the end of the presentation. Switch to Slide Sorter view and select slides 12, 13, and 14. Apply the Title, Text and Content layout. Insert the picture pp02_Student Services in slide 12, the picture pp02_Library in slide 13, and the picture pp02_Fine Arts in slide 14.

l. Check the style of the presentation and make any changes you feel are appropriate. Turn the style check feature off when you are done.

m. Add a Wave custom animation at a medium speed and the Applause sound to the title text on the title slide.

n. Apply the Strips build effect at a medium speed in a Right Down direction to slides 3 through 7, 10, and 11.

o. Run the slide show.

p. Add file documentation and save the presentation as ASU Presentation1. Print slides 1, 2, and 12–15 as handouts (six per page).

Completing the Massage Therapy Presentation ★ ★

2. To complete this problem, you must have completed Step-by-Step Exercise 3 in Lab 1. You have completed the first draft of the presentation on therapeutic massage, but still have some information to add. Additionally, you want to make the presentation look better using many of the PowerPoint design and slide show presentation features. Several slides of the modified presentation are shown here:

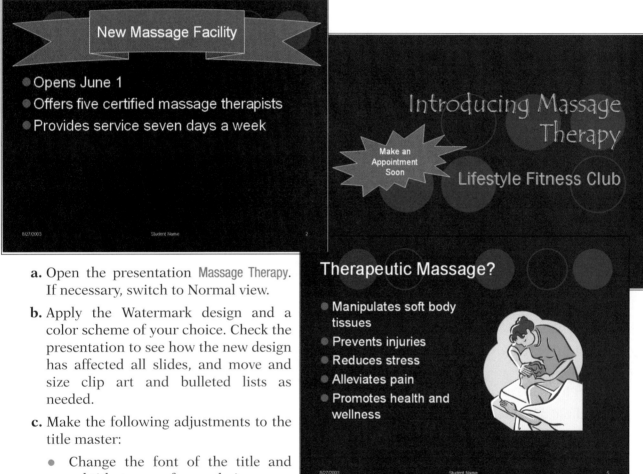

a. Open the presentation Massage Therapy. If necessary, switch to Normal view.

b. Apply the Watermark design and a color scheme of your choice. Check the presentation to see how the new design has affected all slides, and move and size clip art and bulleted lists as needed.

c. Make the following adjustments to the title master:

 • Change the font of the title and subtitle to one of your choice.

 • Change the font color of the title and subtitle to colors of your choice. Add a shadow.

d. On slide 2, replace the slide title with an AutoShape of your choice. Add the text **New Massage Facility** to the AutoShape. Add a medium speed Dissolve In or Out custom animation to the AutoShape. Add a medium speed Fly In custom animation to the bulleted list.

e. Duplicate the title slide and move it to the end of the presentation. Add an AutoShape to this slide that includes the text **Make an Appointment Soon**. Format the object and text appropriately. Move the title and subtitle to accommodate the drawing object.

f. Select an animation scheme of your choice to add transition and build effects to all the slides. Run the slide show.

g. Add the following note to slide 5 in a point size of 18:

Basically, all massages are therapeutic.

h. Add the following note to slide 10 in a point size of 18:

Ask if there are any questions. Pass out brochures.

i. Style-check the presentation and make any necessary changes. Turn off the style-check option when you are done.

j. Add file documentation and save the completed presentation as **Massage Therapy2**.

k. Print the notes page for slide 10. Print slides 1, 5, and 6 as handouts with three slides per page.

Enhancing the Job Fairs Presentation ★ ★

3. To complete this problem, you must have completed Step-by-Step Exercise 5 in Lab 1. Tim has completed the first draft of the presentation for Job Fairs, but he still has some information he wants to add to the presentation. Additionally, he wants to make the presentation look better using many of the PowerPoint design and slide show presentation features. Several slides of the modified presentation are shown here:

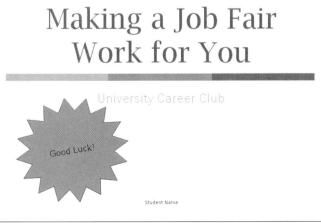

a. Open the presentation Job Fairs. If necessary, switch to Normal view.

b. Change the design template to Levels. Change the color scheme to a color of your choice.

c. Change to Slide Sorter view and check the slide layouts. Make the following adjustments:

- Slide master:
  - — Delete the Date area and Number area placeholders.
  - — Change the font of the title to one of your choice. Increase the font size. Change the font color to a color of your choice.
- Title master:
  - — Change the text color of the subtitle to a color of your choice, bold it, and change it to a font of your choice.

d. Check the slide layouts again in Slide Sorter view and fix the placement and size of the placeholders and pictures as needed.

e. Apply a custom animation to the clip art and bulleted list on slide 3 and add sound effects of your choice.

f. Duplicate the title slide and move it to the end of the presentation. Add a drawing object to this slide that includes the text **Good Luck!**. Format the object and text appropriately.

g. Select an animation scheme of your choice to add transition and build effects to all the slides. Run the slide show.

h. Add the following note to slide 3 in a point size of 18:

You must be able to give a short biography when asked "Tell me about yourself." Practice until you can tell the story smoothly.

i. Style-check the presentation and make any necessary changes. Turn off the style-check feature when you are done.

j. Add file documentation and save the completed presentation as Job Fairs2.

k. Print the notes page for slide 3. Print slides 1, 2, 6, and 8 as handouts with four slides per page.

Enhancing the Triple Crown Presentation ★ ★ ★

4. To complete this problem, you must have completed Step-by-Step Exercise 1 in Lab 1. Logan's work on the Triple Crown Presentation was well received by his supervisor. She would like to see some additional information included in the presentation, including a table of upcoming qualifying hikes. Several of the slides from his updated presentation are shown here:

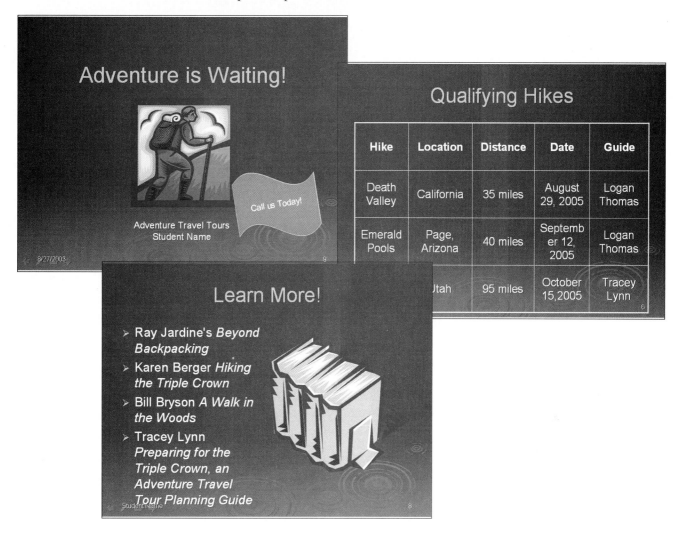

a. Open the file Triple Crown Presentation.

b. Apply a new presentation design and color scheme of your choice to the presentation. Check the presentation to see how the new design has affected all the slides, and move and size graphics and bulleted lists as needed.

c. Modify the text color of the titles using the title and slide masters.

d. Insert a Title and Table slide after slide 6, with 5 columns and 4 rows. Enter the title **Qualifying Hikes**. Enter the following information in the table:

Hike	Location	Distance	Date	Guide
Death Valley	California	35 miles	August 29, 2005	Logan Thomas
Paria Canyon	Page, Arizona	40 miles	September 12, 2005	Logan Thomas
Bryce to Zion	Utah	95 miles	October 15, 2005	Tracey Lynn

e. Size and position the table as shown in the example. Add bold to the table headings. Change the column and row size as needed. Center the table contents vertically and horizontally.

f. Change the border color to one of your choice.

g. Change the layout of slide 6 to Title, Text, and Content. Insert the clip art graphic pp02_Read. Change the coloring of the books from brown and tan to blue.

h. Duplicate slide 1 and place the copy at the end of the presentation. Change the title to **Adventure is Waiting!**.

i. Add a footer that contains your name left-aligned and the slide number right-aligned.

j. Add an AutoShape of your choice to the final slide with the text: **Call us Today!**.

k. Use the Find and Replace command to replace all occurrences of Paria Canyon with **Emerald Pools**.

l. Add the following information to the file properties:

Title: **Triple Crown Presentation2**

Subject: **Lightweight Backpacking Tours**

Author: **Student Name**

Company: **Adventure Travel Tours**

m. Save the file as Triple Crown Presentation2. Print slides 1, 6, 7, and 9 as a handout with all four slides on one page.

Enhancing the Coffee Presentation ★ ★ ★

5. To complete this problem, you must have completed Step-by-Step Exercise 4 in Lab 1. Evan, the owner of the Downtown Internet Cafe, was so impressed with your presentation on coffee that he has decided to run it periodically throughout the day on a large screen in the cafe so customers can see it as well. To "spiff it up," he wants you to convert it to an onscreen presentation with more graphics as well as other design and animation effects. Several slides of the modified presentation are shown here:

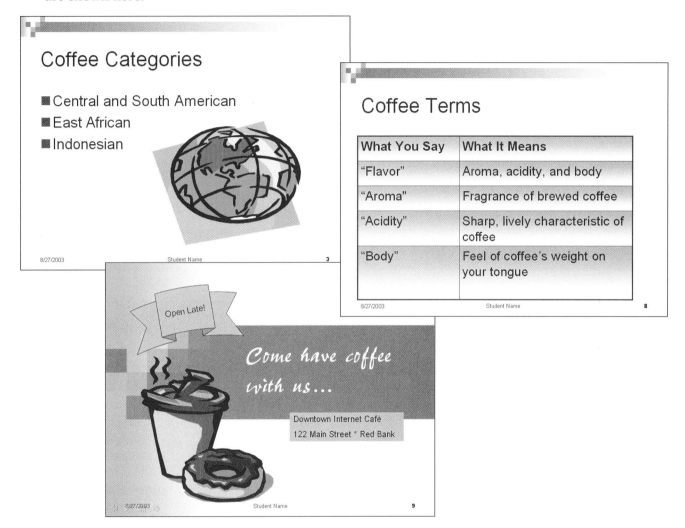

a. Open the file Coffee.

b. Use the Replace feature to replace both instances of the term "Regular Roasts" with **Coffee Categories**. Do the same to replace both instances of the term "Other Offerings" with **Coffee Types**.

c. Change the design template to Pixel or a design of your choice. Select a color scheme of your choice. Check the presentation to see how the new design has affected all slides, and move and size clip art and bulleted lists as needed.

d. Use the slide master to change the font color of all first-level bullet text to a different color.

e. Apply a custom animation and sound of your choice to the coffee cup clip art on slide 2.

f. Change the title of slide 3 to **What's Brewing?**. Delete the clip art.

g. Copy the clip art from slide 2 to slide 3 and size and position it appropriately. Add a third bullet to slide 3 with the text: **Coffee Terms**. Delete slide 2.

h. Insert the graphic pp02_Globe on slide 3. Recolor the background of the picture with colors that match the slide design.

i. Change the title "Central and South American Coffee" on slide 4 to **Coffees from the Americas**.

j. Insert a new slide with a table format after slide 7. Enter the title, **Coffee Terms**. Create the table with 2 columns and 5 rows. Enter **What You Say** as the first column heading and **What It Means** as the second column heading. Copy the terms and definitions from slide 9 into the table. Change the font size of the text as needed. Bold the column headings and put quotation marks around the terms. Center-align the What You Say column. Size the columns and table appropriately. Add a fill color to the table.

k. Delete slide 9.

l. Duplicate the title slide and move the duplicate to the end of the presentation. Change the title to **Come have coffee with us . . .** and delete the subtitle text. Delete the subtitle placeholder.

m. Add the following information in a text box on slide 9:

   Downtown Internet Cafe

   122 Main Street * Red Bank

n. Add a fill color and border to the text box.

o. Insert an AutoShape of your choice on the last slide with the text **Open Late!**.

p. Check the presentation style and make any necessary changes. Turn off the style-check feature when you are done.

q. Set the slide transition to automatically advance after 10 seconds. Run the slide show.

r. Add file documentation information and save the completed presentation as Coffee Show.

s. Print slides 1, 2, 8, and 9 as handouts, four per page.

Successful Interview Techniques ★

1. You work at an employment agency and your manager has asked you to create an onscreen presentation about interview techniques. This presentation will be loaded on all the computers that your company makes available to clients for online job searches, and instructions on how to run the presentation will be posted at each workstation. Select a presentation design that you like and create the presentation using the following notes for reference. Add clip art and build effects where applicable. Add your name to the footer on each slide except the title slide. Set the slide transition so that it automatically advances after an appropriate length of time (long enough for the person viewing the presentation to read each slide's contents). Save the presentation as Interview Techniques. Print all slides of your presentation, six per page.

   - Before a job interview, you should thoroughly research the company (use the library or the Web). For example, what is one event that occurred in the company within the last five years?

   - During the interview, demonstrate your expertise, using a consultant's style of communicating. Create open and clear communication, and effectively respond to open-ended questions. Examples of open-ended questions are: "Tell me about yourself." "What makes you stand out?" "What are your greatest weaknesses?" You should also be ready to answer questions about why you are interviewing with the company and how and where you fit within their organization. You must be prepared to handle both spoken and unspoken objections. And finally, you must justify your salary requirements; don't just negotiate them.

Enhancing the Animal Careers Presentation ★

2. To finish creating the basic Careers with Animals presentation that you began in Lab 1, On Your Own Exercise 5, turn it into an onscreen presentation with a custom design, clip art, sound, transitions, and builds so it will hold your audience's interest. Add speaker notes and rehearse the presentation. When you are done, save the presentation as Animal Careers2, print the presentation as handouts, and print the notes pages for slides containing notes only.

Explaining Fad Diets ★ ★

3. You have been asked to give a lunchbox presentation at the LifeStyle Fitness Club on fad diets. You plan to first describe all fad diets and then end with a summary of the benefits of eating according to the USDA's Food Pyramid and proper exercise. Do some research on the Web to obtain a list of fad diets, including a brief description, pros, and cons. Select an appropriate slide design and include some graphics to liven up the presentation. Add a table that includes some of your data. Include your name in the footer. When you are done, save the presentation as Fad Diets and print the handouts.

Enhancing the Internet Policy Presentation ★ ★ ★

4. After completing the Internet Policy presentation in Lab 1, On Your Own Exercise 1, you decide it needs a bit more sprucing up. First of all, it would be more impressive as an onscreen presentation with a custom design. You also want to add some information about personal computing security. Do some research on the Web to find some helpful tips on protecting personal privacy and safeguarding your computer. Also, add some animated clip art pictures, non-standard bullets, builds, and

transitions to help liven up the content. Make these and any other changes that you think would enhance the presentation. Add a table and check the style consistency of the presentation. Add appropriate documentation to the file. When you are done, save it as Internet Policy2, print the presentation as handouts, and print the notes pages for slides containing notes only.

Sharing Favorite Vacation Spots ★ ★ ★

5. You and your fellow Getaway Travel Club members have decided that each of you should do a presentation on your favorite vacation spot (one you have already been to or one you would like to go to). Pick a location and do some research on the Web and/or visit a local travel agency to get information about your chosen destination. Create a presentation using a custom design and include clip art, animation, sounds, transitions, and build effects to make the presentation more interesting. Include your name as a footer or subtitle on at least one slide. Create and enhance a table. Use speaker notes if necessary to remind yourself of additional information you want to relay that is not included in the slides. Add appropriate documentation to the file. Run the slide show and practice your presentation, then save as Travel Favorites and print your presentation and notes pages.

Working Together 1: Copying, Embedding, and Linking Between Applications

Case Study

Animal Rescue Foundation

The director of the Animal Rescue Foundation has reviewed the PowerPoint presentation you created and has asked you to include a chart showing the adoption success rate that was created using Excel. Additionally, the director has provided a list of dates for the upcoming volunteer orientation meetings that he feels would be good content for another slide.

Frequently you will find that you want to include information that was created using a word processor, spreadsheet, or database application in your slide show. As you will see, you can easily share information between applications, saving you both time and effort by eliminating the need to recreate information that is available in another application. You will learn how to share information between applications while you create the new slides. The new slides containing information from Word and Excel are shown here.

Note: The Working Together section assumes that you already know how to use Office Word and Excel 2003 and that you have completed Lab 2 of PowerPoint. You will need the file Volunteer2, which you saved at the end of Lab 2 of PowerPoint. If this file is not available, use ppwt1_Volunteer2.

Information can be easily copied from a file created in another application, such as Office Word or Excel, and pasted into a PowerPoint slide as a linked or embedded object.

Copying Between Applications

The orientation meeting information has already been entered in a document using Word. All the Microsoft Office System applications have a common user interface, such as similar commands and menu structures. In addition to these obvious features, they have been designed to work together, making it easy to share and exchange information between applications.

Rather than retype the list of orientation meeting dates provided by the director, you will copy it from the Word document into the presentation. You can also use the same commands and procedures to copy information from PowerPoint or other Office applications into Word.

Copying from Word to a PowerPoint Slide

First, you need to modify the PowerPoint presentation to include a new slide for the orientation meeting dates.

1 ● **Start Office PowerPoint 2003.**

● **Open the presentation** Volunteer2 **(saved at the end of Lab 2).**

● **Insert a new slide using the Title Only layout after slide 12.**

● **Close the Slide Layout task pane.**

● **Display the new slide in Normal view.**

Your screen should be similar to Figure 1

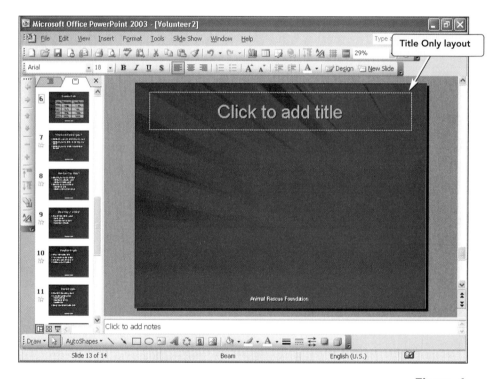

Figure 1

To copy the information from the Word document file into the PowerPoint presentation, you need to open the Word document.

2

● Start Office Word 2003.

● Open the document ppwt1_Orientation Meetings.

Your screen should be similar to Figure 2

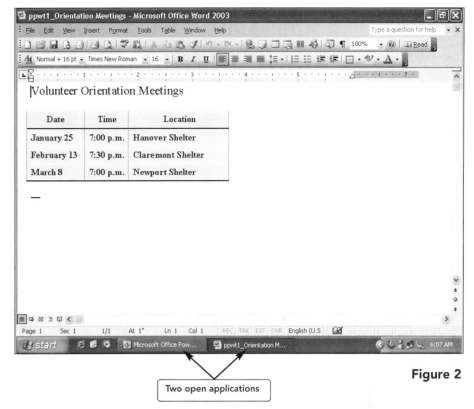

Two open applications

Figure 2

There are now two open applications, Word and PowerPoint. PowerPoint is open in a window behind the Word application window. Both application buttons are displayed in the taskbar. There are also two open files, Orientation Meetings in Word and Volunteer2 in PowerPoint. Word is the active application, and Orientation Meetings is the active file. To make it easier to work with two applications, you will tile the windows to view both on the screen at the same time.

3

● Right-click on a blank area of the taskbar to open the shortcut menu.

● Select Tile Windows **V**ertically

● Click on the Word document window to make it active.

Your screen should be similar to Figure 3

Figure 3

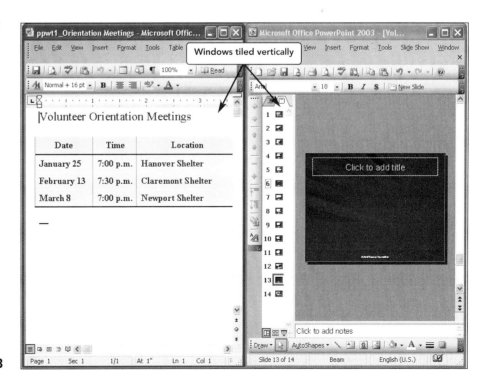

Windows tiled vertically

First, you will copy the title from the Word document into the title placeholder of the slide. While using the Office Word and PowerPoint applications, you have learned how to use cut, copy, and paste to move or copy information within the same document. You can also perform these same operations between documents in the same application and between documents in different applications. The information is pasted in a format that the application can edit, if possible.

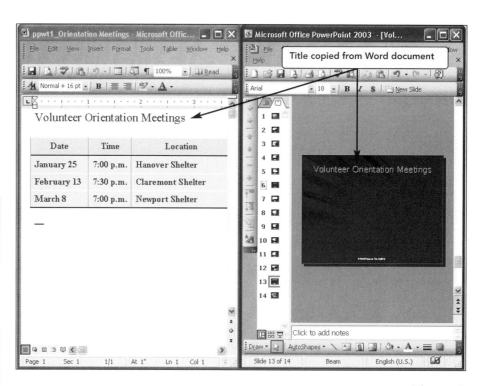

Figure 4

4 ● Select the title "Volunteer Orientation Meetings."

● Drag the selection using the right mouse button to the title placeholder in the slide.

Having Trouble?
If you drag using the left mouse button, the selection is moved instead of copied.

● From the shortcut menu, select Copy.

Another Method
You could also use Copy and Paste to copy the title to the slide.

● Click on the slide to deselect the placeholder.

Your screen should be similar to Figure 4

The title has been copied into the slide and can be edited and manipulated within PowerPoint. The formats associated with the slide master are applied to the copied text. If the copied text included formatting, such as color, it would override the slide master settings, just as if you formatted a slide individually to make it unique.

Embedding a Word Table in a PowerPoint Slide

Next you want to display the table of orientation dates below the title in the slide. You will copy and embed the table in the slide. As you have seen, an object that is embedded is stored in the file that it is inserted into, called the **destination file**, and becomes part of that file. The embedded object can then be edited using features from the source program, the program in which it was created. Since the embedded object is part of the destination file, modifying it does not affect the original file called the **source file**.

1 ● Select the table in the Word document window.

Having Trouble?
Drag to select the entire table or use Table/Select/Table.

● Click 📋 Copy.

● Click on the PowerPoint window.

● Choose **E**dit/Paste **S**pecial.

Your screen should be similar to Figure 5

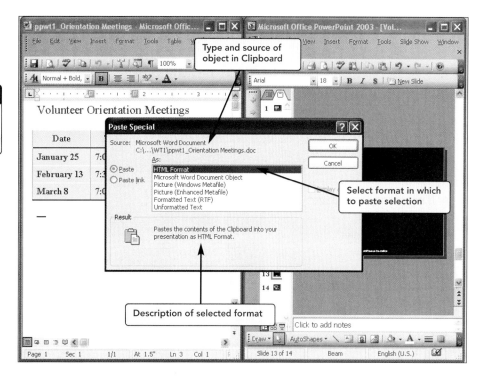

Figure 5

The Paste Special dialog box displays the type of object contained in the Clipboard and its location in the Source area. From the As list box, you select the type of format in which you want the object inserted into the destination file. The default option inserts the copy in HTML (HyperText Markup Language) format. The Result area describes the effect of your selections. In this case, you want the object inserted as a Word Document Object.

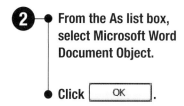

2 ● From the As list box, select Microsoft Word Document Object.

● Click [OK].

Your screen should be similar to Figure 6

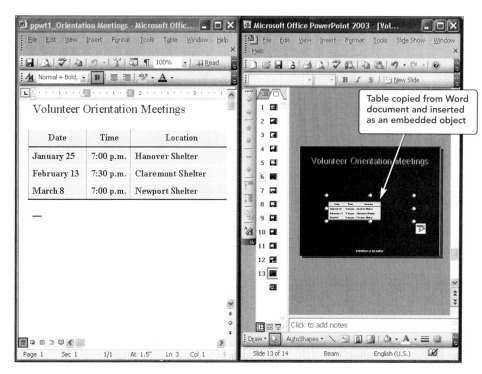

Figure 6

The table, including the table formatting, is copied into the slide as an embedded object that can be manipulated using the Picture toolbar. You will trim or crop the object so that the object size is the same size as the table. Then you will increase the size of the object and position it in the slide.

3 ● Choose <u>U</u>ndo Tile from the taskbar shortcut menu.

● If necessary, maximize the PowerPoint window and select the table.

● Display the Picture toolbar.

● Click 🔲 Crop.

● Position the cropping tool 🔲 over a corner crop mark and drag inward to reduce the size of the object to the same size as the table.

Your screen should be similar to Figure 7

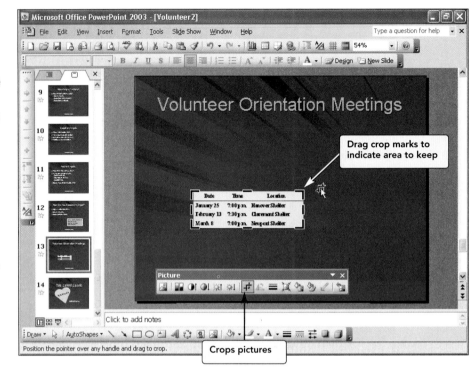

Figure 7

4 ● Click 🔲 Crop to turn off the cropping tool.

● Size and move the table object as in Figure 8.

● Deselect the object.

● Close the Picture toolbar.

Your screen should be similar to Figure 8

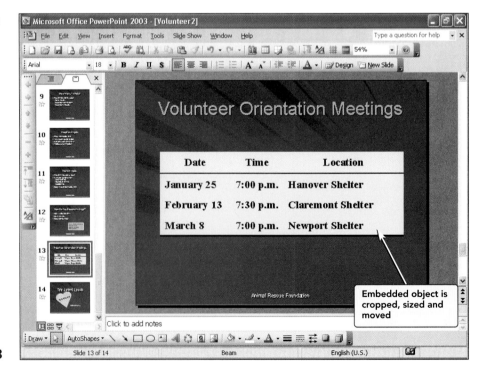

Figure 8

Editing an Embedded Object

As you look at the table, you decide you want to change the appearance of the text in the headings. To do this, you will edit the embedded object using the source program.

Word menus and toolbar

1 ● **Double-click the table.**

Another Method

The menu equivalent is **E**dit/Document **O**bject/**E**dit.

Your screen should be similar to Figure 9

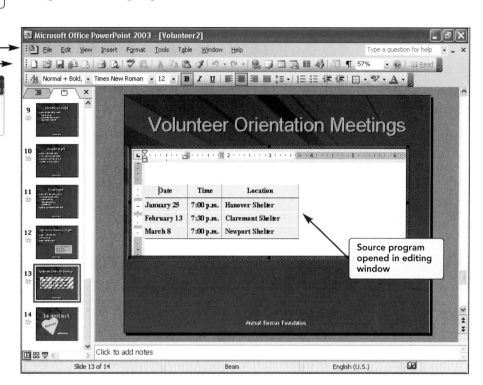

Source program opened in editing window

Figure 9

Additional Information

The user must have the source program on their system to be able to open and edit an embedded object.

The source program, in this case Word, is opened. The Word menus and toolbars replace some of the menus and toolbars in the PowerPoint application window. The embedded object is displayed in an editing window. Now, you can use the Word commands to edit the object.

2
- Change the font color of the three headings to blue.

- Left-align the three headings.

- Close the source program by clicking anywhere outside the object.

Your screen should be similar to Figure 10

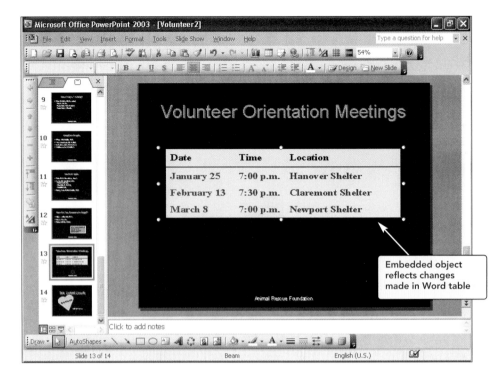

Embedded object reflects changes made in Word table

Figure 10

The embedded object in the PowerPoint slide is updated to reflect the changes you made in the Word table.

3
- Click ▣ Orientation Meetings ... in the taskbar to switch to the Word application.

- Deselect the table and notice that the source file has not been affected by the changes you made to the embedded object.

- Exit Word.

Linking Between Applications

Next you want to copy the chart of the rescue and adoption data into the presentation. You will insert the chart object into the slide as a **linked object**, which is another way to insert information created in one application into a document created by another application. With a linked object, the actual data is stored in the source file (the document in which it was created). A graphic representation or picture of the data is displayed in the destination file (the document in which the object is inserted). A connection between the information in the destination file to the source file is established by creating a link. The link contains references to the location of the source file and the selection within the document that is linked to the destination file.

When changes are made in the source file that affect the linked object, the changes are automatically reflected in the destination file when it is opened. This connection is called a **live link**. When you create linked objects, the date and time on your machine should be accurate. This is because the program refers to the date of the source file to determine whether updates are needed when you open the destination file.

Linking an Excel Chart to a PowerPoint Presentation

The chart of the rescue and adoption data will be inserted into another new slide following slide 6.

- Insert a new slide following slide 6, using the Title Only layout.

- Close the Slide Layout task pane.

- Start Office Excel 2003 and open the workbook ppwt1_RescueData from your data files.

- Tile the application windows vertically.

    Your screen should be similar to Figure 11

Figure 11

The worksheet contains the rescue and adoption data for the past four years as well as a column chart of the data. Again, you have two open applications, PowerPoint and Excel. Next you will copy the second title line from the worksheet into the slide title placeholder.

2 ● Select cell B2.

● Click Copy.

● Select the Title placeholder in the slide.

● Choose **Edit/Paste Special** and select **Formatted Text (RTF)**.

● Click OK .

● Remove the extra blank lines below the title and the extra space at the end of the title.

● If necessary, size the placeholder and position the title appropriately on the slide.

● Click on the slide to deselect the placeholder.

Your screen should be similar to Figure 12

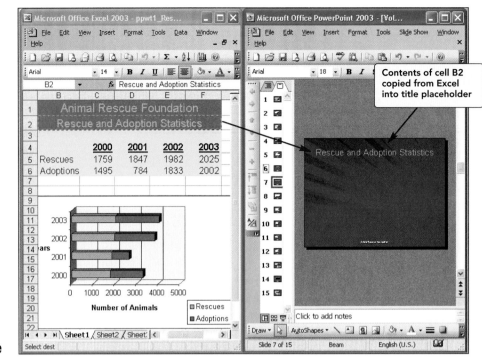

Figure 12

Now, you are ready to copy the chart. By making the chart a linked object, it will be updated automatically if the source file is edited.

3 ● Select the entire chart.

Having Trouble?
Click on the chart to select it when the ScreenTip displays "Chart Area."

● Click 🖹 Copy.

● Click on the slide.

● Choose **E**dit/Paste **S**pecial.

● Select Paste li**n**k.

Your screen should be similar to Figure 13

Figure 13

Again, from the As list box, you select the type of format in which you want the object inserted into the destination file. The only available option for this object is as a Microsoft Excel Chart Object. The Result area describes the effect of your selections. In this case, the object will be inserted as a picture, and a link will be created to the chart in the source file. Selecting the Display as Icon option changes the display of the object from a picture to an icon. Double-clicking the icon displays the object picture. The default selections are appropriate.

4 ● Click [OK].

● Appropriately size and center the linked object on the slide.

● Deselect the object.

Your screen should be similar to Figure 14

Figure 14

Updating a Linked Object

While looking at the chart in the slide, you decide to change the chart type from a column chart to a bar chart. You believe that a bar chart will show the trends more clearly. You also notice the adoption data for 2001 looks very low. After checking the original information, you see that the wrong value was entered in the worksheet and that it should be 1784.

To make these changes, you need to switch back to Excel. Double-clicking on a linked object quickly switches to the open source file. If the source file is not open, it opens the file for you. If the application is not started, it both starts the application and opens the source file.

1 ● **Double-click the chart object in the slide.**

Another Method

The menu equivalent is **E**dit/Linked Worksheet **O**bject/**O**pen.

● **In Excel, right click on one of the columns in the chart and select Chart Type.**

Another Method

The menu equivalent is **C**hart/Chart T**y**pe.

● **Select Column.**

● **Select Clustered column with a 3-D visual effect.**

● **Click** OK .

● **Edit the value in cell D6 to 1784.**

Your screen should be similar to Figure 15

Figure 15

The chart in both applications has changed to a bar chart, and the chart data series has been updated to reflect the change in data. This is because any changes you make in the chart in Excel will be automatically reflected in the linked chart in the slide.

2 ● Untile the application windows.

● Save the revised Excel workbook as RescueData Linked.

● Exit Excel.

● If necessary, maximize the PowerPoint window.

Editing Links

Whenever a document is opened that contains links, the application looks for the source file and automatically updates the linked objects. If there are many links, updating can take a lot of time. Additionally, if you move the source file to another location, or perform other operations that may interfere with the link, your link will not work. To help with situations like these, you can edit the settings associated with links. You will look at how to do this, though you will not actually edit the settings.

1 ● If necessary, select the chart object.

● Choose Edit/Links.

Your screen should be similar to Figure 16

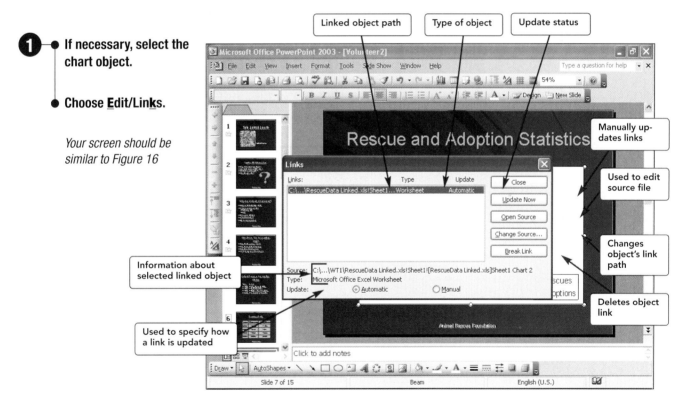

Figure 16

The Links dialog box list box displays information about all links in the document. This includes the path and name of the source file, the range of linked cells or object name, the type of file, and the update status. Below the list box the details for the selected link are displayed. The other options in this dialog box are described in the table on the next page.

Option	Effect
Automatic	Updates the linked object whenever the destination document is opened or the source file changes. This is the default.
Manual	The destination document is not automatically updated, and you must use the Update Now command button to update the link.
Locked	Prevents a linked object from being updated.
Open Source	Opens the source document for the selected link.
Change Source	Used to modify the path to the source document.
Break Link	Breaks the connection between the source document and the active document.

You do not want to make any changes to the link.

2 ● Click .

Linking documents is a very handy feature, particularly in documents whose information is updated frequently. If you include a linked object in a document that you are giving to another person, make sure the user has access to the source file and application. Otherwise the links will not operate correctly.

Printing Selected Slides

Next, you will print the two new slides.

1 ● Switch to Slide Sorter view and select slides 7 and 14.

● Use <u>V</u>iew/<u>H</u>eader and Footer to modify the slide footer to display your name on slides 7 and 14 only.

Having Trouble?

Select the slides you want to modify, use the command, and click [Apply] to apply the new footer to the selected slides only.

● Choose <u>F</u>ile/<u>P</u>rint.

● If necessary, select the printer.

● Select <u>S</u>election as the print range.

● Specify Slides as the type of output.

● Preview the output and change the print to grayscale if necessary.

● Print the slides.

● Save the PowerPoint presentation as Volunteer2 Linked **and** exit PowerPoint.

Your printed output should be similar to that shown here.

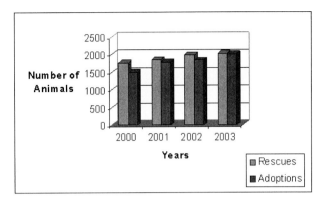

Rescue and Adoption Statistics

Student Name

Volunteer Orientation Meetings

Date	Time	Location
January 25	7:00 p.m.	Hanover Shelter
February 13	7:30 p.m.	Claremont Shelter
March 8	7:00 p.m.	Newport Shelter

Student Name

lab review

WORKING TOGETHER **1**

Copying, Embedding, and Linking Between Applications

key terms

destination file   PPWT1.4
linked object   PPWT1.8
live link   PPWT1.9
source file   PPWT1.4

microsoft office specialist skills

The Microsoft Office Specialist certification program is designed to measure your proficiency in performing basic tasks using the Office 2003 applications. Certification demonstrates that you have the skills and provides a valuable industry credential for employment. After completing this lab, you have learned the following Microsoft Office PowerPoint 2003 Specialist skills:

Skill Sets	Skill Standards	Page
Creating Content	Insert and edit text based content	PPWT1.2
	Insert objects	PPWT1.11
Managing and Delivering Presentations	Organize a presentation	PPWT1.2, 1.9
	Print slides, outlines, handouts, and speaker notes	PPWT1.14

command summary

Command	Action
Edit/Paste **S**pecial/ <Object>	Inserts an item from Clipboard as an embedded object
Edit/Paste **S**pecial/Paste **L**ink	Inserts an item from Clipboard as a linked object
Edit/Lin**k**s	Changes settings associated with linked objects
Edit/Linked Worksheet **O**bject/**O**pen	Opens source application of linked object
Edit/Document Object/Edit	Opens source application of embedded object

lab exercises

rating system

★ Easy

★★ Moderate

★★★ Difficult

step-by-step

Embedding a Table of Massage Prices ★

1. To complete this problem, you must have completed Step-by-Step Exercise 2 in Lab 2. The Massage Therapy presentation is almost complete. You just need to add some information to the presentation about the prices. This information is already in a Word document as a table. You will copy and embed it into a new slide. The completed slide is shown here.

    a. Start Word and open the document ppwt1_MassagePrices.

    b. Start PowerPoint and open the Massage Therapy2 presentation.

    c. Add a new slide after slide 9 using the Title Only layout.

    d. Copy the title from the Word document into the slide title placeholder.

    e. Copy the table into the slide as an embedded object. Exit Word.

    f. Size and position the object on the slide appropriately.

    g. Edit the table to increase the font size as needed.

    h. Change the fill color of the table to match the slide design.

    i. Save the presentation as Massage Therapy3.

    j. Print the new slide.

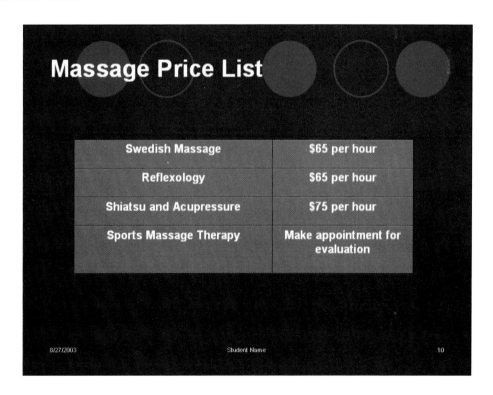

Linking a Table of Coffee Prices ★ ★

2. To complete this problem, you must have completed Step-by-Step Exercise 4 in Lab 2. Evan, owner of the Downtown Internet Cafe, wants you to include information about special prices on coffee beans in the coffee slide show you created. You will link the coffee price information to the presentation, because the prices change frequently with market conditions and good buys. The completed slide is shown here.

a. Start Word and open the document ppwt1_CoffeePrices.

b. Start PowerPoint and open the presentation Coffee Show.

c. Add a new slide at the end of the presentation using the Title Only layout.

d. Enter the slide title ... Or Take Some Home.

e. Copy the table of prices into the slide as a linked object.

f. Copy the text "Roast Coffee Specials" from the Word document into a text box on the slide. Apply a new font color and increase the font size.

g. Size and position the objects appropriately.

h. In the Word document, change the price of Kona to **$14.95**.

i. Save the Word document as Coffee Prices Linked. Exit Word.

j. Save the PowerPoint presentation as Coffee Show Linked.

k. Print the new slide.

...Or Take Some Home

Roast Coffee Specials

Coffee	Description	Cost/Pound
Columbian Blend	Classic body and aroma	$8.50
Kona	Smooth, light bodied	$14.95
Ethiopian	Floral aroma and flavor	$12.00
Sumatra	Dark roasted	$7.95

8/27/2003   Student Name   **10**

Linking a Worksheet on Forest Use ★ ★ ★

3. To complete this problem, you must have completed Step-by-Step Exercise 4 of Lab 2. Logan has found some interesting data on the increase in Americans hiking and wants to include this information in his lecture presentation. The completed slide is shown here.

    a. Start PowerPoint and open the Triple Crown Presentation2 presentation.

    b. Start Excel and open the ppwt1_Forest Use worksheet.

    c. Add a new slide after slide 6 using the Title Only layout.

    d. Enter the title **Most Popular Forest Activities**.

    e. Copy the worksheet range A2 through B6 as a linked object into slide 7. Size and position it appropriately.

    f. You notice that the percentage for hiking in the year 2002 seems low. After checking the original source, you see you entered the value incorrectly. In Excel, change the value in cell B5 to **36.4%**.

    g. Copy the text in cell A8 and paste it into the Notes for slide 7.

    h. Save the worksheet as Forest Use Linked. Exit Excel.

    i. Save the presentation as Triple Crown Presentation3.

    j. Print the new slide.

Command Summary

Command	Shortcut Key	Button	Voice	Action
start /All Programs				Opens program menu
File/**N**ew	Ctrl + N	🗋		Creates new presentation
File/**O**pen	Ctrl + O	📂	Open File open Open file	Opens existing presentation
File/**C**lose		✕	Close presentation	Closes presentation
File/**S**ave	Ctrl + S	💾	Save	Saves presentation
File/Save **A**s				Saves presentation using new file name and/or location
File/Print Pre**v**iew	Ctrl + P	🔍	Print preview	Displays preview of file
File/**P**rint		🖨		Prints presentation
File/Proper**t**ies				Displays statistics and stores information about presentation
File/E**x**it		✕	File exit	Exits PowerPoint program
Edit/**U**ndo	Ctrl + Z	↺ ▾	Undo	Reverses last action
Edit/Cu**t**	Ctrl + X	✂	Cut	Cuts selection to Clipboard
Edit/**P**aste	Ctrl + V	📋	Paste	Pastes item from Clipboard
Edit/Paste **S**pecial/<Object>				Inserts an item from Clipboard as an embedded object
Edit/Paste Special/Paste **L**ink				Inserts an item from Clipboard as a linked object
Edit/Select A**ll**	Ctrl + A			Selects all objects on a slide or all text in an object, or (in Outline pane) an entire outline
Edit/**D**elete Slide	Delete			Deletes selected slide
Edit/**F**ind	Ctrl + F	🔎		Finds specified text
Edit/Replace	Ctrl + H	🔎		Replaces located text with specified replacement text
Edit/Lin**k**s				Changes settings associated with linked objects

Command	Shortcut Key	Button	Voice	Action
Edit/Linked Worksheet **O**bject/**O**pen				Opens source application of linked object
Edit/**D**ocument **O**bject/**E**dit				Opens embedded object for editing by source program
View/**N**ormal		⊞	Normal Normal view	Switches to Normal view
View/Sli**d**e Sorter		⊞⊟	Slide sorter	Switches to Slide Sorter view
View/Slide Sho**w**		⊒	View show Begin slide show Start slide show Slide show view	Runs slide show
View/Notes **P**age		⊡		Displays notes pages
View/**M**aster/**S**lide Master	⇧ Shift + ⊞			Displays slide master for current presentation
View/Tas**k** pane	Ctrl + F1		Task pane Show task pane View task pane Hide task pane	Hides or displays task pane
View/**T**oolbars				Displays or hides selected toolbars
View/**R**uler				Displays or hides ruler
View/**H**eader and Footer				Specifies information that appears as headers and footers on slides, notes, outlines, and handout pages
Insert/**N**ew Slide	Ctrl + M	⊞ New Slide	New slide Insert new slide	Inserts new slide
Insert/**D**uplicate Slide				Inserts duplicate of selected slide
Insert/**P**icture/**C**lip Art		⊠		Opens Clip Organizer and inserts selected clip art
Insert/**P**icture/**F**rom File		⊠		Inserts a picture from file on disk
Insert/**P**icture/**A**utoShapes		⊠		Inserts selected AutoShape object

Command	Shortcut Key	Button	Voice	Action
Insert/Te**x**t Box		[A≡]		Adds a text box
F**o**rmat/**F**ont/**F**ont		[Arial ▾]		Changes font type
F**o**rmat/**F**ont/**S**ize		[18 ▾]		Changes font size
F**o**rmat/**F**ont/F**o**nt Style/Bold	Ctrl + B	**B**	on bold	Adds bold effect to selection
F**o**rmat/**F**ont/F**o**nt Style/Italic	Ctrl + I	*I*	italic	Adds italic effect to selection
F**o**rmat/**F**ont/**C**olor		[A ▾]		Adds color to selection
F**o**rmat/**B**ullets and Numbering/ Bulleted		[≔]		Adds and removes selected bullet styles
F**o**rmat/**A**lignment	Ctrl + L	[≡]	Left justify	Aligns text in a cell or placeholder to left, center, right, or justified
	Ctrl + E	[≡]	Centered	
	Ctrl + R	[≡]	Right justify	
	Ctrl + J	[≡]		
F**o**rmat/Slide **D**esign		[Design]		Changes appearance of slide by applying a different design template
F**o**rmat/**R**eplace Fonts				Finds specified font and replace it with another
F**o**rmat/Slide **L**ayout				Changes layout of an existing or new slide
F**o**rmat/Pi**c**ture/**Re**color		[🖌]		Changes color of a picture
F**o**rmat/**M**aster Layout		[▦]		Selects the placeholder to be added
F**o**rmat/**T**able				Changes table border and fill color
Tools/**S**pelling		[ABC✓]		Spell-checks presentation
Tools/**C**ustomize/**O**ptions/				Shows Standard and Formatting toolbars in two rows
Tools/**O**ptions/Spelling and Style				Sets spelling and style options
Sli**d**e Show/Custo**m** Animation		[A ▾]		Applies custom animation
Sli**d**e Show/Slide **T**ransition		[Transition]		Adds transition effects
Sli**d**e Show/**H**ide Slide		[▨]		Hides selected slide
Slide Show Pointer Options Menu		[✎]		
Arrow	Ctrl + A			Changes pointer to arrow and turns off freehand annotation

Command	Shortcut Key	Button	Voice	Action
Ballpoint Pen	Ctrl + P			Changes pointer to ballpoint pen and turns on freehand annotation
Felt Tip Pen				Changes pointer to felt tip pen and turns on freehand annotation
Highlighter				Changes pointer to a highlighter
Ink **C**olor				Shows color palette for annotation tool
E**r**aser				Changes pointer to eraser
Erase all Ink on Slide	E			Removes all annotations from slide
Slide Show Screen Options Menu		▪		
Go to Slide				Displays hidden slide
S**c**reen/**B**lack Screen	B			Blacks out screen
S**c**reen/**W**hite Screen	W			Whites out screen

Glossary of Key Terms

alignment Controls the position of text entries within a space.

animation Effect that adds action to text and graphics so they move around on the screen.

animation scheme A preset visual effect that can be added to slide text.

AutoCorrect Feature that makes certain types of corrections automatically as you enter text.

AutoShape A ready-made drawing shape supplied with PowerPoint.

build An effect that progressively displays bulleted items as the presentation proceeds.

cell The intersection of a row and column in a table.

character formatting Formatting features that affect the selected characters only.

clip art Professionally drawn images.

current slide The slide that will be affected by any changes you make.

custom dictionary A dictionary you can create to hold words you commonly use but that are not included in the dictionary that is supplied with the program.

default Initial program settings.

demote To move a topic down one level in the outline hierarchy.

design template Professionally created slide design that can be applied to your presentation.

destination file The document receiving the linked or embedded object.

docked toolbar A toolbar fixed to an edge of the window and displays a vertical bar called the move handle, on the left edge of the toolbar.

document window The area of the application window that displays the contents of the open document.

drawing object An object consisting of shapes such as lines and boxes that can be created using the Drawing toolbar.

Drawing toolbar A toolbar that is used to add objects such as lines, circles, and boxes.

embedded object An object that is inserted into another application and becomes part of the document. It can be edited from within the document using the source program.

Find and Replace A feature that allows you to find text in a presentation and replace it with other text.

floating object A graphic object that is inserted into the drawing layer and which can be positioned anywhere on the page.

floating toolbar A toolbar that appears in a separate window and can be moved anywere on the desktop.

font A set of characters with a specific design. Also called a typeface.

font size The height and width of a character, commonly measured in points.

footer Text or graphics that appear on the bottom of each slide.

format To enhance the appearance of a slide to make it more readable or attractive.

Formatting toolbar A toolbar that contains buttons used to modify text.

graphic A non-text element, such as a chart, drawing, picture, or scanned photograph, in a slide.

hyperlink A connection to locations in the current document, other documents, or Web pages. Clicking a hyperlink jumps to the specified location.

keyword A word or phrase that is descriptive of the type of graphic you want to locate.

landscape Orientation of the printed output across the length of the paper.

layout A predefined slide organization that is used to control the placement of elements on a slide.

linked object An object that is created in a source file and linked to a destination file. Edits made to the source file are automatically reflected in the destination file.

live link A link that automatically updates the linked object whenever changes are made to it in the source file.

main dictionary Dictionary that comes with the Office 2003 programs.

master A special slide on which the formatting of all slides in a presentation is defined.

menu bar Located below the title bar, this bar displays the application's program menu.

notes page Printed output that shows a miniature of the slide and provides an area for speaker notes.

object An item on a slide that can be selected and modified.

Outlining toolbar A toolbar that is used to modify the organization of the presentation text and slides.

pane In Normal view, the separate divisions of the window that allow you to work on all aspects of your presentation in one place.

paragraph formatting Formatting features that affect entire paragraphs.

picture An image such as a graphic illustration or a scanned photograph.

picture toolbar A toolbar that is used to modify a graphic.

placeholder Box that is designed to contain objects such as the slide title, bulleted text, charts, tables, and pictures.

point A unit of type measurement. One point equals about 1/72 inch.

portrait Orientation of the printed output across the width of the paper.

promote To move a topic up one level in the outline hierarchy.

rotate handle The ⬚ on the selection rectangle of a selected object that allows you to rotate the object in any direction.

sans serif A font that does not have a flair at the base of each letter, such as Arial or Helvetica.

scroll bar Used with a mouse to bring additional lines of information into view in a window.

selection cursor A colored highlight bar that appears over the selected command.

selection rectangle Hashed border that surrounds a selected placeholder.

serif A font that has a flair at the base of each letter, such as Roman or Times New Roman.

Shortcut menu By right clicking on an item, this menu displays only the options pertaining to that item.

sizing handles Small boxes surrounding selected objects that are used to change the size of the object.

slide An individual page of the presentation.

slide show Used to practice or to present the presentation. It displays each slide in final form.

source file The file from which a linked or embedded object is obtained.

source program The program used to create the linked or embedded object.

spelling checker Locates all misspelled words, duplicate words, and capitalization irregularities as you create and edit a presentation, and proposes possible corrections.

stacking order The order in which objects are inserted into layers in the slide.

Standard toolbar A toolbar that contains buttons that give quick access to the most frequently used program features.

status bar A bar displayed at the bottom of the document window that advises you of the status of different program conditions and features as you use the program.

table An arrangement of horizontal rows and vertical columns.

table reference The letter and number that identifies a table cell.

Task Pane Displayed on the right side of the document window, it provides quick access to features as you are using the application.

template A file that includes predefined settings that can be used as a pattern to create many common types of presentations.

text box A container for text or graphics.

thumbnail A miniature view of a slide.

toolbar Located below the menu bar, they contain buttons that are mouse shortcuts for many of the menu items.

transition An effect that controls how a slide moves off the screen and the next one appears.

typeface A set of characters with a specific design. Also called a font.

view A way of looking at the presentation.

wizard An interactive approach that guides you through the process of performing many complicated tasks.

workspace The large area containing the slide where your presentations are displayed as you create and edit them.

Reference 1

Data File List

Supplied/Used	Created/Saved As
Lab 1	
	Volunteer
pp01_Volunteer1	Volunteer1
pp01_AnimalCare (graphic)	
pp01_Puppy (graphic)	
Step-by-Step	
1. pp01_Triple Crown	Triple Crown Presentation
pp01_Jump (graphic)	
pp01_Stream (graphic)	
2. pp01_Resume	Resume1
pp01_Success (graphic)	
pp01_Cover Letter (graphic)	
3. pp01_Relaxation	Massage Therapy
4. pp01_Logo	Coffee
pp01_Cuppa (graphic)	
pp01_Beans (graphic)	
5. pp01_Resume	Job Fairs
pp01_Biography (graphic)	
pp01_Meeting (graphic)	
pp01_Booth (graphic)	
pp01_Interview (graphic)	
pp01_Follow Up (graphic)	
On Your Own	
1. pp01_Internet Policy	Internet Policy
2. pp01_Memo	Phone Etiquette
3. pp01_Animals	Pet Activities
4.	Placement Services
5. pp01_Animal Careers	Careers with Animals
Lab 2	
pp02_Volunteer2	Volunteer2
pp02_QuestionMark (graphic)	
Step-by-Step	
1. pp02_ASU Presentation	ASU Presentation1
pp02_Arizona (graphic)	
pp02_Student Services (graphic)	
pp02_Library (graphic)	
pp02_Fine Arts (graphic)	
2. Massage Therapy (from Lab 1)	Massage Therapy2
3. Job Fairs (from Lab 1)	Job Fairs2

Supplied/Used	Created/Saved As
4. Triple Crown Presentation (from Lab 1) pp02_Read (graphic)	Triple Crown Presentation2
5. Coffee (from Lab 1) pp02_Globe (graphic)	Coffee Show
On Your Own	
1.	Interview Techniques
2. Careers with Animals (from Lab 1)	Animal Careers2
3.	Fad Diets
4. Internet Policy (from Lab 1)	Internet Policy2
5.	Travel Favorites
Working Together 1	
Volunteer2 (from Lab 2) or ppwt1_Volunteer2	Volunteer2 Linked
ppwt1_OrientationMeetings (Word doc)	
ppwt1_RescueData (Excel chart)	Rescue Data Linked
Step-by-Step	
1. ppwt1_MassagePrices (Word doc) Massage Therapy2 (from Lab 2)	Massage Therapy3
2. ppwt1_Coffee Prices (Word doc) Coffee Show (from Lab 2)	Coffee Prices Linked (Word doc) Coffee Show Linked
3. Triple Crown Presentation2 (from Lab 2) ppwt1_Forest Use (Excel worksheet)	Triple Crown Presentation3 Forest Use Linked (Excel worksheet)

Reference 2

Microsoft Office Specialist Skills

Office PowerPoint 2003 Specialist Certification

Standardized Coding Number	Skill Sets and Skill Standards	Lab	Page	Lab Exercises Step-By-Step	On Your Own
PPO3S-1	**Creating Content**				
PPO3S-1-1	Create new presentations from templates	1	PP1.7	3,4,5	1,2,3,4,5
PPO3S-1-2	Insert and edit text-based content	1	PP1.16	1,2,3,4,5	1,2,3,4,5
		2	PP2.5	1,2,3,4,5	1,2,3,4,5
		WT1	PPWT1.2	1,2,3	
PPO3S-1-3	Insert tables, charts and diagrams	2	PP2.9	4,5	3
PPO3S-1-4	Insert pictures, shapes and graphics	1	PP1.54	1,2,3,4,5	1,2,3,4,5
		2	PP2.23,2.24	1,2,3,4,5	1,2,3,4,5
PPO3S-1-5	Insert objects	WT1	PPWT1.11		
PPO3S-2	**Formatting Content**				
PPO3S-2-1	Format text-based content	1	PP1.49	1,2,3,4,5	1,2,3,4,5
		2	PP2.13,2.15	1,2,3,4,5	1,2,3,4,5
PPO3S-2-2	Format pictures, shapes and graphics	1	PP1.61	1,2,3,4,5	1,2,3,4,5
		2	PP2.22,2.25	1,2,3,4,5	1,2,3,4,5
PPO3S-2-3	Format slides	2	PP2.31,2.33,2.72	1,2,3,4,5	1,2,3,4,5
PPO3S-2-4	Apply animation schemes	2	PP2.54	1,4,5	1,2,3,4
PPO3S-2-5	Apply slide transitions	2	PP2.51		
PPO3S-2-7	Work with masters	2	PP2.38	1,2,3,4,5	1,2,3,4,5
PPO3S-3	**Collaborating**				
PPO3S-4	**Managing and Delivering Presentations**			3,4,5	2,3,4,5
PPO3S-4-1	Organize a presentation	1	PP1.12,1.40–1.45	1,2,3,4,5	1,2,3,4,5
		2	PP2.23,2.63	1,2,3,4,5	1,2,3,4,5
		WT1	PPWT1.2,WT1.9	1,2,3	
PPO3S-4-2	Set up slide shows for delivery	2	PP2.60		
PPO3S-4-4	Deliver presentations	1	PP1.47		
		2	PP2.56		
PPO3S-4-6	Save and publish presentations	1	PP1.31	1,2,3,4,5	1,2,3,4,5
		2	PP2.8	1,2,3,4,5	1,2,3,4,5
PPO3S-4-7	Print slides, outlines, handouts, and speaker notes	1	PP1.62	1,2,3,4,5	1,2,3,4,5
		2	PP2.71	1,2,3,4,5	1,2,3,4,5
		WT1	PPWT1.14	1,2,3	

Index